D1560365

Tracing Women's Romanticism

This book explores a cosmopolitan tradition of nineteenth-century idealist novels written in response to Germaine de Staël's originary novel of the artist as heroine, *Corinne, or Italy*. The author discusses the *Bildungsromane* of Mary Shelley, Bettine von Arnim and George Sand, as responses to Staël's portrait of the artist as abandoned woman, victim of betrayed love.

The first study to consider these major figures from European Romanticism as members of a coherent tradition, *Tracing Women's Romanticism* argues that Staël, Shelley, Arnim, and Sand create proto-feminist visions of spiritual and artistic transcendence that constitute a critique of Romanticism from within. In novels such as *Valperga, Die Günderode* and *Consuelo*, disappointment with Romantic love becomes a catalyst for heightened spiritual, historical and political awareness. This awareness leads to disillusionment with Romanticism's privileging of melancholy, Byronic will and masculinist conceptions of history and *Bildung*.

For these women Romanticists, the search for self-transcendence means rejection of the socially defined limits of individual identity. This abandonment or dissolution of the individual self comes about through historical, artistic, and meditative efforts that culminate in the revelation of the divinity of a collective and potentially revolutionary self.

Kari E. Lokke is Professor of Comparative Literature at the University of California, Davis. She is the author of *Gérard de Nerval: The Poet as Social Visionary* (1987) and co-editor of *Rebellious Hearts: British Women Writers and the French Revolution* (2001).

Routledge studies in romanticism

Tracing Women's Romanticism

Gender, history, and transcendence

Kari E. Lokke

Routledge
Taylor & Francis Group

LONDON AND NEW YORK

First published 2004
by Routledge
2 Park Square, Milton Park, Abingdon, Oxon, OX14 4RN

Simultaneously published in the USA and Canada
by Routledge
270 Madison Ave, New York NY 10016

Routledge is an imprint of the Taylor & Francis Group

Transferred to Digital Printing 2009

Typeset in Baskerville by LaserScript Ltd, Mitcham, Surrey

British Library Cataloguing in Publication Data
A catalogue record for this book is available from the British Library

Library of Congress Cataloging in Publication Data
A catalog record for this book has been requested

ISBN 0-415-33953-7

Contents

Acknowledgments

This book began in the classroom of William H. Gass, whose provocative discussions of the gap between authors' biography and authorial presence in the work of art, between what Gertrude Stein terms Human Nature and Human Mind, presented an intellectual, moral, and spiritual puzzle that has fascinated me since my graduate school days at Washington University in the 1970s. Gass's Kantian meditations on aesthetic disinterest and impersonality troubled and intrigued me, particularly in the form of his purposefully jolting lectures on Ortega y Gasset's *The Dehumanization of Art*. Ortega's prototypical artist, charged with depicting the deathbed scene of a famous man, is utterly detached and ice cold as the body in front of him soon will be. I couldn't help wondering whether if that artist had been a woman, Ortega's book might have turned out quite differently and been entitled instead *The Rehumanization of Art*. This book, in its emphasis on aesthetic transcendence and impersonality in Romantic era women's writings, is an attempt to answer that question. Gass's own writings have also taught me that literary criticism, not doomed to parasitism, can itself be a work of art, inspiring and exhilarating. For that I was and am deeply grateful.

The University of California, Davis has provided support in myriad ways including Committee on Research Travel and Research Grants, a Faculty Development Grant, and a Davis Humanities Institute Fellowship that set this project in motion. Michael Hoffman, then Director of the DHI, offered generous encouragement at a critical time in my academic career. A group of colleagues, convivial and brilliant, from UC Davis and beyond, made that fellowship experience a joy: Joe Boone, Dena Goodman, Anna Kuhn, Valerie Matsumoto, Nancy Paxton, Roger Rouse, Georges Van Den Abbeele, and David Van Leer. Elizabeth Langland, Dean of Humanities, Arts, and Cultural Studies and Barry Klein, Vice Chancellor for Research, provided generous funding for production costs. In merit reviews, confidential readers from the English Department gave the manuscript fair and useful readings. Feminist research group colleagues Alison Berry, Cynthia Brantley, Anna Kuhn, Francesca Miller, Lynn Roller, Stephanie Shields and Vicki Smith offered invaluable chapter-by-chapter feedback, reminding me, as if it were needed, that sisterhood is still powerful. The work of my graduate students assures me that the next generation of scholars will go far beyond what I have written here. Especially relevant for this book are

Tone Brekke's study of the female philosopher and Mariarosa Mettifogo's analysis of the relationship of feminist theory and praxis in George Sand and the Saint-Simoniennes. I am also indebted to research assistants Rebecca Potter, Jeanette Treiber, Sonya Wozniak, Meredith Dutton and Kristin Koster for their efficiency and expertise. Finally, I have benefited more than I can say from the editorial assistance of Brynne Gray who, with her astute mind and eye, rescued me in the final stages of preparing the manuscript for the press.

Dialogues with scholars across the country and encounters with their works have contributed richly and sometimes ineffably to this study. I name here only a few: Frederick Burwick, Madelyn Gutwirth, Diane Hoeveler, Greg Kucich, Lilach Lachman, Tricia Lootens, Anne Mellor, Marjean Purinton, Marlon Ross, Tilottama Rajan, Esther Schor, Juliana Schiesari, Nan Sweet, Sarah Zimmerman. All of us in the field of Romanticism owe an enormous debt to the founders and current officers of three professional organizations: the 18th and 19th Century British Women Writers Association, the International Conference on Romanticism, and the North American Society for the Study of Romanticism.

I thank Liz Thompson, Diane Parker, Joe Whiting, Amrit Bangard, Yeliz Ali, Barbara Archer, David McCarthy, and two anonymous readers at Routledge for expert and thoughtful help in the production process.

Beloved friends, near and far, have made life worth living during the process of writing this book. I particularly wish to thank Nancy Kaiser for providing the ideal blend of professional and personal dialogue in our many years of friendship. Rosemary Kelly, Richard Koepsel, Regina Miesch, and Stacey Shannon offered nourishment for body and soul that has sustained me in moments of self-doubt and questioning. The artistry of my mother, Agnes Lokke, provides me with daily comfort and inspiration. Paul Wurst remains a rare and bright example of one who regularly moves "beyond the impossible" and lives up to his ideals. I thank him for the joy our shared life has given me. Finally, I have benefited immeasurably from the intellectual friendship and personal loyalty, not to mention the wicked humor, of Adriana Craciun and Seth Schein. I dedicate this book to them, knowing that without their encouragement and belief in me, it would never have seen the light of day.

NOTE ON TRANSLATIONS

Quotations from the central novels under discussion – *Corinne*, *Die Günderode* and *Consuelo/La Comtesse de Rudolstadt* – are given both in English and in the original language with the page numbers of the editions used in sequence after the entire block of quoted material. For economy of space, quotations from non-fiction works of Staël, Arnim, and Sand are present only in English translation. I've used published translations where available; otherwise translations are mine.

For Adriana Craciun and Seth Schein

Introduction

Romantic abandon

> Enthusiasm is no passion of the drawing-room, or of the pence-table: its home is
> the heart, and its hope is afar.
>
> Letitia Landon

This project began as a book about sublimity and ended as a book about history.
My original focus on discourses of transcendence shifted gradually to a
recognition of a collective endeavor on the part of women writers of Romanticism
to transform the societies in which they lived. Accordingly, the term sublimity is
supplemented by its feminized and politicized variant, enthusiasm. Thus this
study began as an effort to identify and understand conceptions of aesthetic and
spiritual transcendence in four women writers of the Romantic era – Germaine
de Staël, Mary Shelley, Bettine von Arnim, and George Sand – and concluded
in the realization that these novelists all envisage self-transcendence, both
artistic and spiritual, as participation in historical process. Margaret Fuller, who
in the mid-nineteenth century already saw Staël, Arnim, and Sand as
constituting a coherent group with similar talents, similar aims, and similar
foibles, identifies, in her own inimitable voice, the task of these and all nineteenth-
century women artists as follows: "I would have Woman lay aside all thought,
such as she habitually cherishes, of being taught and led by men."[1] Fuller
continues:

> [W]omen must . . . retire within themselves, and explore the ground-work of
> life till they find their peculiar secret. Then, when they come forth again,
> renovated and baptized, they will know how to turn all dross to gold, and
> will be rich and free though they live in a hut, tranquil if in a crowd. Then
> their sweet singing shall not be from passionate impulse, but the lyrical
> overflow of a divine rapture, and a new music shall be evolved from this
> many-chorded world.
>
> (p. 121)

In this book I trace precisely this development from the self-destructive
emotional excess of Staël's Corinne to the inspired artistic freedom of Sand's

Consuelo. I argue that an idealist and spiritualized understanding of the woman artist's role in historical process made this emancipatory movement possible. Furthermore, the distinctive mysticism of these writers is grounded in their shared experiences as women, just as their collective endeavor to change their respective societies compelled them to discourses of transcendence. Thus, my study seeks to comprehend the many-chorded "new music" that arose from novelistic portraits of female creativity in women's roles as poets, philosophers, and prophets at a time when nineteenth-century European women sought to establish themselves as artistic professionals.

Accordingly, I examine here meditative, mystical, and utopian visions of religious and artistic transcendence in the novels of women Romanticists as vehicles for the representation of a gendered subjectivity that seeks detachment and distance from the interests and strictures of the existing patriarchal social and cultural order. My position, in its recognition of the oppositional nature of these novelists' spiritual commitments, accords with that of Naomi Schor whose *George Sand and Idealism* is one of the few critical works to address this strain of nineteenth-century women's writing. Schor writes:

> [I]dealism, as it is appropriated by Sand, signified her refusal to reproduce mimetically and hence to legitimate a social order inimical to the disenfranchised, among them women. Idealism for Sand is finally the only alternative representational mode available to those who do not enjoy the privileges of subjecthood in the real.[2]

Yet whereas Schor focuses upon the implications of the politics of idealist representation for novelistic style and genre, my interest here shifts to the idealist novel as a privileged locus of nineteenth-century women's historiography and as a central contribution of women writers to the visionary Romantic tradition from which literary critics have so often excluded them.

It is thus also my hope that this comparatist study – certainly one of the first of its kind to treat English, French, and German women novelists of the nineteenth century – will enrich the terrain of Romantic studies by revealing the significance of hitherto unexamined contributions on the part of women authors to landscapes of Romantic transcendence. Whereas critics as varied as Margaret Homans, Marlon Ross, Anne Mellor, and Stuart Curran have asserted that traditional and restrictive associations of women with nature, immanence, and the body in Western culture exclude them from the discourse of transcendence that forms the heart of Romantic aesthetics and metaphysics, I argue that these novelists create feminine and (proto-)feminist visions of spiritual and artistic transcendence that constitute a critique of Romanticism from within.[3] Despite its title, then, this book does not seek to set up gender-complementary models of Romanticism or to suggest that Romantic philosophy and art were inherently inimical to women's values and interests. Rather, I hope to shed light on women's contributions to Romantic aesthetics, historiography, and novelistic practice in order to encourage reconfigurations of Romantic studies that acknowledge women's vital and as yet insufficiently understood contributions to the central cultural debates of the day.

Furthermore, my choice to focus on the novel, rather than on poetry, as an exemplary Romantic genre, counters and questions the privileging of poetry in both the traditionalist, masculinist criticism of Abrams, de Man, and Bloom *and* those aforementioned critics writing against them in their re-evaluations of the cultural meaning of Romantic transcendence. This emphasis on poetry as the quintessential Romantic genre crosses national boundaries, moving beyond the focus on the six canonical poets of British Romanticism, and is reflected in the prestige of Hölderlin studies, for example, within the field of *Germanistik* and the prominence of Baudelaire in French Romantic studies. My aim here is not to undermine the significance of the recent (re)discovery and re-evaluation of the women poets of the Romantic period, critical efforts which I believe have produced the most exciting and significant work of the last decade in the field of Romantic studies. Rather, I wish to highlight the breadth of women writers' previously unacknowledged contributions to European Romanticism in the realms of the aesthetic theory and historiography encompassed by the genres of the *Künstlerroman* and the historical novel respectively. Focus on the novel furthermore illuminates women's contributions to the most socially influential literary genre of the nineteenth century, one in which, as Mellor has shown in *Mothers of the Nation*, women had already achieved pre-eminence by the end of the eighteenth century.[4]

My study, then, is complementary to the work of these previously mentioned critics whose writings reveal the power of nineteenth-century female genius to create *within* what Stuart Curran terms "the hegemony of male values" (p. 207). I choose a different emphasis for my analysis: the metaphors and textual strategies through which these writers did in fact assert their right to direct communion with divinity, their right to membership in a visionary company, and, perhaps most importantly, to historical agency. In asserting these rights and expressing their anger, sorrow, and frustration at the devaluation of their talents, beliefs, and accomplishments, female Romanticists participated not only in the redefinition of feminine sensibility but also in the reconceptualization of the relation of body to spirit, thought to action, myth to history, as well as the rethinking of concepts of vision and transcendence, of divinity itself. There have been few comparative studies of women Romanticists, and as yet no books seeking to establish communalities of experience and expression among women Romanticists of different nationalities.[5] I envisage the task of this study, then, as the delineation of an international and cosmopolitan women's Romanticism that intersects with, but is also distinct from, that Romanticism which, up until the last two decades, scholars have conceived of as eminently and almost exclusively masculine.

Thus this book also seeks to comprehend and illuminate the quasi-mystical language in which these novelistic portraits of the female artist and visionary are drawn, as well as the relation of that language to idealist conceptions of history that informed the Romantic era. Furthermore, the artistic and professional efforts of the nineteenth-century novelists under discussion here inevitably are set against the backdrop of the aftermath of the French Revolution and culminate in the work of Arnim and Sand written in the decade leading up to the Revolutions of 1848. Beginning with Staël's disillusionment with the Napoleonic outcome of the French Revolution, this book comes full circle to conclude with Sand's novel *Consuelo* set in the decades prior to the 1789 Revolution, a novel suggesting both the inevitability of that Revolution and the possibility that its outcome might have been different had artists such as Sand's Consuelo been politically active in that social upheaval.

As their titles reveal, the four novels at the heart of this study make female development their focus: *Corinne* (1807), *Valperga* (1823), *Die Günderode* (1840), and *Consuelo* (1842–4). As female *Bildungsromane*, each of these novels takes a female character from youth into maturity, teaching her hard-won lessons along the way. More explicitly and specifically, as portraits of female artistry and creativity, each of these novels belongs to a subgenre of the *Bildungsroman*, the *Künstlerroman*. Though it is hardly necessary, this study reminds us once again that for nineteenth-century women artists, Staël's *Corinne, or Italy* (1807) unquestionably establishes itself as the originary portrait of European female genius. Clearly, the novels of Shelley, Arnim, and Sand constitute responses to the overwhelming emotional power and cultural resonance of this novel and its self-destructive heroine that are not always easy for us to understand today.[6] Whereas *Valperga* and *Consuelo* represent conscious novelistic revisions of *Corinne*, Arnim's autobiographical *Die Günderode* seeks to come to terms with the story of her friend the poet Karoline von Günderode, whose fate mirrored that of the fictional Corinne, by suppressing that tragic narrative and replacing it with the story of her own life-affirming artistic development.

The traditional *Bildungsroman* is, of course, a fundamentally conservative form, narrating, as it does, the growth of the middle-class young man from callow and idealistic youth to his integration into the societal status quo through bourgeois marriage and proper professional placement. Like Goethe's prototypical Wilhelm Meister, the hero survives disappointment and disillusionment by compromising with the societal powers that be. As Franco Moretti writes in *The Way of the World: The Bildungsroman in European Culture*, compromise is "not surprisingly, the novel's most celebrated theme."[7] Furthermore, this genre is politically as well as culturally conservative; "the classical *Bildungsroman* narrates 'how the French Revolution could have been avoided'" (p. 64) and disavows that Revolution, seeking to deny "the irreversibility of its effects" (p. 73). The novels under discussion here, on the other hand, seek to envisage how the world might look had the Revolution succeeded in implementing its original republican and egalitarian aims and to imagine the collective psychic changes that would be necessary for that implementation.

Corinne, *Die Günderode*, and *Consuelo*, then, were all clearly written as retorts to the political and social complacency of Goethe's *Wilhelm Meister* (1795–6). In her opening improvisation, Staël's Corinne prophetically echoes the doomed Mignon's "do you know the land where orange trees bloom...?" from the

Lehrjahre, thus inviting her public to reread Goethe's novel from the perspective of its sacrificial victim.[8] And Arnim, whose notorious stylization of herself as Mignon in *Goethe's Correspondence with a Child* (1835) was read even at the time as an implicit attack on his Olympian aloofness, creates in her subsequent narrative persona, Bettine, a figure who claims to be that earlier character now reincarnated and full of exuberant life. Finally, Sand's *Consuelo* rewrites the sequel to the *Lehrjahre*, *Wilhelm Meisters Wanderjahre* (1821), replacing the middle-class Wilhelm with its "gypsy" heroine Consuelo and substituting utopian socialism for the conservative and authoritarian ideology of Goethe's prototype.

As female *Bildungsromane*, then, these novels inevitably follow a different path from that of the traditional *Bildungsroman*, a narrative path that bears comparison to that delineated in such studies as *The Voyage In: Fictions of Female Development*, edited by Elizabeth Abel *et al.*, Susan Fraiman's *Unbecoming Women: British Women Writers and the Novel of Development*, and Lorna Ellis's *Appearing to Diminish: Female Development and the British Bildungsroman*, 1750–1850.[9] At the same time, however, the female *Künstlerromane* that I examine here also exhibit crucial differences from the larger category of female *Bildungsromane*, works such as *Pride and Prejudice*, *Emma*, *Jane Eyre*, *The Mill on the Floss*, that are the subject of these earlier studies. Indeed one of the central purposes of this study is to shed light on a number of remarkable examples of this little-known and little-studied genre so that it will no longer be possible for critics to claim that "the woman artist is a missing character in fiction" or to bemoan the absence of "serious literary work" by women depicting their artistic struggles.[10] Such assertions reveal the Anglophone bias of much feminist criticism of modern fiction in their obliviousness to the work of such authors as Staël, Caroline Auguste Fischer, Caroline Pichler, Lou Andreas-Salomé, Sibilla Aleramo, and Isak Dinesen, an imbalance this comparatist study seeks to redress.[11] A notable exception to this Anglophone limitation is Evy Varsamopoulou's *The Poetics of the Künstlerinroman and the Aesthetics of the Sublime* which traces the twentieth-century legacy of Staël's Corinne from H.D. to Christa Wolf and Marguerite Duras and thus continues from the modernist era where mine concludes. Though couched in Freudian and Lacanian psychoanalytic theory, Varsamopoulou's conclusions bear comparison to my own emphasis upon these writers' sense of participation in a historical and artistic process beyond the individual: "The protagonists' and narrators' relation to their literary forerunners (male or female) is characterized by a desire to prolong, repeat and participate in their own and others' literary art and discourse on the sublime, perceived as a virtual *venue*."[12]

As the aforementioned feminist critics of the genre have emphasized, earlier studies of the *Bildungsroman* assumed a male protagonist and a masculine pattern of development; they describe "'human development' in exclusively male terms" and generally follow one central hero in his process of maturation and social integration.[13] If this social integration involves, for the masculine hero, marriage and a fitting middle-class profession, the four novels under discussion here, as *Künstlerromane*, present an obvious and direct challenge to such a narrative pattern. One cannot, of course, in any real sense, speak of professional choice for any European woman in the first half of the nineteenth century, and novels from Mary Hays's *Memoirs of Emma Courtney* (1796), Mary Wollstonecraft's *Maria, or the Wrongs of Woman* (1797), and Mary Robinson's *The Natural Daughter* (1799) to Charlotte Brontë's *Jane Eyre* (1847) and *Villette* (1853) address this issue explicitly. In the case of the female artist, however, the conflict between aspiration toward public, creative self-expression and marriage/domesticity is extreme in the utmost degree. Indeed, for the woman artist, marriage and professional development are mutually exclusive. This absolute conflict, then, accounts for the radicalism of these novels, a radicalism that Linda Huf, in *The Portrait of the Artist as a Young Woman*, finds in the female *Künstlerroman* even today.[14] Indeed, as a subgenre of the *Bildungsroman*, the female *Künstlerroman* represents a profound critique of that genre from within. If the novel devoted to the male artist also critiques bourgeois society, it does so from a much more individualistic, even anti-social, perspective that diverges radically from the female tradition I am exploring here. One need only think of the German tradition that ranges from Wackenroder and Tieck's artist heroes, tormented by, but unable to escape, their own self-absorption, and E.T.A. Hoffmann's obsessive *Ritter Gluck* (1809) or *Councillor Krespel* (1819) to Thomas Mann's *Death in Venice* (1911) or *Tonio Kröger* (1903) for obvious examples of this striking divergence between male and female traditions.[15]

Ultimately, the heroines of Staël's, Shelley's, and Arnim's novels reject marriage explicitly and consciously; the compromise that characterizes the traditional *Bildungsroman* is unknown to them. In the novels studied here, none of the heroines accepts the necessity of the manipulation of appearances that Lorna Ellis suggests is crucial to the maturation process of the protagonists of the female novel of development if they are to "manipulate societal expectation in order to promote their own welfare" (p. 23) "to find a compromise between self and society, [and] to form a bridge between their views of themselves and those of the men they love" (p. 33). Sexually experienced before she meets Oswald, Corinne makes it clear that she wishes to be his lover and companion, but it is not at all apparent at the outset that she wants to be his wife. Shelley's Euthanasia chooses her republican ideals over marriage to her betrothed once he becomes her political enemy. And Bettine von Arnim's protagonist prefers female friendship and the mentorship of an elderly Jew to what she fiercely terms "the moth-eaten joys of domestic bliss." Finally, Sand's Consuelo marries the aristocratic Albert, Count Rudolstadt at the conclusion of that novel only when it is clear that he is dying and that their union will never be consummated. And in the sequel, *La Comtesse de Rudolstadt*, once Albert has symbolically died and come back to life a new man, this Catholic ceremony is nullified by and replaced with an egalitarian union, celebrated under the auspices of the secret revolutionary society of Invisibles whose only female leader demands a radical redefinition of bourgeois marriage. The political prescience of these novels is rendered evident by the fact that they undoubtedly anticipate the genre that Rita Felski has recently described as "most clearly identified with contemporary feminist writing ... the narrative of female self-discovery, in which access to self-knowledge is seen to require an explicit refusal of the heterosexual romance plot."[16]

This radical refusal of compromise inevitably carries a heavy cost for the protagonists of these nineteenth-century novels, and the depiction of the high price these women artists pay for freedom is one of the central tasks of these four authors. For Corinne, the price of freedom is ultimately life itself, as Oswald's rejection of her in favor of her blonde, virginal, and domestic half-sister Lucile precipitates her self-willed demise at the conclusion of the novel. Like the powerful brightness of Staël's vision of female genius, the intensity of the pall that Corinne's abandonment and melodramatic death cast over future nineteenth-century depictions of the artist heroine is difficult to describe and hard to fathom.[17] Yet, if the costs are high, so, ultimately, Shelley, Arnim, and Sand reveal in their responses to Staël, are the rewards of freedom. Indeed, I read the representations of spiritual and aesthetic transcendence in this cosmopolitan tradition of women's idealist novels as responses to the ubiquitous cultural presence of Staël's portrait of the artist as abandoned woman. Whereas nineteenth-century poets such as Felicia Hemans, Letitia Landon, Marceline Desbordes-Valmore, and Karolina Pavlova exploited this persona of the lovelorn female, victim of betrayed love, to the fullest, even as they covertly challenged it, female fiction and prose writers were explicitly and pointedly critical of the myth of the woman artist as Ariadne abandoned by Theseus, Sappho betrayed by Phaon, or Dido by Aeneas.[18]

This, then, is the central argument of this book: that in the *Künstlerromane* of Staël, Shelley, Arnim, and Sand, disappointment with Romantic passionate love becomes a catalyst for the cultivation of heightened political, spiritual, and historical awareness. This disappointment becomes as well a synecdoche for disillusionment with (masculinist) Romanticism itself and its obsessions with melancholy, Byronic, Promethean will, and masculinist conceptions of culture and *Bildung*. For these women writers of Romanticism, Romantic transcendence means not self-aggrandizement as it does for Wordsworth, Byron, Chateaubriand, or Musset but rather an abandonment or dissolution of the individual self through historical, political, and spiritual efforts that culminate in a revelation of the divinity of collective selfhood.

Accordingly, these novels tell the tale, not of one central character's development into maturity but of the interplay of double or multiple narratives that tell the stories of several women's interconnected lives. In *The Voyage In*, Abel *et al.* argue that female novels of development frequently reveal "a disjunction between a surface plot, which affirms social conventions, and a submerged plot which encodes rebellion; ... a plot that charts development and a plot that unravels it" (p. 12). Similarly, Susan Fraiman, in *Unbecoming Women*, demonstrates convincingly that multiple, divided, and split narratives play a key role in the female *Bildungsroman*, and that, alongside the conventional marriage plots, these novels tell other stories "in a spirit of protest, challenging the myth of courtship as education, railing against the belittlement of women, willing to hazard the distasteful and the indecorous" (p. xi). According to Fraiman, these counter-narratives – the story of Bertha Mason in *Jane Eyre*, to name the most obvious example – "account for growing up female as a deformation, a gothic disorientation, a loss of authority, an abandonment of goals" (p. xi) even as they are ultimately subsumed into the traditional marriage plot.

In the female *Künstlerroman*, these submerged, defiant stories take front and center stage as the plot opens up to multiple narratives of several women's lives and the focus shifts – sometimes subtly, sometimes dramatically – from male–female relationships to relations among women. Mentorship of women by women is thus central to female development in each of these texts as their authors seek to move beyond the traditional courtship and marriage plot where, frequently, as in *Emma*, it is the husband to be who mentors his young fiancée. Clearly, then, in their demonstrations that women, and women artists in particular, must find their *own* ways out of imprisoning patriarchal strictures, these four novels embody their authors' individual understandings of Margaret Fuller's exhortation that women should "lay aside all thought . . . of being taught and led by men" (p. 121). Rather than highlighting recognition of individual accomplishment and genius, the focus on mentorship valorizes influence on the future, even at the cost of abandoning self-interest and accepting anonymity.

Thus the interactions of Corinne, her half-sister Lucile, and Juliette, Lucile's daughter by Oswald, dominate the conclusion of Staël's novel, overshadowing the heroine's bitter reproaches of her weak and unfaithful lover. Before dying, Corinne passes on the legacy of her own female genius to Juliette, suggesting the possibility of unifying her sister and herself, the light and the dark, the domestic and the artistic, the private and the public, the spiritual and the passionate, in one woman, as well as revealing Staël's own recognition of her vital role in a tradition of Western female artists. Though troubling and self-contradictory, the conclusion of *Corinne* at least holds out the hope that growing up female for the young Juliette will not have to entail a "deformation" and "an abandonment of goals" (Fraiman, p. xi).

Similarly, Shelley's *Valperga: or, The Life and Adventures of Castruccio, Prince of Lucca* (1823) tells the tale of three extravagantly named female characters, Euthanasia, Countess of Valperga, Beatrice, and Mandragola who correspond to the archetypes of Mother, Maiden, and Crone and may be said to represent the collective and mythic development of women throughout European history. These three fictional figures are connected to each other through their relationships to the historical figure of Castruccio Castracani, the fourteenth-century prince whose life and rise to political power is documented in Machiavelli and Sismondi. Though the novel opens with Castruccio's rise to power and his love for both Beatrice and Euthanasia, the story of the relationship between these two women soon supplants the courtship plot and becomes the heart of the novel as Euthanasia seeks to comfort and counsel Beatrice after her seduction and abandonment by Castruccio. Beatrice's fate reads quite literally as a gothic "deformation" of that destiny traditionally granted to a protagonist like Wilhelm, for both her taking of a lover (Castruccio) and her travels (an expiatory pilgrimage` to Rome) – obligatory moves for the male hero of the *Bildungsroman* – are ultimately figured as horrific psychic and physical rapes that destroy her spirit. At the conclusion of *Valperga*, however, Shelley offers Euthanasia's wisdom as a direct answer to the gothic horror and despair of Beatrice when Euthanasia seeks to enlighten Beatrice, who has become a Paterin heretic cursing God as the principle of evil in her response to abandonment by Castruccio, with a [proto-] feminist parable of the cave. In this scene of female instruction, Euthanasia elucidates a vision of meditative transcendence guided by an "inner light" that determines the regulation of mental faculties termed "powers"; thus she internalizes the power struggles that are the narrative and thematic key to *Valperga* and suggests that the only true power one can ever claim is power over oneself.

Arnim's 1840 autobiographical and lyrical *Briefroman Die Günderode* is also built upon the mirroring of the lives of two young women in their mutual development toward creative self-expression. Ostensibly the record of Bettine's admiration and love for the poet Karoline who clearly serves as her counselor and mentor in the opening letters, the novel also records, like *Valperga*, the opposition between one woman's victimization by masculinist cultural norms and another's firm and defiant self-assertion. Never mentioning or even hinting at the historical Karoline's tragic abandonment by her married lover Friedrich Creuzer, Arnim portrays *her* Karoline's melancholy vulnerability as the product of her unrealized artistic ambition and her fears that she will never achieve and be recognized for artistic greatness, never join the ranks of canonical (male) greatness. Thus it is not erotic but cultural abandonment that she dreads. Her internalization of masculinist norms of artistic accomplishment and recognition dooms her. And it is fear of societal censure and bourgeois hegemony – astutely figured by Karoline as a many-headed hydra – that renders her incapable of living up to the ideals that she and Bettine advocate in their newly conceived *Schwebe-Religion*, a revolutionary religion of female courage and activism.

In Sand's *Consuelo* (1842–4), the doubling of the female development narrative takes the form of a merciless critique of Corinne and her author, as Sand's gifted and innocent heroine is set in contrast to the (pointedly named) prima donna Corilla, who, in her uncontrolled emotionality, her promiscuity, and vanity, sells herself body and soul to her profession. More interestingly and generously, Sand reveals female mentorship and guidance to be crucial to Consuelo's development in two relationships fundamental to the novel. First, Consuelo's Freemasonic/ Illuminist initiation includes a pivotal encounter with a spiritual elder of Les Invisibles who turns out to be the mother of Consuelo's betrothed Albert who has taken refuge in this revolutionary society from an unhappy, stultifying marriage. Echoing the political programs of Sand's feminist contemporaries, the Saint-Simoniennes, this sibylline figure states unequivocally to Consuelo that she has a right to sexual fulfillment in her marriage and that acceptance of union without physical passion would be spiritually destructive and wrong. Her entire message to Consuelo is grounded in the precept of the "divine equality of man and woman" as she furthermore makes it clear that it will be Consuelo's task, as a member of Les Invisibles, to educate women in particular, women of all classes and countries, about their vital part in the battle to destroy intellectual and economic tyranny, the goal toward which this secret society strives. Even more radically and originally, Sand's narrative reveals that the occult marriage celebrated at the conclusion of *La Comtesse de Rudolstadt* will be fulfilling because Consuelo is, in reality, marrying a feminized man who has himself fully lived the experience of Romantic abandonment, and who, even more importantly, has evinced the capacity to serve as a nurturer and a maternal protector of his beloved. Albert is significantly and repeatedly associated with Consuelo's mother, the wandering musician whose spirit has guided her daughter throughout the novel. Marriage, Sand seems to be suggesting, will be mutually satisfying when men become (like) women!

The shared counsel of the female characters central to these novels is rooted in a meditative and often mystical consciousness that finds its source in a temporary withdrawal from worldly engagement that corresponds quite precisely to Margaret Fuller's Transcendentalist admonitions to her female contemporaries that they "retire within themselves, and explore the groundwork of life till they find their peculiar secret" so that they can "come forth again, renovated and baptized," *and*, ultimately, free. This movement within also resembles the exploration of the inner self – the spiritual, moral, and emotional development that Marianne Hirsch, in "Spiritual Bildung," sees as distinguishing the fate of the female protagonist of the *Bildungsroman* from her more worldly male counterpart. For Hirsch, however, the "exclusively spiritual development" of the heroines of *Wilhelm Meister*, *The Mill on the Floss*, *Effi Briest*, and *The Awakening* constitutes a diminution, an acquiescence to patriarchal limitation, and, in the final analysis, "a death warrant" (p. 26) for the self as a whole. She writes:

> Like Eurydice, our four nineteenth-century protagonists remain forever trapped and lost in their underworld caverns. For them, inwardness affords no sustained insight, introspection no more than glimpses of self-knowledge. Subjectivity is not an assertion of individual identity and imaginative power, but a dissolution, an extinction. The inner life thus becomes not a locus of knowledge and power but the place, in the words of Jane Austen, of "feelings unemployed."
>
> (p. 47)

The plot of the female *Bildungsroman*, telling the story of "the potential artist who fails to make it" (p. 28), is for Hirsch cyclic, entropic, repetitive, and profoundly ahistorical.

In contrast, the novels under discussion here clearly represent introspection as indeed leading to insight, self-knowledge and ultimately to historical agency, though that agency is *not* predicated solely upon *individual* identity or imaginative power. In both their congruence with and ultimate departure from Hirsch's narrative, these female *Künstlerromane*, a subcategory of the novels she discusses, confirm the power of her analysis at the same time that they also show how explicit focus on the even partially realized female artist enables a certain liberatory movement toward collective knowledge and power, toward historical intervention. In order to depict the historical agency of the female artist, these novelists must of necessity *rewrite* history, since previous historiography, focusing on public and political realms, had excluded women a priori. Each of these texts, then, makes a significant contribution to nineteenth-century historiography as it was practiced by women who were excluded from formal, academic writing of history.[19]

Seeking simultaneously to [re]animate exempla of past political or aesthetic agency and to project them into the future, these novelists belong to that category of historian defined, according to Michel de Certeau, by their claim "to reencounter lived experience, exhumed by virtue of a knowledge of the past."[20] Their Orphic efforts, mirrored by the journeys of their characters, bring to light a rich cast of beloved Eurydices, both male and female, historical and fictional. Indeed, Romantic women writers' historiographical premises and motivations imply a narrative technique, in de Certeau's terms, or, in this case, a novelistic method. This historiographic "tendency valorizes the relation the historian keeps with a lived experience, that is, with the possibility of resuscitating or 'reviving' a past. It would like to restore the forgotten and to meet again men [sic] of the past amidst the traces they have left. It also implies a particular literary genre, narrative" (pp. 35–6). For Staël and her descendants, this narrative exists in an intense and conflicted, love–hate relation to the narrative of Enlightenment progress typified by Kant's *Idea for a Universal History with a Cosmopolitan Purpose* (1784) and *Conflict of the Faculties* (1795–9) and transcendentalized in Schiller's *Naïve and Sentimental Poetry* (1795). The idealism of the writers featured in this study is inevitably shadowed by a dark knowledge peculiar to a woman's perspective. Hence the prevalence of Gothic or uncanny moments in each of these novels, moments haunted by revivified ghosts of both the near and painful as well as the distant and abysmal past. The other type of history delineated by de Certeau "ponders what is comprehensible and what are the conditions of understanding," bringing "historians back to the methodological hypotheses of their work, ... to principles of intelligibility that might produce relevance and even 'facts,' and finally, back to their epistemological situation, present in all research characteristics of the society in which they are working" (p. 35). This type of history is perhaps best represented in the eighteenth and nineteenth centuries by empiricist and positivist histories from which woman, as both subject and object, was largely excluded as "other."

De Certeau's categorizations help us understand the affinities, at first perhaps puzzling, between women's historiography and the rationalist/idealist traditions of Kant, Godwin, and Hegel, as opposed to the empiricism grounded in Locke and Hume. The faith in the power of pure thought that is evinced in these novels, a faith typical of idealist philosophy, is certainly also understandable in feminist terms, given the contrast between the freedom of thought open to these women and the restrictions placed upon their "objective" experience. Indeed the rationalist Godwin's fascinating essay "On History and Romance" (1797) provides intriguing parallels to the treatment accorded history in the novels studied here. Explicitly attacking the historical writings of Hume and Voltaire, and seeking to defend the novel or romance as he terms it from charges of effeminacy and frivolity, Godwin boldly asserts that "[i]t must be admitted indeed that all history bears too near a resemblance to fable" and that "[n]othing is more uncertain, more contradictory, more unsatisfactory than the evidence of facts."[21] The answer of Wollstonecraft's lover and Mary Shelley's father to Hume and Voltaire is, fittingly, historical romance, grounded in the knowledge of individual character and leaving aside abstractions to study human "passions and peculiarities" (p. 361). The tables are now turned: "the writer of romance then is to be considered as the writer of real history; while he who was formerly called the historian, must be contented to step down into the place of his rival, with this disadvantage, that he is a romance writer, without the arduous, the enthusiastic and the sublime license of the imagination, that belong to that species of composition" (p. 372).

Certainly, *Valperga* and *Consuelo* belong to Godwin's category of historical romances and are also historical novels in the strict sense of the term in that they place their fictional female characters in relation to prominent historical figures and represent the political realities of their times as determining their heroines' fates. These novels clearly demonstrate women's commitment to and expertise in this genre that dates back to the decade that produced Godwin's essay – the 1790s – and women novelists' strong contemporaneous responses to the French Revolution, well before Sir Walter Scott's *Waverley* (1814) that is generally identified as originating this genre.[22] *Corinne* and *Die Günderode* are also grounded in extensive meditations on history, both as it was lived and represented, and as it informs the heroines' fundamental values and choices – moral, aesthetic, and political.

In the initially puzzling conclusion to Godwin's essay, individual history is subsumed into the kind of collective vision that is the aim of the novelists studied here. The tables are turned once again as this collective history of "successive multitudes," the necessitarian Godwin suggests, becomes the province of the historian/scientist after all:

> Here then the historian in some degree, though imperfectly, seems to recover his advantage upon the writer of romance. He indeed does not understand the character he exhibits, but the events are taken out of his hands and determined by the system of the universe, and therefore, as far as his information extends, must be true. The romance writer, on the other hand, is continually straining at a foresight to which his faculties are incompetent, and continually fails. ... That principle only which holds the planets in their course, is competent to produce that majestic series of events which characterizes flux, and successive multitudes.
>
> (p. 372)

Significantly, whereas the atheist Godwin denies the capacity of foresight to the novelist, the spiritual orientations of the women writers featured here lead them to claim a kind of prophetic vision and to depict their heroines as mystically comprehending the "system of the universe" in moments of enthusiasm that allow concourse with historical ghosts.[23]

Jon Mee has cogently argued that British discourse on enthusiasm remained remarkably consistent from Hobbes through Hunt in its suspicion and disparagement of the term as connoting an excess of passion and religious zeal that threatened the stability and integrity of individual subjectivity and body politic.[24] If this is the case, then the cosmopolitan tradition of Romantic women novelists I am tracing here, in its overwhelmingly positive presentation of enthusiasm, constitutes a radical departure from such British discourse. For Staël, as I will argue, enthusiasm represents the attainment of a transcendent and God-like perspective of philosophic wisdom and detachment from passion that brings forth an almost supernatural eloquence in her heroine, the *improvisatrice* Corinne. Mee makes clear the association of enthusiasm with the religious fanaticism and monomania that "allowed individuals or the crowd to be swept up in a single idea" (p. 52). In contrast, Staël aligns melancholy with monomania or obsession and enthusiasm with a liberatory multiplicity of inspirations and perspectives. Strongly influenced by Staël's recuperation of enthusiasm, which was itself indebted to Shaftesbury and Rousseau, Shelley similarly accords her heroine Euthanasia poetic and political talents that are inseparable from her ruling passion of enthusiasm for liberty.

Furthermore, in both *Corinne* and *Valperga*, enthusiasm clearly functions as a code word for French Revolutionary sympathies, as they are articulated not by the mob but by women who are members of an elite intelligentsia. Later in the century, Arnim democratizes the German variant of enthusiasm, *Begeisterung*, by applying it to her youthful alter-ego Bettine whose proposed revolutionary religion is founded in order to sanctify even the most mundane happenings in obscure young girls' lives. Significantly, the English reviews of her work highlight her girlish "enthusiasm."[25] This process of democratization is, in a sense, quite spectacularly completed in Sand's *La Comtesse de Rudolstadt* with its glorification of mass underground revolutionary movements, open to leaders of both sexes and all social classes, as manifestations of a sacred enthusiasm. Finally, the novelists discussed here, perhaps in an effort to distance themselves from ancient conceptions of the female body as vulnerable to hysterical possession, link enthusiasm with a meditative, introspective consciousness that enables the heroine to maintain self-possession and philosophical detachment in the face of overwhelming emotion.[26] If, as Mee suggests, "the confusion of the bodily and spiritual was liable to be identified with an improperly regulated enthusiasm" (p. 14), then these Romantic women writers challenged the dualism on which that judgment was based. And if enthusiasm does submit to a regulatory function in the texts discussed here, to use Mee's Foucauldian terms, that function is not so much to stifle passion or repress revolt as it is to sublimate these forces into art and ideals that will survive the death of the individual female body, sometimes quite uncannily and mysteriously, and be passed on from generation to generation as agents of inspiration for social change.

Thus Staël's concept of enthusiasm, a transcendent aesthetic and spiritual state embodied in the *improvisatrice* Corinne at the beginning of the novel, is inseparable from the impersonal, meditative response that Staël sees as essential to the perpetuation of the ideals of the French Revolution in the wake of its bloody betrayal of those goals. Enthusiasm, for Staël, is an elevated state of mind, beyond personal emotion and holding all the connotations of inspiriting divinity and doubling of self found in that word's etymology. It unites Corinne in a passionate dialogue with her friends and her audience about human destiny, duties, and affections and is precisely analogous to the perspective that Staël, throughout her life, counsels her contemporaries to seek in response to their thwarted revolutionary efforts. Thus, the concluding chapter of *On Germany*, with its celebration of enthusiasm, compares historical process – and progress – to the effort, both material and spiritual, of building the Mayan pyramids, effort based upon the labor of generations of countless anonymous individuals and proof that "there are centuries for the good that can be done by truth" (p. 324).[27] From this perspective, the artistic legacy passed on to Juliette by Corinne at the conclusion of the novel is a significant step, albeit an overdetermined and conflicted one, toward the revelation of the truth of women's artistic and creative potential.

The city of Rome, the backdrop for Corinne's artistic triumphs, literalizes the historical record that forms the subtext of Staël's novel and is the source of its ameliorative vision of collective human fate. The intrusion of Roman ruins into the realms of the ordinary and the mundane provokes a kind of shock, that, according to Staël, "reminds you that there is an eternal power in man, a divine spark, and that you must never grow weary of lighting it in yourself or of rekindling it in others. ... The Forum, so tightly enclosed, witness to so many astonishing things, is striking proof of man's moral grandeur. ... Honor then, eternal honor, to brave and free peoples because they so fascinate the gaze of posterity" (p. 65). Rome in the days of the Republic, the site of "great actions" (p. 65), serves as a model for the future of Italian government (implicitly) beyond the tyranny of Napoleon.

In honor of Madame de Staël (certainly brave and ever seeking to be free), and the fascination she represented to "the gaze of posterity," Shelley takes her Florentine heroine Euthanasia on a youthful voyage to Rome which she describes in language that both intensifies and complicates her predecessor's historical narrative by celebrating the power of historical memory and yet acknowledging her own sense of limitation in relation to that power. Euthanasia's experience of the Pantheon by moonlight provokes a response of Staëlean "wild enthusiasm," rising to a pitch of "mute ecstasy" that allegorizes the nineteenth-century woman artist's spiritualized and ambivalent relation to historical agency. This experience of the historical sublime – as Euthanasia describes it, combining "the universal graspings of my own mind" and "the sure tokens of other spiritual existences" (p. 150) – suggests at first a failed sublime in that its expression seems to presuppose dissolution of the individual self when she imagines her own death as a consequence of expressing this "overwhelming ecstacy" (p. 150). Yet Euthanasia concludes her meditations on this epiphany by depicting her retrospective vision of Rome as "a burning cloud of sunset in the deep azure of the sky," a time "on which my intellectual eye rests with emotion, pleasurable now" (p. 151). The sense of inadequacy and failure disappears into the eloquent calm of this memorable description of the historical reality and contemporaneous presence of the spirits of the dead.

Furthermore, surviving the harrowing trials to which she is subjected throughout the novel with her dignity and integrity intact, Euthanasia does indeed gain the maturity and presence of mind that enable her to achieve the seemingly elusive goals stated above. In communicating her parable of the cave to Beatrice, with its mapping out of realms of female subjectivity, of "content of mind," she does clearly achieve the goals she sets for herself in her Roman meditations: disclosing "the secret operations" of the soul at work within her and "lay[ing] bare the vitals of [her own] being" (p. 151). Finally, when Euthanasia drowns on her journey of exile to Sicily, and she is depicted as asleep in "the oozy cavern of the ocean" (p. 438), we are encouraged to believe that she does not die, but lives on in a manner analogous to those historical entities who visited her in her moonlit experience of the Pantheon. Her posthumous existence, then, is dramatically different from that of Castruccio, her former betrothed, who has defeated her militarily and sent her into this fatal exile, for the epitaph on his tombstone reads, "I live and shall live, by the fame of my deeds, [and] the glory of Italian soldiery" (n60, pp. 467–8). Ultimately, I will argue that Mary Shelley, in a sense, resuscitates her heroine when she begins her subsequent novel, *The Last Man* (1826), with a preface that depicts a journey by its author-editor to such an underwater sea cave holding the kind of wisdom and beauty embodied in Euthanasia in the lost sibylline leaves of centuries of female writers so that they can be made accessible to collective consciousness. The Orphic efforts of future women writers, after the fashion of de Certeau's definition of the historian, will prevent this Euthanasia-Eurydice from being "forever trapped and lost" in her underworld cavern, as are the heroines of Hirsch's female *Bildungsromane*. Furthermore, Shelley herself sustained this progressive effort in her later historiographical contributions to Dionysius Lardner's *Cabinet Cyclopedia* in biographical essays devoted to such prominent women as Staël and Madame Roland. As Greg Kucich has argued, given the enormous popularity of Lardner's volumes, this "form of feminist historiography" constituted "one of the most potentially influential contributions she could ever make to the gender reform movements of her time."[28]

Similarly, *Die Günderode* offers clear examples of feminist historiographical theory and practice as Arnim resuscitates Karoline von Günderode through the inclusion of her writings in their fictionalized correspondence and rescues her from the cultural abandonment to which she had been doomed as an author since her suicide in 1806. This lyrical novel features numerous explicit dialogues on academic, masculinist historiography that are highly critical of its positivist tendencies, its blind focus on wars and governmental strife, and its exclusion of women. Their sense of exclusion from heroic, public action impels the friends Karoline and Bettine to their mutual revolutionary and utopian project of "Weltumstürzen" (turning the world on its head), that culminates in a proposal for a new religion, a religion of female courage and activism termed a *Schwebe-Religion*. This religion of "floating" or "hovering" suggests a transcendent free flight with utopian political and spiritual function. Withdrawal into herself in her solitary visits to an isolated tower where she holds dialogues with the stars makes possible participation in this radical and utopian conversation for Bettine, a conversation first held with her friend Karoline and then later opened up to her mentor, the Jewish tutor Ephraim. Ultimately, Bettine's consciousness is dispersed, through the agency of her tutor, to generations of his students to come. The fictional Bettine's author realized this dream of historical influence in her key role as cultural heroine for young left Hegelians like Gutzkow and Börne and for generations of feminist scholars and activists down to the present day.

Consuelo is an explicitly historical novel set in the decades prior to the French Revolution of 1789. It provides the reader a panoramic view of European culture and politics during the pre-revolutionary era, a perspective that surveys the Venetian opera scene, the realms of protorevolutionary illuminism and occultism, and the courts of Frederick the Great and Maria Theresa. Its cast of characters includes, among many others, the historical figures of Haydn, Metastasio, Porpora, Voltaire, Cagliostro, Saint-Germain and Adam Weishaupt. Both *Consuelo* and *La Comtesse de Rudolstadt* turn on Orphic spiritual journeys by the heroine, the first, in a significant role reversal, bringing to light her entombed fiancé, Albert and the second illuminating the record of oppression and slaughter that has been European history. Similarly, in her remarkable contemporaneous work *Jean Ziska* (1843), devoted to the fifteenth-century Protestant insurrectionary and follower of Jean Huss, translator of Wycliffe and Lollardism into the Slavic world, Sand draws forceful analogies between the erasure of women's history and official Church silencing of heretical expression.

Jean Ziska offers a compelling theoretical framework for the idealist histories written by the Romantic novelists discussed here and deserves recognition as a major nineteenth-century treatise of feminist historiography. Sand opens her treatise with the rejection of all previous academic, official, and ecclesiastical histories regarding Ziska's heretical exploits, declaring that "nothing is more obscure or complicated than the certainty of past fact."[29] The history of religious conflict remains for Sand "a shadowy abyss" (p. 17), obscured and deformed by the interests of Church and State, by religious and temporal power. Yet Sand is no post-modernist. Rather, she is a child of the French Revolutions of 1789 and 1830, looking forward, we now know, to the Revolution of 1848 and the Paris Commune of 1871. Instead of asserting the relative, fragmentary, or discursive nature of historical reality, Sand advocates the search for what she cryptically terms "the ideal fact" (p. 15). Thus understanding of history must involve the determination of the moral causes of events as well as the augmentation of erudition with sentiment and divination.

We are never in doubt, from beginning to end of Sand's essay, that she is directing her words to her fellow women, whom she directly addresses, in a relaxed tone of intimacy and confidentiality. Reflecting the notorious ambivalence toward members of her own sex that has so vexed contemporary feminist commentators on her work, Sand nevertheless does find her way clear to a valorization of qualities she considers specifically feminine, the product of women's educational and social upbringing. She writes:

> Women, when I recall that it is for you that I write, I feel my heart more at ease, for I have never doubted that, despite your vices, your faults, your notorious laziness, your absurd coquetry, your frivolous puerility, there is not in you, something pure, enthusiastic, candid, great and generous, that men have lost or not yet attained.
>
> (pp. 18–19)

We are furthermore never in any doubt that Sand intends this treatise as an emancipatory rallying cry to encourage women's intellectual, political, and above all spiritual development. Nowhere is this clearer than in the following emphatic, direct address to her female readers, pitting them unequivocally against the oppressive authority of the Catholic Church: "You are all daughters of heresy, you are all heretics, everyone of you protests in your heart, everyone of you protests in vain" (p. 19). Sand provides here a historical framework for understanding the prominence of the figure of the witch in the tradition under discussion here. The history of women, then, becomes the history of heresy, as Sand proclaims all women heretics, rendered paupers by the laws of marriage and the family, and by necessity disciples of John the Baptist and Saint Francis, as well as other great "apostles of the ideal" (p. 19).

Sand defines an idealism here, as Naomi Schor has argued, that is "a politics as much as an aesthetics," and that compels our rethinking of the term as "a way of reclaiming its utopian dimension, the ability of an ideal to empower and to mobilize the disenfranchised" (p. 14). But how exactly does Sand define the oxymoronic concept of "the ideal fact" upon which she seeks to base future histories? For Sand, this truth is the fundamentally life-affirming constitution of a divinely created humanity that acts, through Providence and despite all appearances, in the name of truth and justice. Examining the relation of these women writers to canonical Romanticism will help us understand the nature and historical function of these feminist ideals.

The crucial focus in each of these novels on the dissolution of the individual artist into future collective historical and spiritual effort defines these authors' relation to canonical, masculine Romanticism as well as to the French Revolution without which Romanticism cannot be conceived. I am using the treacherous term Romanticism in this book to mean the late eighteenth- and early nineteenth-century European cultural movement defined by a historicization of aesthetic standards and represented, in theoretical terms, most clearly by Schiller's *Naïve and Sentimental Poetry* (1795) and Staël's *On Literature* (1800) and *On Germany* (1810). The first two works were written directly in response to the French Revolution as were Schiller's *Aesthetic Letters*. At least since Sainte-Beuve, scholars have conceived of *On Literature* as a kind of prospectus for Romanticism.[30] Staël's later *On Germany* was, of course, a protest against Napoleonic empire and despotism that took the form of a celebration of German Romantic art and philosophy.

As Hans Robert Jauß has shown, *Naïve and Sentimental Poetry* moves beyond the sterile impasse of the *querelle des anciens et des modernes* through the development of a philosophy of history that renders that debate in a sense irrelevant by emphasizing the inevitability of cultural change and suggesting the affinities of a work of art for the era in which it originated.[31] Informed by Montesquieu's *The Spirit of Laws* (1748) and influenced by Schiller, *On Literature* is an even more explicitly historicist sociology of literature that clearly states its aim as the study of literature in relation to specific political and religious institutions, cultural mores, and nationalities.[32] The opposition naïve/sentimental in Schiller corresponds to the distinction between ancient and modern, nature and culture, sense and spirit, Homer and Goethe's *Werther* that in *On Literature* becomes the opposition South/North, Pagan/Christian, *joie de vivre/mélancolie*. The central role of Goethe's *Sorrows of Young Werther* (1774) in each of these taxonomies serves to highlight their striking similarities. For Schiller, the character Werther embodies the sentimental idealist to perfection as he is created by the naïve realist Goethe; for Staël, the novel *Werther* represents the highest achievement of Northern literature, in its sublime portrait of "self-reflecting passion" and its "truthful portrayal of the aberrations of enthusiasm" (p. 183). The deep connection of continental Romanticism to English literature becomes evident as well when we remember that Goethe, in *Dichtung und Wahrheit* (1814), characterizes that notorious novel as written in response to the melancholy English poetry of Young, Gray, and Goldsmith, and of course Ossian/MacPherson.

Influenced by his brother Friedrich's conception of the romantic in his *Athenaeum Fragments* (1798) and *Dialogue on Poetry* (1799), Staël's friend August Wilhelm Schlegel then labeled this pairing of naïve/sentimental, South/North as "*Klassik/Romantik*" and canonized that opposition in his influential *Lectures on Drama* given in 1808 and first published in 1809. It is A.W. Schlegel's lectures as well as Staël's version of German culture, mediated, publicized, and politicized through her acclaimed and notorious *On Germany*, that define the term Romantic as it is reiterated in various forms in later important theoretical works of French and German Romanticism: Stendhal's *Racine and Shakespeare* (1823), Hugo's *Preface to Cromwell* (1827), Baudelaire's *Salon of 1846*, Heine's early and appreciative essay "Die Romantik" (1820), and his later hostile polemic *The Romantic School* (1832–3). Even though the work of Schiller and Schlegel strongly influenced the literary historical writings of Coleridge, and Shelley's *Defence of Poetry* borrows significantly from Staël, neither critic chose the term "romantic" to define contemporary art.[33] One must turn to Germany and France for emphasis upon the word "romantic" simultaneous with the literary development now given that name and for extended theorizing of that "movement" by its contemporaries – a sign, perhaps, of that English resistance to theory that David Simpson has so convincingly delineated in *Romanticism, Nationalism, and the Revolt Against Theory*.[34]

For the purposes of my discussion of women writers of Romanticism and historiography, what is crucial in this definition of the movement by its *own* members is the repeated emphasis upon historical development or telos as infinite striving, a movement away from concrete, objective, sensuous representation toward the ideal, ineffable, and sublime. The disappointments of the French Revolution, then, clearly necessitate some form of transcendentalizing of the familiar Enlightenment narrative of progress in both male and female writers. In Schiller, this means the inevitable privileging of the sentimental and modern over the naïve and ancient, despite his repeated efforts to reject comparisons of these incommensurable kinds of art. The naïve, a product of a closeness to nature, "obtains its value by the absolute achievement of a finite," the sentimental, born of reflection and withdrawal into the self, "by approximation to an infinite greatness," the naïve by "absolute representation," the sentimental by "representation of an absolute."[35] For Schiller, the superiority of the sentimental is inseparable from the notion of progress, though that teleological aim is abstracted from any clear political or social goal: "Insofar as the ultimate object of mankind is not otherwise to be attained than by that progress ... there cannot therefore be any question to which of the two the advantage accrues with reference to the ultimate object" (p. 113). Indeed, for Schiller, the appeal of the sentimental or the sublime is its ineffability which is that of the infinitely receding horizon. With Baudelaire's *Salon of 1846*, the terms of the distinction between naïve and sentimental, now labeled classic and romantic, have changed but little despite their translation into French and the passage of 50 years: "Whoever says romanticism says modern art – that is intimacy, spirituality, color, aspiration toward the infinite."[36] Famously, the divided modern self for Schiller produces a melancholy longing, like "the feeling of an invalid for health" (p. 105) or analogous to the adult Wordsworthian consciousness of the innocence and "glad animal movements" of childhood, forever out of reach. Half a century later, Baudelaire labels this wounded self, now Christianized, Romantic: "Romanticism is a kind of grace, celestial or infernal, to which we owe eternal stigmata" (p. 22).

I emphasize the stability of this contemporaneous conception of Romanticism in order to demonstrate the existence of a clearly articulated idea of this cultural movement within which and/or against which women writers positioned themselves. Each chapter of this book takes as its focus the proto-feminist critique performed by a woman writer of Romanticism on a crucial paradigm of that literary movement and its obsession with the relation of history to infinite striving and perpetual dissatisfaction: first, Romantic melancholy or the *mal du siècle*, Schiller's longing of the sick for the healthy, the sentimental for the naïve; second, the Promethean, Byronic, infinitely striving hero whose quest risks, again according to Schiller, "an infinite fall into a bottomless abyss" (p. 190) and, finally, the telos of Romantic *Bildung* (i.e. the transcendentalized narrative of Enlightenment perfectibility). In Chapter 1, Germaine de Staël's *Corinne* challenges an entropic Romantic melancholy with the life-affirming concept of enthusiasm. Staël's *On Literature*, in contrast to Schiller's elegiac melancholy and Baudelaire's splenetic pessimism, emphasizes the millennial, seemingly interminable quality of historical process in order to hold out hope for the fulfillment of specific political ideals promulgated by the French Revolution and betrayed by its current practitioners. Historical process, rather than merely embodying the infinitely receding horizon of the unapproachable ideal, becomes a rich field of social endeavor and political praxis. Its generous, indeed infinite, vistas are not merely mirages; rather they hold out the possibility that progressive, even utopian, goals may indeed be realized.

Staël's faith in the future is vindicated in the recent resurgence of scholarly interest in Staël and in particular the growing appreciation of her gifts as a historian after more than a century of what Claire Gaspard has termed the "great silence" of nineteenth-century historians on Staël's vital role as witness and recorder of the French Revolution and the Napoleonic empire.[37] This faith also sustains Staël in times of deep sadness, moments when she is compelled to acknowledge that she labors not for her disappointing contemporaries but for elusive and anonymous descendants, "strangers very far from us, unknown to us, men whose image and memory cannot be drawn in our minds" (p. 174). Despite this sadness, the Conclusion of *On Literature* affirms her commitment to the enactment of revolutionary goals, a process that will take not decades, but centuries: "When one accuses philosophy of the crimes of the revolution, one attaches shameful actions to great thoughts, the judgment of which is still pending in the face of future centuries" (p. 420; my translation). *Corinne* stages the conflict between the conservative disillusionment and melancholy embodied in the Scottish Lord Nelville and Corinne's enthusiasm, an aestheticized and spiritualized translation of her Enlightenment faith as expressed in *On Literature*. And if Corinne herself is ultimately vanquished by the cultural prestige of Romantic melancholy, Staël intimates that her author and future readers will not be. Jean-François Lyotard's compelling meditation, in "The Sign of History," on enthusiasm as a political force still vital today suggests that Staël was right.[38]

Similarly, in Chapter 2, Mary Shelley's *Valperga* counters the destructive potentialities of the self-obsessed Promethean and Byronic hero with a heroine who embodies a dispassionate and impersonal meditative consciousness that Shelley deems a prerequisite for effective and progressive political praxis. In essence, Shelley both affirms and questions the paradigm of Enlightenment perfectibility celebrated in *On Literature*, emphasizing that without introspection and vigilant self-knowledge, no beneficial political or social action is possible. Shelley's subsequent novel, the autobiographical *The Last Man*, exposes the will to power behind the dialectic of Enlightenment and underlines Shelley's praise for meditative consciousness as it is embodied in the heroine of the earlier novel in a particularly succinct fashion. Through the vehicle of the novel's first person narrator, her alter ego Lionel Verney, Shelley depicts the Byronic Raymond, who, in his quest for power and world domination, ultimately unleashes a plague that destroys the entire human race: "Thus, while Raymond had been wrapt in visions of power and fame, while he looked forward to entire dominion over the elements and the mind of man, the territory of his own heart escaped his notice; and from that unthought of source arose the mighty torrent that overwhelmed his will, and carried to the oblivious sea, fame, hope and happiness."[39] The Promethean will to power of *Valperga*'s Castruccio acquires metaphysical, cataclysmic dimensions in *The Last Man*, revealing this conflict to be a lifelong preoccupation for Shelley and taking this tension between psychic and spiritual awareness and reckless political action to an apocalyptic extreme.

If *Corinne* (1807) challenges the moral and aesthetic authority of Romantic melancholy with the emancipatory potential of poetic enthusiasm, and *Valperga* (1823) attacks Napoleonic/Byronic self-will with self-knowledge and self-respect, Bettine von Arnim offers a critique of the unconsciously masculinist and hierarchical concepts of history and *Bildung* developed by Kant, Schiller, Goethe, and the German Romantics, as I demonstrate in Chapter 3. *Die Günderode* (1840) questions the driven, teleological and potentially oppressive nature of Romantic *Bildung* as represented by Kant, Schiller, and Goethe with a critique that prefigures Horkheimer and Adorno's *Dialectic of Enlightenment*. Her female philosophers envisage a new religion of female freedom and courage termed, as previously mentioned, a *Schwebe-Religion*, a floating or hovering faith that precludes domination and oppression by its rejection of fixity and clear social position. By choosing women, Jews, and other disenfranchised members of nineteenth-century German society as exemplary embodiments of self-realization and enlightenment, *Die Günderode* takes the concept of *Bildung* out of the realm of theory and demands that it be put into praxis, thus radically transforming it into a utopian effort to create a society in which there would be no need or desire for female suicide.

In Chapter 4, George Sand's monumental masterpiece, *Consuelo*, and its sequel *La Comtesse de Rudolstadt*, written and published serially from 1842 to 1844, constitute a kind of compendium of the questions raised by my study as a whole concerning the relation of the woman writer to canonical Romanticism. Sand's *Consuelo*, as ideal artist, is set against the backdrop of her critique of previous models of Romantic genius, both female and male: the abandoned woman based upon Corinne, the Promethean titan, and the self-absorbed and self-destructive melancholiac. In the Venetian chapters that open the novel, when Consuelo herself is betrayed by her fiancé Anzoleto, Consuelo chooses the free and independent life of the artist rather than indulging in a self-destructive performance of the role of the abandoned woman.

In the Bohemian chapters of *Consuelo*, Sand represents Albert, Count Rudolstadt as an other-worldly musician and violinist modeled on Frederic Chopin and the Polish nationalist poet Adam Mickiewicz as an embodiment of Romantic melancholy. Sand furthermore offers a socio-political diagnosis of this *mal du siècle*, revealing it to be caused in Albert's case by his guilt over bloody campaigns he waged in his previous incarnation as Jean Ziska, Protestant heretic and Slavic insurrectionary against German and Papal conquerors. In essence, through the metaphor of metempsychosis and her explorations of the multiple incarnations of Albert, Sand reveals Romantic melancholy to be rooted in guilt occasioned by the French Revolution which in turn is inseparable from Romantic glorification of the titanic individual. In place of these models of Romantic genius, Sand concludes her novel with a vision of the artist that incorporates socialist and proto-feminist elements of the early nineteenth-century utopian movements of Saint-Simon, Fourier, Enfantin, and Leroux. With her husband Albert, Consuelo wanders anonymously as a gypsy artist, an artist ministering to the people, helping them to create the profound and revolutionary change to come. Consuelo thus demonstrates most clearly the explicitly historical and activist role given by Sand to *Bildung* and to its ultimate aim of spiritual enlightenment or transcendence. The revolutionary potential accorded Corinne by Germaine de Staël is finally vindicated by, and realized in, her descendant Consuelo.

As the female *Künstlerroman* or *Künstlernovelle* moves into the twentieth century, it experiences a subtle shift away from history toward myth, away from open partisan political engagement toward ever more complex explorations of female subjectivity. The conflicted relationship to enlightenment teleologies of progress so evident in Staël, Shelley, Arnim, and Sand is resolved in favor of participation in post-Nietzschean mythic narratives that celebrate pantheistic or anarchic ideals rather than privileging progress and perfectibility. Thus the oppositional nature of women modernists' meditations on female creativity lies in their exploration of a free-floating, multivalent creative and spiritual self, already prefigured in the novels of women writers of Romanticism. For modernist women writers, however, this self is dissolved into labyrinthine genealogies and mythic cycles rather than historical effort, the distinction between these categories, of course, being not always easy to maintain. These meditations on female subjectivity reach a kind of climax of clarity and intensity in the theoretical speculations of early twentieth-century writers like Gertrude Stein, Virginia Woolf, and Isak Dinesen. My Epilogue, then, explores Isak Dinesen's creative manifesto from *Seven Gothic Tales* (1934), *The Dreamers*, whose central character the prima donna Pellegrina Leoni, clearly an avatar of Corinne and Consuelo, exemplifies female transcendence illuminated by a modernist sensibility, as the melodramatic and tragic Staëlean heroine takes flight into the lightness and delicacy of Dinesen's tragi-comedy.

1 "The vast tableau of destinies"

Germaine de Staël's *Corinne*, enthusiasm, and melancholy

> What can the ethics of an intellectual be, if not this: to make oneself permanently capable of detaching oneself from oneself?
>
> Michel Foucault

> No Sibyls have existed like those of Michel Angelo; those of Raphael are the true brides of a God, but not themselves divine. It is easy for women to be heroic in action, but when it comes to interrogating God, the universe, the soul and, above all, trying to live above their own hearts, they dart down to their nests like so many larks, and if they cannot find them, fret like the French Corinne.[1]
>
> Margaret Fuller

Such is the judgment of Margaret Fuller on the sibylline heroine of Germaine de Staël's novel *Corinne, or Italy* (1807). Herself termed a Yankee Corinna by her contemporaries, Fuller nevertheless saw Corinne, and by extension her creator, as incapable of true philosophic introspection and courage, as out of her element in elevated thought and imprisoned by emotional worries and expectations of domesticity. Though in *Woman in the Nineteenth Century*, Fuller writes vividly and beautifully of the beams of Staël's intellect rendering "the obscurest school-house in New England warmer and lighter to the little rugged girls who are gathered together on its wooden bench,"[2] she also cannot help charging Staël with excessive emotionalism and vanity. Now imagining the author as an eagle, Fuller writes: "She could not forget the Woman in the thought; while she was instructing you as a mind, she wished to be admired as a Woman; sentimental tears often dimmed the eagle glance" (p. 94). Staël, Fuller suggests with her bird metaphors, is incapable of the wisdom gained from the sustained flight of philosophic meditation because she cannot live "above [her] own heart" or above her socially defined identity as a woman.

Similarly, Mary Shelley in her chapter on Staël for the Cabinet Cyclopaedia's *Eminent Literary and Scientific Men of France* (1839), expresses her disappointment in Staël's second novel, though she does describe it as possessing a "charm ... that stamps it as coming from the hand of genius."[3] In conclusion, however, Shelley, like Fuller, charges Staël with a lack of self-control and fortitude in creating a heroine who dies as a consequence of her sorrow over betrayal in love:

> The authoress ... might wish to impress on men an idea of the misery which their falsehood produces. ... For the dignity of womanhood, it were better to teach how one, as highly gifted as Corinne, could find resignation or fortitude enough to endure a too common lot, and rise wiser and better from the trial.
>
> (p. 332)

As a writer and as a novelist in particular, Germaine de Staël has suffered harsh criticism.[4] The decline in Staël's reputation since her death in 1817 and the inability of critics to separate the author from her heroines have been well documented as an example of contravention and male bias in scholarly criticism by Madelyn Gutwirth (1978) in *Germaine de Staël, Novelist: The Emergence of the Artist as Woman*.[5] In complete agreement with Gutwirth's assessment of the history of Staëlean criticism, I must nevertheless also ask why it is that women writers such as Fuller and Shelley, sympathetic to the cause of women's rights and freedoms, have felt compelled to join the chorus of voices so critical of Germaine de Staël. Clearly George Eliot's Maggie Tulliver is not the only strong woman who has felt like putting *Corinne* down for good with the entrance of Lucile, the heroine's blonde angelic half-sister who will inevitably become the wife of Corinne's beloved.

It is as if Staël gives us a woman of genius in Corinne, certainly one of the first such heroines in European literature, and then takes that gift away, revealing that Corinne is no genius after all but only a self-indulgent, vengeful, and excessively emotional woman, little more than a stereotype, unable to endure what Mary Shelley tersely terms "a too common lot," the loss of her unfaithful lover.[6] Certainly, as Shelley suggests, Staël was seeking to impress upon men – upon Benjamin Constant and Prosper de Barante in particular – the unhappiness caused by their faithlessness.

Yet if one moves beyond the biographical origins of *Corinne*, as one *must* to be fair to its author, the novel becomes first and foremost a study in conflict between the seemingly unlimited potentialities of female genius and the psychosocial environment that works relentlessly to thwart and defeat it. As Gutwirth writes:

> [Germaine de Staël] sought to move woman via the immanent to the transcendent realm and to lay claim to a place for her there. This was a very fragile enterprise, for it challenged every notion of woman's nature and her place. ... Here is a statement that says, "Woman possesses genius." It is for this unspeakable pretension that posterity has never forgiven *Corinne*.
>
> (p. 301)

And it is for holding out this hope and then seeming to destroy it in the self-willed demise of its heroine that future women novelists have also found it hard to forgive Staël. Yet from a contemporary feminist perspective Staël's refusal to "forget the Woman in the thought," as Fuller put it, is perhaps not a weakness but a sign of honesty and strength, for she does not seek to mask women's struggles under a false veil of universal humanity somehow beyond sex and gender. If Germaine de Staël does indeed depict women as capable of genius and of transcendence, what does she mean by these terms? And how does she conceptualize female creativity, "a womanly model of transcendence" (p. 310), as Gutwirth puts it, and the relation of this gift to the patriarchal society that thwarts it? Such questions are essential to an understanding of Staël's Romanticism and her strong influence on future generations of women writers. Contemporary feminist criticism is thus compelled to ask with Nancy K. Miller whether Maggie Tulliver was indeed justified in refusing to finish Staël's *Corinne*.[7]

This chapter seeks to elucidate the significance – political, ethical, aesthetic, and spiritual – of Staël's model of female genius and its potentially transformative role in nineteenth-century European history. In order to demonstrate the central importance of Staël's philosophy of transcendence to her work as a whole, I first trace the development of this philosophy as represented by the concept of enthusiasm in her non-fiction writings throughout her entire literary career. While Staël's early writings depict women as mired in vanity and emotionality and thus incapable of the sustained detachment from self that for her constitutes genius and enthusiasm, Staël eventually comes to see women as quintessential figures of self-doubling or transcendence, of self-possession as opposed to self-absorption. Furthermore, melancholy, for Staël, clearly constitutes a political response to the thwarting of French Revolutionary ideals, a defeatist response that she counters with a vision of perfectibility linked to the historical role of (female) genius and enthusiasm. The heroine of *Corinne*, set in opposition to the melancholy Oswald, then, incarnates this enthusiasm, its vulnerability as well as its emancipatory potential in post-revolutionary, Napoleonic Europe. Finally, Corinne's demise at the conclusion of the novel represents her seduction by Oswald's melancholy and morbid self-preoccupation, an affective state which functions for Staël as a synecdoche for patriarchal values and cultural traditions.

Transcendence: enthusiasm, self-possession, and pleasurable abstraction

If one examines Staël's oeuvre in its entirety, it becomes clear that, in her non-fiction works, the conceptions of transcendence, selfhood, and creativity remain consistent throughout her life. In no sense is her vision of genius or wisdom a vision of uninhibited emotionality and expression of feeling as unsympathetic critics like René Wellek have suggested. Rather, from *The Influence of the Passions on the Happiness of Individuals and Nations* (1796) and *On Literature Considered in its Relationship to Social Institutions* (1800) to *On Germany* (1810) and *Reflections on Suicide* (1813), Staël advocates a detached, impersonal perspective as the essence of aesthetic form and philosophic wisdom.[8] She terms this state of mind enthusiasm, and, especially in her later works, it holds all the connotations of inspiriting divinity and doubling of self that the word etymologically implies. Her chapters on enthusiasm in *On Germany*, for example, define it, in opposition to fanaticism, as tolerance, openness, and philosophic calm. Clearly aware of the predominantly negative connotations of the English use of the term in its association with excess of religious zeal, Staël pointedly gives the term a purely positive valence. From the beginning, Staël's meditations on enthusiasm are political in origin. Just as in the English context, as Jon Mee has shown, enthusiasm is closely associated with the Protestant sectarians of the Civil Wars, so in Staël's France it cannot be separated from support for the French Revolution.[9] *The Influence of the Passions* is Staël's response to that cataclysmic eruption of violent emotion into the French Revolution, the Reign of Terror, as well as her attempt to hold fast to the Revolution's ideals while condemning its bloody excesses:

> [The reader] should be able to imagine that enthusiasm for certain ideas is not mutually exclusive with contempt for certain men, and that hope for the future may be reconciled with hatred for the past. Then, even though the heart is forever torn by its wounds, the mind can still, after a while, rise to general meditations.
>
> (p. 152)

Intellectual detachment, described metaphorically as a kind of spiritual elevation, is figured as balm to the eternally open wound to the heart inflicted by the Revolution's betrayal of its ideals. Here Staël describes two states of mind – enthusiasm and a painful sense of wounding, later termed melancholy – that will remain concepts central to her ethical, aesthetic, and religious thought throughout her entire life.[10] Indeed *Corinne* will represent this conflict between melancholy and enthusiasm as an historical allegory for the contest over the political fate of post-Revolutionary, Napoleonic Europe. Seeking to "disengage [her mind] from every momentary impression" (p. 153), Staël states her thesis clearly and succinctly in her essay on the passions, once again stressing that her point is political as well as psychological: "The real obstacle to individual and political happiness is the impulsive force of the passions, sweeping man away quite independently of his own will" (p. 153). The answer to the suffering of "passionate souls" is philosophical detachment achieved through moral courage, intellectual discipline, and profound meditation, for our thoughts are the only events we can truly control: "We must place ourselves above ourselves in order to control ourselves, and above others in order to expect nothing of them" (p. 165). Clearly and explicitly she distinguishes self-control from any effort to dominate or control others.

   Staël is not advocating insensitivity to or a numbing repression of pain and feeling. Rather, she suggests focusing a clear and self-conscious eye on one's passions and desires, thus acknowledging their power and then, through an act of will, freeing oneself from them. "In a kind of pleasurable abstraction, we rise some distance above ourselves, watching ourselves think and live. . . . We are now placing ourselves in relation to our own consciousness, instead of to fate" (p. 168).

Transcendence of passions and of the desire to control others brings about a self-possession and independence of mind that is not egoism but rather selflessness, for through detachment, we begin to see ourselves as part of a larger whole, to witness "the intention of nature" and take part in "the calm of the order of the universe" (p. 167). For Staël, then, freedom, not self-abnegation, is the ultimate aim of philosophy:

> The self-possession acquired through meditation offers a satisfaction which is completely different from the pleasures of the man interested in his own personal self. The selfish man needs other people; he is demanding; he suffers every wound impatiently; he is dominated by his egoism, and if that feeling were capable of energy it would bear all the characteristic marks of a great passion; but the happiness a philosopher finds in self-possession is the feeling that gives real independence.
>
> (p. 168)

Furthermore, instead of railing against fate we accept it, taking pleasure in the change and chance that is life itself, developing the capacity of philosophic flight, letting one's life "drift at the will of the wind":

> What would really lead us to think of life as a voyage is that there never seems to be any preordained place to rest. Just try to fix your life to the absolute power of one idea or one feeling – it all turns into obstacles or misfortunes at every step. ... When the events of our lives are not heralded by burning desires or followed by bitter regrets, we are able to find enough happiness in the isolated pleasures aimlessly distributed by chance.
>
> (p. 166)

In *Corinne*, rejection of the "absolute power" of one idea or feeling will come to serve as a program for political and socio-cultural liberation as well.

Ultimately, for Staël, the true disposition of the human heart, the truest human feeling, is the sweet or pleasant calm that results from the effort to view individual human destiny, lost in collectivity, first in the light of historical process and ultimately through the mysterious eyes of infinity. Summarizing her *Influence of the Passions*, she writes, "I tried to discover whether the painful sharpness of personal experience was not blunted a little if we placed ourselves in the vast tableau of destinies, where everyone is lost in his century, the century lost in time, and time lost in the incomprehensible" (p. 170). The idea of a tableau suggests a picture and the presence of order and design, even if the design is not evident to the individual human spectator. Historical perfectibility and spiritual liberation are, for Staël, inseparable.[11]

Almost 15 years after her work on the passions, in *On Germany* Staël expands her idea of philosophical detachment and vague melancholy into the concept of enthusiasm in order to accommodate her increasingly spiritual worldview and to elucidate her understanding that religious and aesthetic emotion is sublimated personal passion. The chapters on enthusiasm, the concluding chapters of *On Germany*, significantly ranked by Mary Shelley as the finest of Staël's writings, are, as Staël herself asserts, the résumé of the entire work.[12] For Staël, the capacity for enthusiasm means battling self-interest and egoism in order to open oneself to the eternal and the divine.[13] The chapter entitled "The Influence of Enthusiasm on the Enlightenment" demonstrates the manner in which Enlightenment and Romantic thought dovetail in Staël's mind and clarify her role as an intermediary between eighteenth- and nineteenth-century worldviews.[14] "Enthusiasm lends life to invisible things, and interest to things without immediate bearing on our worldly prosperity" (p. 321); it means love of knowledge in and for itself, tolerance in place of fanaticism. Rather than leading to error, as empiricists would suggest, enthusiasm gives us wings and arouses us to reach "to the heart of things," for "we come across the truth only when our souls are elevated" (p. 322). Thus, as in her treatise on passion, Staël again asserts the necessity of striving for a bird's-eye perspective and eloquently elucidates the concept of a sublime that is anything but egotistical: "Physical nature follows its unvarying course through the destruction of individuals; man's thought becomes sublime when he succeeds in thinking of himself from a universal point of view. He then quietly contributes to the triumph of truth" (p. 322). Transmutation of personal suffering into spiritual understanding is the goal of both individual and collective human development. True to her enlightenment roots, Staël has no doubt of the ultimate triumph and progress of truth as the product of a proverbial, collective effort, though her proverb is displaced into ancient Mayan culture, perhaps to indicate the long journey necessary to European culture before it reaches this goal:

> Whatever the surrounding atmosphere, a sincere word is never completely lost; success may have its day, but there are centuries for the good that can be done by truth.
>   Each of the inhabitants of Mexico carries a little stone along the main highway to add to the great pyramid they are building in the middle of their country. It will bear no one's name, but every one of them will have contributed to a monument that will last longer than them all.
>
> (p. 324)

Finally, in *Reflections on Suicide* (1813), Staël reiterates her assertion that social ambition encourages humanity to attach "too much importance to the chain of circumstances of which his individual history is composed."[15] In place of personal striving and ambition she advises, as a means of cultivating happiness, the power of contemplation: "We are so bounded in ourselves, so many circumstances agitate and wound us, that we have incessant need for plunging into that ocean of boundless thought, which like the Styx may render us if not invulnerable, at least resigned" (p. 33).

Staël rejects suicide as the consequence of self-indulgent passion and as repugnant to the spirit of "true enthusiasm" and in its place recommends a delicate balance of self-will and resignation as a response to life's adversity which she poignantly describes as a long shipwreck, from which fragments of friendship, fame, and love wash up on the shore (p. 33). Furthermore, the woman who battled Napoleonic tyranny her entire adult life cannot emphasize strongly enough that "we cannot confound resignation to the will of God, with condescension to the power of man" (p. 69) and that acceptance of divine will is not to be equated with acceptance of political oppression. She draws a firm line between the heroic martyrdom of a Socrates or a Thomas More and the suicide born of frustrated passion or despair. For Staël, spiritual and political progress go hand in hand. This distinction between suicide as political protest and suicide born of frustrated passion is inevitably a gendered one, since Staël claims that "there is one cause of suicide which interests almost every human heart, and this is love" (p. 20). As we will see later, *Corinne* collapses this distinction in a highly problematical fashion, as suicide becomes both an act of passion and a political statement.

Accordingly, and with intriguing consequences for an understanding of her novelistic plots, she refines her concept, developed in her earlier writings, of destiny or Providence as a spiritual teacher; indeed in *Reflections on Suicide* fate takes the form of a proto-Freudian repetition compulsion and mirror of the psyche:

> So far ... from being blind, fortune appears to make us the objects of her penetrating scrutiny, and seldom fails to attack us in that weakness where we are most susceptible. In her we find the secret tribunal, to whose sentence we must submit without appeal. Yet, if its decisions should appear unjust, we perhaps, and we only, are conscious what truths they intimate, or what lessons they prescribe.
>
> (p. 15)

Only by taking "large and comprehensive views" (p. 14), by distancing ourselves from our trials and sufferings so that we begin to see a pattern in them, will we be able to learn the lessons that Providence is trying to teach us, so that suffering becomes a salutary moral process of amelioration and our characters are refined and perfected by the test. Thus, in contrast to Freud's *Beyond the Pleasure Principle* (1920), the repetition compulsion does not inevitably lead to regression and death, but can instead lead to change and growth for the individual psyche and to historical progress for the collective.

"Living outside oneself": toward a feminist model of transcendence

If Staël's moral and aesthetic ideal of philosophical detachment and transcendent vision effected by self-conscious doubling of the self remains relatively clear and consistent throughout her life, her representation of woman's relation to this ideal is much more troubled and complex. I discuss the history of the development of Staël's conception of female genius and transcendence in detail because this history provides an exemplary record of the obstacles facing a nineteenth-century woman artist at the same time that it elaborates possible philosophical and proto-feminist means for surmounting those barriers. Thus, the importance of her aesthetic theory for an understanding of nineteenth-century concepts of female genius cannot be overemphasized.

Staël herself is the first to acknowledge her own limitations in relation to her philosophy of transcendence. Thus she concludes *The Influence of the Passions* with a naïve admission of, and an apology for, her own difficulties in applying her philosophy in her own life: "I am not sure I succeeded in this first attempt to try my doctrine out on myself. Am I the best person, then, to affirm its power?" (p. 170). Generations of literary critics have thought not. Furthermore, the novella *Zulma*, originally intended for *The Influence of the Passions* as the chapter on love, is a kind of apology for a crime of jealous and possessive passion committed by a woman who murders her faithless lover. Clearly at this time in her life, Staël's analytical work seeks transcendence of emotion whereas her fiction explores to the limit the expression and consequences of passion.

The chapter "On Vanity" cuts to the heart of the problem. Here, a decade before *Corinne*, she formulates the tensions and conflicts central to the tragedy of that novel, though with the essential difference that in *Corinne* the narrative voice is sympathetic to the woman of genius whereas here the narrator speaks from the perspective of societal convention.[16] Prevented by "their destiny" – a word that for Staël means a mysterious combination of biology and metaphysical essence – from laying claim to power and glory, women are confined to ephemeral and insignificant triumphs that spring from vanity. "In women everything is either love or vanity" (p. 159), Staël writes, convinced that it is her task to guide women away from "the misfortune of taking themselves as the object of their own efforts" (p. 160) in order that they may devote themselves to love. They should not strive for the selflessness of heroic action or philosophic detachment; only through love will they achieve true transcendence of the limitations of egoism and individuality. Staël is clearly concerned for woman's happiness in a man's world, for she asserts that men, like Pygmalion, bow down only to their own work and do not want a superior, independent woman. "Chance provides a few exceptions; if there are souls carried away by their talent or their character, they may escape the common law – a few laurels may someday crown them. Even so, these women cannot escape the inevitable unhappiness which invariably clings to their destiny" (p. 160). Foreseeing her own future unhappiness and the tragedy of her character Corinne, she reiterates the clichés that imprison her rather than challenging them:

> A woman cannot exist by herself alone. Even glory does not give her enough support. The insurmountable weakness of her nature and her situation in the social order have placed her in a daily dependency from which even immortal genius would not be enough to rescue her. In any case, nothing eradicates the distinguishing characteristics of women's nature.
>
> (p. 160)

Her position here is radically essentialist. Great women like Sappho or Elizabeth I only prove her point, she claims, for Sappho committed suicide over unrequited love and Elizabeth "died a victim to her passion for the Earl of Essex" (p. 162). She concludes her discussion of women and their vain search for glory with a warning:

> Before women begin a glorious career, whether aimed at Caesar's throne or the crown of literary genius, they must realize that to gain this glory they have to renounce the happiness and peace of the destiny of their sex – and that in this career there are very few fates which are worth the most obscure life of a beloved wife and happy mother.
>
> (p. 162)

Thus "On Vanity" provides a disturbingly clear picture of Germaine de Staël's internalization of the most inhibiting sexual stereotypes of her day. She is clearly vulnerable to the power of men like her father who belittled her writing and made fun of her by nicknaming her "Monsieur de Saint-Écritoire" when she was seventeen and Napoleon who told her that the woman he most admired would be the one who had given birth to the largest number of children. "On Vanity" also provides the plot summary for *Corinne* – the female artist blessed with a "crown of literary genius," a blessing that becomes a curse in the realm of personal happiness.

Similarly in the chapter "On Women Writers" from *On Literature* written in 1800, four years after *The Influence of the Passions*, Staël speaks of the "dreadful destiny" (p. 206), the "torture of [the] useless superiority" (p. 205) of the woman "seduced by intellectual celebrity and insistent on achieving it!" (p. 205). Staël, who had sought the social spotlight ever since she was a precocious child in her mother's salon, is still ostensibly tormented by the notion that superiority in a woman is "out of line with the destiny of her sex" (p. 204) and that the public woman has ripped a veil of privacy from herself that she will ever after long for in vain. "Women feel there is something pure and delicate in their nature, quickly withered by the very gaze of the public. Wit, talent, passion in the soul may make them emerge from this mist which should always be surrounding them, but they will always yearn for it as their true refuge" (p. 207).[17]

In this essay, nevertheless, the balance has begun to tip away from emphasis on woman's essential nature and destiny to her place in a potentially changeable social reality: "Examine the social order ...; you will soon see it up in arms against any woman trying to raise herself to the height of masculine reputation" (p. 206). Increasingly aware of the calumny and mockery that has been the public response to her own relentless drive to express herself intellectually and artistically, Staël composes "On Women Writers" ostensibly as a plea for sympathy. More importantly it is also a clear if covert demand for emancipation of women through improvement of their educational opportunities along the lines of Mary Wollstonecraft's *Vindication of the Rights of Woman* (1792). Like Wollstonecraft, Staël, aware that her audience is largely male, designs her argument accordingly;

she argues that better educated women will make better mothers and more appealing and interesting wives, that more liberty for women would benefit society as a whole:

> If the situation in civil society is so imperfect, what we must work toward is the improvement of their lot, not the degradation of their minds. For women to pay attention to the development of mind and reason would promote both enlightenment and the happiness of society in general.
>
> (p. 205)

Staël's increased focus in this essay upon the societal restrictions that shape women's temperaments and limit their opportunities enables her to reach some startlingly modern conclusions about the anomalous, as she terms it, "uncertain" position of women in her time, particularly since the Revolution. Anticipating such twentieth-century feminist analyses as Elaine Showalter's "Feminist Criticism in the Wilderness," she asserts that European women belong neither to the realm of nature nor to the realm of culture: "At present ... most women belong neither to the natural nor to the social order" (p. 201).[18] Staël thus makes a pioneering contribution to what Teresa de Lauretis sees as the vital task of feminism still today: the "effort to create new spaces of discourse, to rewrite cultural narratives, and to define the terms of another perspective – a view from 'elsewhere.'"[19]

This outsider status becomes the source of an invaluable moral vision expressed and idealized in terms that prefigure Virginia Woolf's *Three Guineas* (1938) or Adrienne Rich's *Of Woman Born* (1986):

> [W]omen are the ones at the heart of everything relating to humanity, generosity, delicacy. Women are the only human beings outside the realm of political interest and the career of ambition, able to pour scorn on base actions, point out ingratitude, and honor even disgrace if that disgrace is caused by noble sentiments.
>
> (p. 204)

One must of course smile at this immensely powerful woman's assertion of her political ineffectuality; she would later be named, for example, by Mme de Chastenay, alongside Russia and England, as one of three major opponents to Bonaparte. In fact, Staël is already in 1800 becoming stronger in her sense of self and her sense of the worth of her sex. Woman is no longer simply the vain and ineffectual creature she was in "On Vanity." And the superior or "extraordinary" woman is doubly an outsider, a pariah, for "[s]he lacks both the sympathy inspired by a woman and the power protecting a man" (p. 208). Not only self-indulgent but also dissembling, this plea for sympathy suggests that Staël wishes to hide her own strength, her power, and her demand for social change behind a disarming assertion of her own vulnerability. More importantly, however, when Staël's emphasis upon the pain caused by the woman writer's status as societal pariah is placed alongside the chapter's epigraph, a clear picture of Staël's vision of woman's transcendence comes into view. The epigraph, taken from *The Indian Hut* (1790) by Bernardin de Saint-Pierre, reads as follows: "Unhappiness is like the black mountain of Bember, at the edge of the blazing kingdom of Lahor. As long as you are climbing it, you see nothing ahead of you but sterile rocks; but once you are at the peak, heaven is at your head, and at your feet the kingdom of Cashmere" (p. 201). The unhappiness and suffering which ostracization from and exclusion by conventional society cause the woman writer call forth and compel the detached and clear philosophic perspective which from beginning to end of her work Staël exalts as the highest moral and aesthetic value.

Finally, ten years later in the chapter devoted to women from *On Germany*, Staël extends this characterization to include all women whose destiny, "created by women's souls alone," is relatively "untouched by the influence of political circumstances" (p. 294). She has come 180 degrees from the judgments of "On Vanity" to a celebration of the uniqueness of female spirituality, a spirituality that is culturally constructed as much as it is an expression of women's bodies:

> Nature and society make women quite accustomed to suffering, and I think it is clear that most women today are better than men. In an age when the universal malady is egoism, men are necessarily less generous and sensitive than women: all practical interests relate to them. Women are related to life only by the ties of the heart; even when they go astray, they are misled by sentiment. Their personality is always double, whereas the only goal of men's personality is that personality itself.
>
> (p. 294)

This doubling of selfhood in women enables them the distance and detachment from personal identity – in the name not just of feelings but also of ideas and virtues – that for Staël is the essence of wisdom and understanding:

> The most beautiful virtue, devotion, is women's pleasure as well as their destiny: no happiness exists for them except through the reflected glory and reflected good fortune of someone else. In the end, living outside oneself – whether through ideas, feelings, or virtues – makes the soul accustomed to a sense of elevation.
>
> (p. 294)

Staël is of course making a virtue of necessity and glorifying the self-denial and self-sacrifice that have been imposed upon women since the origin of patriarchal society, seemingly even complicit in denying women (and her celebrated heroine Corinne in particular) the right to self-assertion and pride in their own accomplishments. Nevertheless she proceeds to a vehement attack on the sexual double standard in terms reminiscent of Wollstonecraft's *Vindication*, and she cleverly and perhaps also disingenuously describes her terms for accepting the exclusion of women from the public sphere, terms she must know will never be met:

> It is right to exclude women from political and civil affairs: anything that puts women in competition with men goes against their natural vocation. Fame itself is only a brilliant way to bury the happiness of a woman. However, if women's destiny is to be one continuous devotion to conjugal love, the reward for this devotion will have to be the scrupulous fidelity of any man who is the object of it.
>
> (p. 318)

Rather than justifying the oppression of women here, Staël is, I think, most importantly suggesting that the exclusion of women from positions of governmental and institutional power has enabled them to develop spiritual faculties that should in fact be emulated by all humankind, for the capacity to "live outside oneself" is, as we have seen, the quality she values most highly from beginning to end of her *oeuvre* as the ultimate spiritual goal of humanity. Staël is perhaps also suggesting that if her terms for women's exclusion from the public sphere are not met, women should refuse to accept such marginalization and instead infuse their own values into that public sphere, with potentially transformative, revolutionary consequences. Seen in this light, women's subjectivity becomes a model, with clear socio-political implications, for the future perfectibility of humankind, which, for Staël as enlightenment thinker, is the highest good.

Germaine de Staël, then, advocates an ethics and aesthetics of selflessness, a relinquishing of personality for openness to a collective or universal selfhood beyond the individual ego. As Jean Starobinski has suggested, Staël's recognition of the futility of the search for personal happiness and the fulfillment of passionate desire leads her in *Reflections on Suicide* to promulgate "moral suicide," renunciation of individuality, as an ethical and aesthetic ideal. It is, in fact, according to Starobinski, Staël's recognition of the necessary self-destruction, the "death" of the personal author as a precondition of artistic creation, that accounts for the remarkable and prescient modernity of Staël's moral and aesthetic theories:

> Mme de Staël defined precisely, in striking formulas, a rupture that will be the essential act of the great writers of the nineteenth century. The entry into literature presupposes the sacrifice of the man in favor of the work, the abolition of personal, empirical existence ... for the benefit of the second existence that he pursues in his work.[20]

Yet, if Staël has permitted us to witness this "very modern separation of the realm of *life* and that of *l'écriture*" (p. 251; my translation), she never wishes this separation to be complete as do writers like Flaubert, Mallarmé, and Valéry. If we do always see Germaine de Staël in Corinne and Delphine, as Starobinski asserts, it is because Staël is self-consciously and purposefully calling our attention to them as women who are victims of oppression, because her ideal of moral suicide is a political as well as spiritual ideal. Staël's ideal of self-transcendence through doubling and detachment functions analogously to and as the ideal substitution for the literal suicide so prevalent in Staël's fiction and which Margaret Higonnet in her essay "Suicide as Self-Construction" defines as "a condition for freedom," as the expression of a "desire for self-definition" and a gesture of self-assertion in the lives of women who feel themselves denied any other means of self-expression.[21] In not forgetting the "woman in the thought" as Margaret Fuller and perhaps Starobinski would wish her to, Staël creates an aesthetic and ethical philosophy that is a double-edged sword cutting through to an honest recognition of both the specific burdens and the specific opportunities which her societal position presents to nineteenth-century woman. Her self-transcendence enables a clear vision of both "heaven ... and ... the kingdom of Cashmere," both spiritual and social reality.

Lawrence Lipking in *Abandoned Women and Poetic Tradition* eloquently defends Staël against the charge that her art is excessively personal or emotional, recognizing the originality and the power of Staël's theoretical and fictional texts and indeed suggesting that they form the basis of a woman's aesthetics that has yet to be fully elucidated.[22] If the art of Staël and other women is considered too personal, Lipking asserts, it is because impersonal has meant masculine. Certainly feminists since Mary Wollstonecraft have made this argument, but what is significant about Lipking's essay is his recognition – like that of Starobinski – of the pivotal importance of Staël's ethics and aesthetics in literary history and his assertion that their vehemently personal quality be held up as a kind of model for women's art. Lipking, then, in an unfortunately condescending formulation, reduces this "poetics of abandonment" to "a poetics of need," "like the unsatisfied craving of children who cry to be held" (p. 78), a reaction to woman's abandonment by male love and male justice. Thus for all his perspicacity, Lipking, it seems to me, has taken the plot of Staël's fiction for her poetics, has followed Staël only halfway in her aesthetic and spiritual quest, for what she ultimately asserts over and over again is that women's emotional abandonment, in both its senses, serves as a kind of catalyst for the triumph over and detachment from emotion, need, and desire that is humanity's highest spiritual achievement. It is ultimately that abandon of self called enthusiasm – a strength rather than a need – that Staël celebrates, for she conceives it as the emblem of women's true liberation, intellectual, spiritual, and political.

Corinne and melancholy: maternal inspiration/ paternal authority

Corinne possesses this strength fully at the beginning of her novel, but is bereft of it at the end, and this is the challenge she represents to contemporary feminist criticism. This body of criticism has read Corinne's self-destruction both as a protest against the restrictions of patriarchal society and an embodiment of a brilliant woman's self-destructive internalization of the values of that society. My own argument builds on prior feminist criticism to examine Staël's concept of female genius and the potential within that concept for a revolutionary and feminist conception of art, subjectivity, and spirituality.

As Deborah Heller asserts in "Tragedy, Sisterhood, and Revenge in *Corinne*," Staël's novel belongs to a woman's plot familiar in nineteenth-century novels which pits woman's potential against "narrow social conventions and expecta- tions" or, as George Eliot puts it in the "Prelude" to *Middlemarch*, "a certain spiritual grandeur ill-matched with the meanness of opportunity."[23] Significantly, however, as Heller points out, *Corinne* "is immediately distinguishable from later, more typical nineteenth-century treatments of this theme by its unremitting insistence on the *fulfilled* genius of its heroine; when we first see Corinne she is being crowned for her artistic achievement at the Capitol in Rome" (p. 214). Thus *Corinne* provides a picture not only of the restrictive psychosocial forces that bring about the demise of Staël's nineteenth-century woman artist, but more importantly, it also suggests, in revolutionary fashion, an alternative and potentially feminist model of subjectivity, religion, morality, and aesthetics before Corinne succumbs to paternal judgment at the end of the novel.

The key to understanding Corinne's vision of a radically original art, morality and religion is the concept of enthusiasm elucidated in the first half of this chapter, which, as Corinne asserts to her lover, Oswald, is the fountainhead of all that she most values in human culture and which she sees as bringing that culture into concord with nature. "Poetry, love, religion – everything related to enthusiasm – is in harmony with nature" ("La poésie, l'amour, la religion, tout ce qui tient à l'enthousiasme enfin est en harmonie avec la nature") she exclaims passionately to him.[24] For Corinne "there are only two distinct classes of men on earth: those who feel enthusiasm and those who scorn it; all other differences are the work of society" ("Il n'y a que deux classes d'hommes distinctes sur la terre, celle qui sent l'enthousiasme, et celle qui le méprise: toutes les autres différences sont le travail de la société"; p. 183; p. 188). In her theoretical works, Staël presents enthusiasm in a kind of dialectical relation with melancholy, so that the emotional experience of melancholy is necessary to but ultimately sublated by the privileged state of enthusiasm. The melancholy induced by reflection on the past and on human finitude is transformed through meditation into the spiritual and forward-looking state of enthusiasm. In *Corinne*, Staël's treatment of enthusiasm is not systematic and the term is at times associated with Oswald as well as Corinne.[25] Furthermore, enthusiasm can suggest both Italian sensuousness as opposed to Northern repression of the body *and* an ideal union of body and spirit, naïve and sentimental, South and North represented by the Italian-English Corinne. Nevertheless, on the whole, melancholy and enthusiasm in *Corinne* stand in opposition and form a pair that is explicitly gendered, as Marie-Claire Vallois acutely observes, "translated in fiction in terms of an opposition between masculine and feminine characters."[26] Thus, according to Vallois, *Corinne* represents "a strategy for escaping the romantic (male) schema," through a demonstration of the "failure of the romantic quest inscribed in the mode of melancholy" (p. 93).

Vallois reveals the manner in which Corinne's female voice and performance art represent a critique of a masculinist aesthetic of monumentality. My analysis builds on the groundwork established by Vallois and other feminist critics to theorize the tension in Staël's work between conflicting models of subjectivity, morality, and spirituality that mirror the Staëlean opposition between masculine and feminine aesthetics and the corresponding emotional states of melancholy and enthusiasm. And by feminine aesthetics here, I mean art that makes room for the form and content of women's experiences and subjectivities rather than any identifiable stylistic traits such as French feminist Hélène Cixous delineates. Just as John Isbell's *The Birth of European Romanticism* illuminates the scope and coherence of Staël's attack on Napoleonic ideology in *On Germany* in its synthesis of artistic, political, and spiritual realms, so my analysis of *Corinne* emphasizes the far-reaching and all-encompassing nature of this novelistic critique of patriarchal values and hierarchies by elucidating the alternative aesthetic, psychological, religious, and political ideals promulgated by the heroine before her lapse into melancholy. Furthermore, and perhaps most important for our understanding of Staël's relation to Romanticism and her influence on future women writers, a picture of the shadow cast by the masculinist cultural history of melancholy on this novel and its heroine will clarify the novel's painful conclusion and help us comprehend Staël's refusal or inability to create a female character who sustains her inspiration in the face of paternal abandonment, rejection, and condemnation. For in her encounter with the melancholy Oswald, Corinne comes face-to-face with a powerful Western cultural tradition that, as Juliana Schiesari has shown in *The Gendering of Melancholia*, empowers men associated with this affective state as emblems of intellectual and artistic superiority even as it ignores or excludes women.[27]

Italian enthusiasm and British melancholy: Corinne and the *mal du siècle*

Corinne enters the novel as an embodiment of enthusiasm only to be overwhelmed by the melancholy that destroys her through the agency of her beloved Scottish Oswald, Lord Nelvil. Thus *Corinne* begins and ends not with its heroine but with Oswald whose name entitles the first chapter as if to indicate his dominance of the social and temporal world of the novel. Oswald is immediately presented as the classic melancholiac, so much so that he might have served as a model for Freud's "Mourning and Melancholia," a text that, like *The Uncanny*, reminds us of his affinity for and roots in the ideology of European Romanticism. Freud asserts that "dissatisfaction with the self on moral grounds" is by far the most outstanding feature of melancholia.[28] Oswald is ill with grief over his father's death, suffering from "remorse stirred by a meticulous conscience" (p. 3). Other symptoms, according to Freud, include:

[a] profoundly painful dejection, abrogation of interest in the outside world, loss of the capacity to love, inhibition of all activity, and a lowering of the

self-regarding feelings to a degree that finds utterance in self-reproaches and self-revilings, and culminates in a delusional expectation of punishment.

(p. 153)

Indeed, this list represents a precise outline of Oswald's character. At twenty-five he is "wearied of life" ("découragé de la vie"; p. 3; p. 3), "no longer in touch with the objects around him" ("ils n'étaient plus en relation avec les objets qui l'environnaient"; p. 3; p. 4), "his wounded sensibility no longer had any taste for the illusions of the heart" ("Il était lassé de tout"; p. 4; p. 5), and he is "hesitant to confront fate" ("timide envers la destinée"; p. 4; p. 4). He is profoundly self-destructive, risking his life recklessly at least four times in the novel, thus exhibiting what Freud terms the "overthrow, psychologically very remarkable, of that instinct which constrains every living thing to cling to life" (p. 156).

Most significantly, however, he is overwhelmed by the "fall in self-esteem" (p. 153), the "dissatisfaction with the self on moral grounds" that for Freud distinguishes melancholy from "normal" mourning. "[Oswald] was spitting blood, yet he looked after himself as little as possible, for believing himself guilty, he was excessively severe in his self-judgment" ("[Oswald] crachait le sang, et se soignait le moins qu'il était possible; car il se croyait coupable, et s'accusait lui-même d'une trop grande sévérité"; p. 7; p. 7). Oswald even calls himself a murderer and takes responsibility for the death of his father, which occurred during the Revolutionary years when he remained in France to protect an aristocratic French woman against his father's wishes. Staël is perhaps suggesting here the double bind that support of counter-revolutionary France placed upon the liberal, nationalistic English. Oswald's self-condemnation takes on further political and metaphysical dimensions as the individual father becomes identified with fatherland and spiritual authority: "Alas!", Oswald exclaims. "While he was still alive, did not an incredible set of circumstances convince him that I had betrayed his affection, that I had rebelled against my country, against his will, against everything sacred on earth?" ("Hélas! Quand il vivait, un concours d'événements inouïs n'a-t-il pas dû lui persuader que j'avais trahi sa tendresse, que j'étais rebelle à ma patrie, à la volonté paternelle, à tout ce qu'il y a de sacré sur la terre?"; p. 4; pp. 4–5). Indeed, one of the most remarkable aspects of Staël's portrayal of melancholy is the explicitness of her recognition that it is the product of a patriarchal moral and social order. The specifically nineteenth-century nature of Oswald's melancholy is evident when one sees that *Corinne* provides a portrait, through a woman's eyes, of the feminized *mal du siècle* hero of male novelists such as Chateaubriand and Constant. This hero who is described by Margaret Waller as "alienated from the patriarchal status quo" by a seemingly inextricable emotional bondage to a woman is revealed by Staël "not as a sad exception to patriarchal rule but as the latest incarnation of the law of the fathers."[29] Indeed, Oswald is doubly bound, in a kind of repetition compulsion, by transgressive women – first to the French seductress and then to Corinne who haunts him even after his marriage to Lucile, his father's choice, so that he is compelled to leave his fatherland and be near Corinne at her death.

If England is associated with patriarchy and with melancholy, Italy is the land of Corinne's mother, a land that fosters inspiration and enthusiasm. When we meet Corinne, she is dressed as Domenichino's Sibyl, being crowned with laurels in Rome like Tasso and Petrarch before her. As feminist critics since Ellen Moers have noted, the nature of her triumph as "a woman renowned only for the gifts of genius" (p. 22) is an implicit critique of Napoleonic militarism: "her triumphal chariot had cost not a single tear to anyone; and neither remorse nor fear checked admiration for these most beautiful gifts of nature: imagination, feeling, and thought" ("[U]ne femme illustrée seulement par les dons du génie; son char de victoire ne coûtait de larmes à personne; et nul regret, comme nulle crainte, n'empêchait d'admirer les plus beaux dons de la nature, l'imagination, le sentiment et la pensée"; p. 22; p. 23).[30] Hence it is the presumably apolitical nature of her discourse that constitutes it as a political critique. Her loyal friend Prince Castel-Forte pays tribute to her "grace and gaiety, a gaiety with no trace of mockery, owed only to a lively mind and radiant imagination" ("la grâce et la gaîté de Corinne, cette gaîté qui ne tenait en rien à la moquerie, mais seulement à la vivacité de l'esprit, à la fraîcheur de l'imagination"; p. 23; p. 24). Her eloquence is an "all-powerful force," her improvisational poetry "an intellectual melody" ("une mélodie intellectuelle"; p. 24; p. 25). The source of her eloquence is enthusiasm that Castel-Forte calls an "inexhaustible well of feelings and ideas" ("l'inépuisable source des sentiments et des idées, l'enthousiasme"; p. 24; p. 25). Thus Corinne represents joy and inexhaustible life in the face of Oswald's dejection and longing for death. In contrast to Oswald's withdrawal into the self, her soul seems at one with the universe; describing Italy, she exclaims, "Here sense impressions blend with ideas, all life draws from the same wellspring, and the soul – like the air – fills space to the outer limits of heaven and earth" ("Ici, les sensations se confondent avec les idées; la vie se puise tout entière à la même source, et l'âme, comme l'air, occupe les confines de la terre et du ciel"; p. 29; p. 31).

In place of Oswald's punitive father God, she worships a gentle and comforting divinity, both male and female:

> And so [nature] always brings redress, and all wounds are cured by her helping hand. Here even the heart's anguish is consoled by wonder at a God of goodness and by insight into the secret of His love. The passing misfortunes of our transitory life are dispersed into the fertile and majestic bosom of the immortal universe.
>
> (p. 30)

> Ainsi, toujours [la nature] répare, et sa main secourable guérit toutes les blessures. Ici l'on se console des peines mêmes du cœur, en admirant un Dieu de bonté, en pénétrant le secret de son amour: les revers passagers de notre vie éphémère se perdent dans le sein fécond et majestueux de l'immortel univers.
>
> (p. 31)

Here Corinne celebrates the ability to see oneself in "the vast tableau of destinies," both human and natural, that Staël envisages in her early essay on the passions. Once again it is enthusiasm that allows Corinne to stand outside herself, to double herself and be both woman and sibyl, both earthly being and "genius endowed with splendid wings" ("un génie doué de si brillantes ailes"; p. 39; p. 41). "She had just spoken, filling her soul with the noblest thoughts, and through the power of enthusiasm she was not timid anymore. No longer a fearful woman, she was an inspired priestess, joyously devoting herself to the cult of genius" ("[L]'enthousiasme l'emportait sur la timidité. Ce n'était plus une femme craintive, mais une prêtresse inspirée, qui se consacrait avec joie au culte du génie"; p. 32; p. 34).

"Intellectual melody": art as self-abandon

This state of enthusiasm is the heart of an aesthetic of impersonality and disinterestedness that Corinne elucidates eloquently and explicitly in the novel thanks to the fact, as Castel-Forte puts it, that she is "good at both enthusiasm and analysis, gifted as an artist and able to see herself objectively" ("à la fois susceptible d'enthousiasme et d'analyse, douée comme un artiste, et capable de s'observer elle-même"; p. 43; p. 45). Describing her improvisations, Corinne makes clear that they are impersonal in that they are like "a lively conversation" and are the result of collective efforts of expression:

> [I]t is to my friends that I owe most of my talent, particularly in this genre. Sometimes when people have spoken of the great and noble questions of man's moral life, his destiny, his goal, his duties, his affections – the conversation inspires my passionate interest. At times the interest lifts me beyond my own powers, brings me to discover in nature and in my own heart bold truths and language full of life that solitary thought would not have brought into being.
>
> (pp. 44–5)

> [C]est à mes amis que je dois surtout en ce genre la plus grande partie de mon talent. Quelquefois l'intérêt passionné que m'inspire un entretien où l'on a parlé des grandes et nobles questions qui concernent l'existence morale de l'homme, sa destinée, son but, ses devoirs, ses affections; quelquefois cet intérêt m'élève au-dessus de mes forces, me fait découvrir dans la nature, dans mon propre cœur, des vérités audacieuses, des expressions pleines de vie, que la réflexion solitaire n'aurait pas fait naître.
>
> (pp. 46–7)

So much for the solitary Romantic genius composing in his garret or on his mountaintop. Above all, it is transcendence of personal identity that, for Corinne, creates true poetry:

At such times it seems to me that I am experiencing a supernatural enthusiasm, and I sense full well that what is speaking through me has a value beyond myself. ... Ultimately I feel I am a poet not only when a happy choice of rhymes or harmonious syllables, or a favorite cluster of images dazzles my listeners, but also when my soul rises up, when from on high it disdains what is selfish and base – in a word, when a splendid act would be easier for me: it is then that my verses are better. I am a poet when I admire, when I scorn, when I hate – not out of personal feelings, not for my own cause, but for the dignity of the human race and the glory of the world.

(p. 45)

Je crois éprouver alors un enthousiasme surnaturel; et je sens bien que ce qui parle en moi vaut mieux que moi-même: ... Enfin je me sens poète, non pas seulement quand un heureux choix de rimes ou de syllabes harmonieuses, quand une heureuse réunion d'images éblouit les auditeurs, mais quand mon âme s'élève, quand elle dédaigne de plus haut l'égoïsme et la bassesse; enfin, quand une belle action me serait plus facile: c'est alors que mes vers sont meilleurs. Je suis poète, lorsque j'admire, lorsque je méprise, lorsque je hais, non par des sentiments personnels, non pour ma propre cause, mais pour la dignité de l'espèce humaine et la gloire du monde.

(p. 47)

Thus Corinne's portrayal of Shakespeare's Juliet depends upon detachment from personal emotions. She is glad that Oswald does not play Romeo, for in that case, truth would have destroyed the authority of art. Georges Poulet, then, is, I think, mistaken when he asserts, making no distinction between Corinne and Staël and fostering the cliché of Staël's uncontrolled emotionalism, that

> [it] is immediately obvious that such a manner of acting (and communicating) is diametrically opposed to Diderot's paradox of the actor. Mme de Staël in no way seeks to remain immune to the emotional disquiet that seizes her in the course of a dramatic portrayal. She does not, for the sake of a better performance, endeavor to maintain a detached calm.[31]

As we have just seen, this detachment is precisely what she does seek, though it is the doubling of self that results from the exaltation that she believes art alone can inspire rather than the more calculated repetition of coded gestures that characterizes Diderot's paradigmatic actors. Instead, it is Nelvil who becomes overly emotional, who can't distinguish art from life and who has to be dragged moaning, in a frenzy, from the hall when he believes Juliet/Corinne dead!

As a manifestation of enthusiasm, art, for Staël, is privileged over social morality which is inevitably linked to a specific socio-political status quo. Thus to use literature to advance a political goal, though it be the noblest possible goal, is a perversion of the imagination (p. 121). Anticipating Percy Shelley's *Defence of*

Poetry (1821), which she likely influenced, Staël sees art as enabling the spontaneous conception of "splendid acts" not yet encompassed by social reality and its systematic moralities. Speaking of music, Staël elucidates the profound and subtle manner in which art breaks old patterns and stimulates movement, change, and growth: "Music alone speaks to the inner spring of existence, wresting it free of its set position. What has been said of divine grace suddenly transforming hearts, may – on a human level – be applied to the power of melody. . . ." ("[C]elui-là seul s'adresse à la source intime de l'existence, et change en entier la disposition intérieure. Ce qu'on a dit de la grâce divine qui tout-à-coup transforme les cœurs, peut, humainement parlant, s'appliquer à la puissance de la mélodie"; p. 165; p. 169). Thus Staël figures aesthetic transcendence as movement and flexibility rather than as a fixed or changeless absolute. Music, indeed, is a cure for melancholy because of its capacity – once again – to double the self and allow detached expression of emotion:

> Music doubles our idea of the faculties of our soul. When we hear it, we feel capable of nobler endeavors. . . . In the language of music, unhappiness itself is without bitterness, without wrenching pain, without unpleasantness. Music gently lifts the weight almost always pressing on the heart of one capable of serious and deep affection, a weight causing such uninterrupted pain that it sometimes blends in with our very sense of existence.
>
> (p. 165)

> La musique double l'idée que nous avons des facultés de notre âme; quand on l'entend, on se sent capable des plus nobles efforts. . . . Le malheur même, dans le langage de la musique, est sans amertume, sans déchirement, sans irritation. La musique soulève doucement le poids qu'on a presque toujours sur le cœur, quand on est capable d'affections sérieuses et profondes; ce poids qui se confond quelquefois avec le sentiment même de l'existence, tant la douleur qu'il cause est habituelle.
>
> (pp. 169–70)

The religious life: battle or hymn?

Indeed such an aesthetic does threaten Oswald's "very sense of existence," his attachment to guilt and melancholy as the very foundation of his being. As Corinne acutely observes: "You, my dear Oswald, do not love the arts in themselves. . . . You are moved only by what suggests the heart's suffering to you" ("Vous, mon cher Oswald, . . . vous n'aimez pas les arts en eux-mêmes, mais seulement à cause de leurs rapports avec le sentiment ou l'esprit. Vous n'êtes ému que par ce qui vous retrace les peines du cœur"; pp. 148–9; p. 153). Thus Oswald can see in the Colosseum, for Corinne Rome's most beautiful ruin, "only the master's wealth and the slave's blood" ("[I]l ne voyait dans ces lieux que le luxe du maître et le sang des esclaves"; p. 67; p. 69). In the place of Corinne's aesthetics of joy and freedom Oswald "looked for moral feeling everywhere, and all the magic of the arts could never satisfy him" ("Il cherchait partout un sentiment moral, et toute la magie des arts ne pouvoit jamais lui suffire"; p. 68; p. 70). In keeping with his excessively meticulous and judgmental conscience, he asserts a cruel ethic of sacrifice that sends shudders through Corinne's being when he exclaims that "any sacrifice at all is more beautiful than all the outpourings of soul and thought" ("un sacrifice, quel qu'il soit, est plus beau, plus difficile, que tous les élans de l'âme et de la pensée") and advocates a violence of repression in which "celestial might subdue[s] the mortal man in us" ("une puissance céleste subjugue en nous l'homme mortel"; p. 68; p. 70).

For Oswald, violence, sacrifice, and guilt are the essence of religion and spirituality. He accepts the definition – political and potentially militaristic – of religion bequeathed to him by his father: "religion – that final treaty of alliance between fathers and children, between death and life…" ("[L]a religion, ce dernier traité d'alliance entre les pères et les enfants, entre la mort et la vie"; p. 138; p. 142). Thus like his father, he judges Corinne's imaginative genius harshly:

> The poetic enthusiasm that makes you so charming is not … the most salutary form of devoutness. Corinne, with nothing but that inspiration, how could a person be expected to prepare for the innumerable sacrifices duty requires of us? … You describe the existence of the blessed, and not of mortals. The religious life is a battle and not a hymn.
>
> (pp. 184–5)

> L'enthousiasme poétique, qui vous donne tant de charmes, n'est pas … la dévotion la plus salutaire. Corinne, comment pourrait-on se préparer par cette disposition aux sacrifices sans nombre qu'exige de nous le devoir? … [V]ous décrivez l'existence des bienheureux, et non pas celle des mortels. La vie religieuse est un combat, et non pas un hymne.
>
> (p. 189)

For Corinne, religion, like art, has its sources and its expression beyond morality, in what she terms religious enthusiasm. "If religion meant only strict adherence to morality, what more would it have than philosophy and reason?" "It is the power to love and to feel compassion" ("Si la religion consistait seulement dans la stricte observation de la morale, qu'aurait-elle de plus que la philosophie et la raison? … c'est la puissance d'aimer et de plaindre"; p. 182; p. 187). In an intellectual move that anticipates Kierkegaard, Staël explicitly separates morality from religion and gives the spiritual priority as an expression of a non-rational and higher faculty.

However, Staël's religion and art are ultimately one, in contrast to the profound dualism of Kierkegaard which is founded in a mind/body split. Accordingly, Corinne follows the Italian custom, shocking to Oswald, of painting his likeness and placing it opposite that of the Virgin Mary, meditating on these images in preparation for her retreat to a convent during Lent. "The image of the loved one face to face with a symbol of the divine" ("l'image de celui qu'on aime vis-à-vis d'un emblème de la Divinité"; p. 168; p. 172) links eros with a female symbol of agape. For Corinne, the ideal of selflessness is not equivalent to asceticism or to self-sacrifice, both of which are associated with Nelvil and Lady Edgermond in the novel. Indeed, Corinne abandons England when she comes of age and returns to Italy in search of happiness which she explicitly defines as "the development of our abilities" ("le développement de nos facultés"; p. 254; p. 259), equating the smothering of one's mind and soul with suicide. The heart of Corinne's creed, eloquently expressed, is a union of the sensuous and the spiritual, a coexistence of rather than a battle between the earthly and divine: "So, dear Oswald, allow us to mix everything together: love, religion, genius, and sun, and perfumes, and music, and poetry. There is no atheism save in coldness, selfishness, vile behavior" ("Cher Oswald, laissez-nous donc tout confondre, amour, religion, génie, et le soleil et les parfums, et la musique et la poésie; il n'y a d'athéisme que dans la froideur, l'égoïsme, la bassesse"; p. 184; p. 188).

Subjectivity as multiplicity: the enigma of the feminine

Corinne's ability to "mix everything together," the seemingly self-contradictory nature of her subjectivity, is as troubling and challenging to Oswald as is her aesthetic and religious vision:

> He wondered whether it was inconsistency or superiority that tied together so many contradictory qualities, whether it was the power to feel everything or to successively forget that explained her moving almost instantaneously from melancholy to gaiety, from depth to charm, from the most amazingly knowledgeable or thought-filled conversation to the coquetry of a woman who seeks to please and wants to captivate. But her coquetry was so perfectly dignified that it compelled as much respect as the strictest reserve!
>
> (p. 38)

> [I]l se demandait si le lien de tant de qualités presque opposées était l'inconséquence ou la supériorité; si c'était à force de tout sentir, ou parce qu'elle oubliait tout successivement, qu'elle passait ainsi, presque dans un même instant, de la mélancolie à la gaîté, de la profondeur à la grâce, de la conversation la plus étonnante et par les connaissances et par les idées, à la coquetterie d'une femme qui cherche à plaire et veut captiver: mais il y avait dans cette coquetterie une noblesse si parfaite, qu'elle imposait autant de respect que la réserve la plus sévère.
>
> (p. 40)

Unable to accept the richness and multiplicity of Corinne's psyche, Oswald fears her and seeks to typecast her just as his father had done when he rejected Corinne as a potential bride for his son and called her "one of those beautiful Greeks who bewitched the world and held it in their sway" ("une de ces belles

Grecques qui enchantaient et subjugaient le monde"; p. 329; p. 335): "Was there some magic in her charm or was it poetic inspiration? Was she Armida or Sappho?" ("Son charme tenait-t-il de la magie, ou de l'inspiration poétique? Était ce Armide ou Sapho?"; p. 39; p. 41); "Who are you? Where did you get so many different charms that would seem to be mutually exclusive – sensitivity, depth, gaiety, grace, spontaneity, modesty? Are you an illusion?" ("[Q]ui donc êtes-vous? où avez-vous pris tant de charmes divers qui sembleraient devoir s'exclure? Sensibilité, gaîté, profondeur, grâce, abandon, modestie; êtes-vous une illusion?"; p. 51; p. 53). For her part Corinne explains her seductive secret quite rationally, expressing her own acceptance of the contradictions and multiplicity within her:

> What you like to call "magic" in me is a spontaneity that sometimes gives free rein to different feelings and contradictory thoughts without making any effort to harmonize them; for that harmony, when it exists, is almost always artificial, while genuine character is largely inconsistent.
>
> (p. 100)

> [C]e qu'il vous plaît d'appeler en moi de la magie, c'est un naturel sans contrainte, qui laisse voir quelque-fois des sentiments divers et des pensées opposées, sans travailler à les mettre d'accord; car cet accord, quand il existe, est presque toujours factice, et la plupart des caractères vrais sont inconséquents.
>
> (p. 103)

Though fascinated with Corinne's self-knowledge, Oswald ultimately sees it as transgressive, for it is born of experience and wisdom, both sexual and worldly, that he finds unacceptable in a woman. When Corinne confesses that she has known "the illusion of love" before meeting him, he responds with a judgment in the name of his father: "She is the most attractive of women but she is Italian and has not the shy, innocent heart unknown to itself which is doubtless possessed by the young Englishwoman my father intended for me" ("C'est la plus séduisante des femmes, mais c'est une Italienne; et ce n'est pas ce cœur timide, innocent, à lui-même inconnu, que possède sans doute la jeune Anglaise à laquelle mon père me destinait"; p. 52; p. 54). Furthermore, Corinne makes it clear that she does not really wish to marry Oswald, though she wants to be his lover. Corinne's psychic complexity and emotional spontaneity stand in opposition to female "purity" and sexual monogamy which even Corinne herself self-destructively internalizes as the feminine ideal. Praising a young Roman woman who died young and lived "a life without stain," Corinne exclaims, "How enviable the fate of a woman who has managed to retain the most perfect oneness in her destiny, and who carries only one memory off to the grave!" ("[Q]u'il est digne d'envie le sort de la femme qui peut avoir ainsi conservé la plus parfaite unité dans sa destinée, et qui n'emporte au tombeau qu'un souvenir!"; p. 80; p. 82).

Thus the concept of the unity of self becomes a metaphysical construct profoundly destructive to Corinne's sense of self-worth and self-knowledge.

Oswald is even more extreme in his rejection of the multiplicity of experience offered by life as he reveals the paternal image associated with unnatural and untimely death at the core of his ideal of self-sacrifice and repression: "Happy, happy are the children who die in their father's arms ... and who meet death held in the bosom of the one who gave them life" ("Heureux, dit Oswald, heureux les enfants qui meurent dans les bras de leur père, et qui reçoivent la mort dans le sein qui leur donna la vie!"; p. 80; pp. 81–2).

Ironically, Corinne does carry only one memory to her grave: the melancholy sense of her loss of and abandonment by Oswald. The novel's sympathetic narrator raises the inevitable question posed by the novel: "Must a single feeling so despoil an entire life?" ("Et faut-il qu'un seul sentiment dépouille ainsi toute la vie?"; p. 351; p. 357). After losing Oswald, Corinne's emotional fluidity and spontaneity as well as her capacity for detachment vanish along with her gift for improvisation:

> Unable to divert her thoughts from her own plight, she portrayed her suffering. But no longer were there any general ideas or universal feelings that correspond to all men's hearts; it was the cry of grief, ultimately monotonous as the cry of birds in the night, too fervent in expression, too vehement, too lacking in subtlety: unhappiness it was, but it was not talent.
>
> (p. 368)

> Se sentant alors incapable de détourner sa pensée de sa propre situation, elle peignait ce qu'elle souffrait; mais ce n'étaient plus ces idées générales, ces sentiments universels qui répondent au cœur de tous les hommes: c'était le cri de la douleur, cri monotone à la longue, comme celui des oiseaux de la nuit; il y avait trop d'ardeur dans les expressions, trop d'impétuosité, trop peu de nuances: d'était le malheur, mais ce n'était plus le talent.
>
> (p. 375)

Monomania, obsession, and repetition compulsion replace inspiration. "True grief is not naturally fruitful: it produces only a somber restlessness that incessantly leads back to the same thoughts. Thus did the knight, pursued by a lamentable fate, vainly wander around and about a thousand times, only to return always to the same place" ("La véritable douleur n'a point de fécondité naturelle: ce qu'elle produit n'est qu'une agitation sombre qui ramène sans cesse aux mêmes pensées. Ainsi, ce chevalier poursuivi par un sort funeste, parcourait en vain mille détours, et se retrouvait toujours à la même place"; p. 368; p. 375).

The triumph of melancholy

At the conclusion of the novel, then, Corinne succumbs to the power of melancholy. The history of Corinne's seduction by Oswald's melancholy is a key to understanding Corinne's inability to maintain her capacity for inspiration and enthusiasm despite the fact that they are supported in her mind by consistent and carefully articulated models of subjectivity, art, and religion with great emancipatory potential. Melancholy is figured in the novel as a kind of contagious but prestigious disease that Oswald passes on to Corinne. However, rather than enhancing her intellectual and artistic gifts as it does for such figures as Tasso who haunts the text from beginning to end, melancholy reduces Corinne to a pitiable and inarticulate grief.[32] For as Schiesari convincingly argues, the "prestigious pathos" of melancholy is reserved for men; in women it is devalued and labeled depression.

> Nothing more eloquently expresses what I call the gendering of melancholia than this split between a higher-valued form understood as male and a lower-valued one coded as female. Moreover, the "higher" form (melancholia) is made to represent a sensitive or exquisite illness characterized by representation itself, whereas the "lower" form (depression) remains characterized by an incapacity to translate symptoms into a language beyond its own self-referentiality as depression.
>
> (p. 16)

"Far from being inspired to express themselves in some heightened artistic way, women melancholiacs – especially those who by lack of a husband are most alienated from phallic authority – lapse into utter inarticulateness and can no longer find a place in the symbolic order's prime system, language" (p. 15). During her first improvisation at the opening of the novel, Oswald is immediately figured as a punishing instance who "seemed to chide her gently" so that "she was impelled to meet his need by talking of happiness with less certainty, by devoting a few verses to death in the midst of celebration" ("semblait lui faire doucement des reproches; elle ... se sentait le besoin de le satisfaire, en parlant du bonheur avec moins d'assurance, en consacrant à la mort quelques vers au milieu d'une fête"; p. 30; p. 32). Her second attempt to improvise for Oswald fails completely as she loses "the presence of mind required for the gift of improvisation"; her feelings for Oswald "subdu[ed] her mind completely" ("la présence d'esprit nécessaire pour le talent d'improviser"; "le sentiment avait subjugué tout-à-fait son esprit"; p. 110; p. 113). Finally, she is reduced at the end of the novel to communication in fragments, mourning the loss of her gifts: "My talent no longer exists, and I mourn for it" ("Mon talent n'existe plus: je le regrette"; p. 369; p. 376). The woman who had once incarnated Gozzi's Amazon Queen, Semiramide, *la figlia dell'aria*, ruling over men and the elements, has now completely withdrawn from the world into herself, waiting for death.

Corinne, then, despite her acute self-knowledge and inspirational gifts, is unable to sustain her enthusiasm and falls victim to Oswald, "the Spirit of Sorrow" ("Génie de la douleur"; p. 145; p. 149) because she – or perhaps her creator – is overwhelmed by the power of Romantic melancholy as a cultural emblem of aesthetic elitism and, even more importantly, moral authority. Her home faces the temple consecrated to the Sibyl, her garden perfumed by flowers and the ringing of windharps. Yet one has only to look at the subjects of the paintings that Corinne has chosen for her home to register the depth of her vulnerability to the physical and emotional violence of patriarchal cultural tradition: Brutus the Elder sending his sons off to be executed, Dido and Aeneas, Tancred and the dying Clorinda, Hippolytus and Phaedra, and finally Macbeth! Furthermore, Staël represents Corinne as vulnerable to melancholy through her English paternal heritage which she represses when she leaves England and abandons her patronym for the name of Pindar's (legendary) mentor, Corinne. But almost as soon as she meets Oswald they enter into a kind of contest to see which one has greater claim to sensitivity and suffering. Corinne tells Nelvil, "Of all my gifts, the most powerful is the gift for suffering" ("de toutes mes facultés, la plus puissante c'est la faculté de souffrir"; p. 75; p. 78), and he soon begins to see "a melancholy look in Corinne's eyes instead of their natural interest and fire" ("une expression de mélancolie dans les regards de Corinne, naturellement si pleins d'intérêts et de flamme"; p. 78; p. 80). And when it is Corinne and not the frail consumptive Oswald who succumbs to the Roman sickness midway through the novel one senses that the contagion of Oswald's spiritual malady is complete, despite or perhaps even because of the fact that he nurses her back to health. Staël expresses his effect upon Corinne with a phallic metaphor representative of his pernicious influence: "Corinne recovered, but another ill penetrated her heart even deeper than ever" ("Corinne en guérit; mais un autre mal pénétra plus avant que jamais dans son cœur"; p. 284; pp. 289–90).

What Corinne and perhaps Staël herself do not fully realize is that the rules of the game change when one moves from the cultural significance of male suffering to the meaning of female suffering. Culturally sanctioned female suffering comes in the name of love rather than in the name of art and this passion removes rather than heightens genius in Corinne. Thus when she admits her growing preference for northern (Scottish) rather than southern (Italian) art, for art that yields to "mystery's terror, to the melancholy prompted by the uncertain and the unknown" ("à l'effroi du mystère, à la mélancolie qu'inspirent l'incertain et l'inconnu"; p. 301; p. 307), Oswald is flattered but also concerned to think that his influence may have "dimmed [her] brilliant imagination" ("flétri [sa] belle imagination"; p. 301; p. 307). Corinne answers by suggesting that for women love and artistic genius are incompatible: "Deep passion stands accused, not you. Talent requires inner independence that true love never allows" ("Ce n'est pas vous qu'il faut en accuser … mais une passion profonde. Le talent a besoin d'une indépendance intérieure, que l'amour véritable ne permet jamais"; p. 301; p. 307). Oswald's response is a chilling summary of the novel as a whole, an emblematic stifling of Corinne's imagination and a silencing of her voice: "Ah! if that is so, may your genius be hushed, and may your heart be all mine!" ("Ah! S'il est ainsi … que ton génie se taise, et que ton cœur soit tout à moi"; p. 302; p. 307). Complicit in her own oppression, Corinne "did not dare reply [to his words] for fear of disturbing their sweet effect" ("n'osa répondre, de peur de troubler en rien la douce impression qu'elle éprouvait"; p. 302; p. 307).

In the end Corinne allows herself to be dominated and silenced by Oswald because he represents a moral authority and stands in for a patriarchal social order toward which she comes to direct all her emotion and passion in an effort to seek approval and love. For Corinne, Oswald becomes the supreme embodiment of celestial virtue, as she tells him when he is on the verge of abandoning her for England and military duty: "I see you as an angelic being, as the purest and noblest in character to have appeared on earth" ("Je vous regarde comme un être angélique, comme le caractère le plus pur et le plus noble qui ait paru sur la terre"; p. 309; p. 315). It is as if Oswald brings to life within Corinne the English father(s) whom she had repressed in her flight to Italy and in her life as an independent artist. For Oswald is constantly asking himself, in a manner ludicrous to a post-Freudian reader, whether or not his father would have approved of his beloved, and when he learns the truth, determines never to marry against his father's wishes. Furthermore, when Corinne restores from memory the portrait of Oswald's father, the man who had branded her a witch, damaged during Oswald's rescue of a drowning old man, Staël figures Corinne's internalization of his image and of his judgmental morality. The patriarch does not die; instead, he is constantly revived in the psyches of the next generation.

Feminist critics Gutwirth, Heller, Waller, and Peel have all illuminated significant facets of this self-destructive acceptance of the patriarchal value system that ultimately kills Corinne. My focus here is the hegemonic power of the masculinist paradigm of Romantic melancholy – the degree to which it defines Oswald's aesthetic, political, and religious vision as well as the manner in which Corinne's seduction by its glamour means that her demise fits almost precisely the psychic patterns delineated in Freud's "Mourning and Melancholia." My point is not that Freud's essay theorizes a universal psychic pattern essential to human nature and hence applicable to Corinne, but rather that Freud's essay looks back on the same centuries of cultural representation of melancholia as does *Corinne* and distills these constructs into the patterns that he then detects in the patients he diagnoses in his essay. For Freud the crucial mechanism is the over-zealous conscience that is produced when "one part of the ego sets itself against the other, judges it critically, and as it were, looks upon it as an object" (p. 157). This occurs, according to Freud, when the response to the loss of the love object results in "an identification with the abandoned object" (p. 159):

> Thus the shadow of the object fell upon the ego, so that the latter could henceforth be criticized by a special mental faculty like an object, like the forsaken object. In this way the loss of the object became transformed into a loss in the ego, and the conflict between the ego and the loved person transformed into a cleavage between the criticizing faculty of the ego and ego as altered by the identification.
>
> (p. 159)

This is precisely what happens with Oswald at the death of his father; he internalizes his father's standards and wishes, refuses to marry anyone who does not correspond to them, and ultimately conceives of his marriage to Lucile as expiation of his crime against the father.[33] Furthermore, his self-torture and self-destructiveness can be read as a desire for revenge against the internalized father who denies him any pleasure in life. Thus Freud describes the melancholiac as "taking revenge by the circuitous path of self-punishment" on the original loved object, without having to express anger and hatred directly.

More provocatively and disturbingly, when she meets Oswald, the same mechanisms begin to gain power over Corinne and finally take control of her when he abandons her for Lucile. As the novel progresses, Staël takes from Corinne her alternative aesthetic and spiritual vision and replaces it with a moral order based on paternal judgment, guilt, and retribution. Indeed the cleavage of self that Freud attributes to the melancholiac is analogous to the doubling of self so central to the affective state of enthusiasm, with a crucial difference. In the state of enthusiasm, the self takes a kind of detached, intellectual pleasure in its observation of the actions of the ego and may even, as Staël later comes to recognize in *Reflections on Suicide*, discover patterns of behavior that it has the power to change. The melancholiac, on the other hand, judges, punishes, and ultimately condemns the self to repetition compulsion and to death. When Oswald leaves her, Corinne leans her head "against her father's portrait." "At that moment, her whole life must have passed before her eyes, her conscience exaggerated her sins and she feared she did not deserve divine mercy" ("contre le portrait de son père"; "en ce moment sa vie passée s'offrait en entièr à elle; sa conscience exagéra toutes ses fautes, elle craignit de ne pas mériter la miséricorde divine"; p. 313; p. 319). Following Oswald to England and surreptitiously attending a play where Oswald and Lucile are also present, Corinne has been transformed from a celebrated performer into an obscure spectator. The narrator's commentary on the tragedy's suicidal conclusion mirrors the sado-masochism that Freud sees as central to the melancholiac's self-punishment: "How dreadful is the heart's suffering, when it gives rise to such barbaric joy, when the sight of its own blood yields the fierce satisfaction of the savage enemy who takes vengeance!" ("Qu'elle est terrible la souffrance du cœur, quand elle inspire une si barbare joie, quand elle donne, à l'aspect de son propre sang, le contentement féroce d'un sauvage ennemi qui se serait vengé"; p. 341; p. 347).[34]

In the end it is as if Corinne, or perhaps Staël herself, is overwhelmed by the discrepancy between the plethora of prestigious cultural models representing the moral authority of melancholy and the lack of cultural support for her own spirituality and art based in compassion, pleasure, and love. Thus when Corinne, dressed in widow's weeds, approaches Oswald at her father's castle in Scotland, Staël calls forth that foremost melancholiac Hamlet: "As in the tragedy of Hamlet, one might have thought ghosts were roaming outside the palace where banquets were being held" ("[C]omme dans la tragédie de Hamlet, les ombres erraient autour du palais où se donnaient les festins"; p. 354; p. 360). Corinne's transformation is complete; no longer an embodiment of joy and enthusiasm, she is now a ghost, the supreme emblem of the guilty conscience. Yet in the next lines Corinne is not even allowed the dignity of an identification with Hamlet or his father (presumably reserved only for men); instead she becomes Ophelia, as she imagines plunging herself into a stream so that Oswald will stumble upon her body the next day and she will be avenged.

This scene at her father's estate – concluding appropriately at her father's grave – is the climactic scene in the novel, the decisive moment when she anonymously returns Oswald's ring to him, freeing him to marry Lucile. Here Staël's symbolism is powerfully explicit in its assertion that it is not Corinne's relation to Oswald, to Oswald's father, or even to her own father that destroys her, but rather her relation to a ubiquitous and condemnatory patriarchal society and value system. Making the "sacred pilgrimage" to her father's grave, she is nevertheless a complete outsider and outcast, by virtue of her history as an independent woman and artist in Italy: "she felt a stranger now – though on paternal soil, a person isolated – though near the man she had hoped to marry. The ground gave way under her feet, and there was only the ferment of grief to give her strength" ("[Elle] se sentait étrangère sur le sol paternel, isolée près de celui qu'elle avait espéré pour époux . . . ; [l]a terre manquait sous ses pas; et l'agitation de la douleur lui tenait seule lieu de force"; pp. 353–4; p. 360). Significantly, she now desires that her relation to Oswald be sanctioned by marriage. A sense of closeness to her father – the paternal soil – provides no support, only pain and mourning for her status as outcast, as pariah. As she stands before the grave of her father, "the barriers between [herself and Nelvil] appeared stronger than ever in her mind . . . it seemed that her father was joining forces with Oswald's, and that the whole of paternal authority condemned her love" ("[L]es obstacles qui la séparaient de lui s'étaient offerts à sa réflexion avec plus de force que jamais; . . . il lui sembla que [son père] aussi s'unissait à celui d'Oswald, et que l'autorité paternelle tout entière condamnait son amour"; p. 357; pp. 363–4).

At this moment she sacrifices herself to unhappiness and melancholy in the name of Lucile's purity and innocence and in so doing ensures the misery of Lucile and Oswald as well. From this moment on, once Nelvil learns the truth about Corinne's decision, she functions as a punishing conscience or super-ego, in effect replacing his father as the triumphant agent of punishment and emotional vengeance. Her "Last Song" is motivated by a desire to shame Oswald: "she wanted the ungrateful man who had deserted her to feel once more that he had given the deathblow to the woman who in her time knew best how to love and how to think" ("elle désira que l'ingrat qui l'avait abandonnée sentît encore une fois que c'étoit à la femme de son temps qui savait le mieux aimer et penser, qu'il avait donné la mort"; p. 414; p. 421). Thus her moral victory is profoundly hollow and ironic, for it comes at the expense not only of her art but also of her spiritual and political values as she appropriates the sado-masochistic psychic mechanisms shown by Freud to be at the heart of melancholia, perhaps the only effective weapons against a character like Oswald. Though she claims to forgive Oswald and to eschew any desire for revenge, her last letter to him says something very different as she seeks to deny him all happiness, in the name of a master–slave dynamic, just as his father had done:

Do you know that I would have served you like a slave? Do you know that had you loved me faithfully, I would have bowed down before you as before a messenger from heaven? Well, what have you done with so much love? What have you done with an affection unique in this world? With an unhappiness just as unique? Therefore do not lay claim to happiness, do not offend me by thinking you may win it still.

(p. 409)

Savez-vous que je vous aurais servi comme une esclave? Savez-vous que je me serais prosternée devant vous comme devant un envoyé du ciel, si vous m'aviez fidèlement aimée? Eh bien! qu'avez-vous fait de tant d'amour? qu'avez-vous fait de cette affection unique en ce monde? un malheur unique comme elle? Ne prétendez donc plus au bonheur; ne m'offensez pas en croyant l'obtenir.

(p. 415)

Corinne becomes a substitute father, demanding and receiving from Oswald the self-punishment and self-destruction that he enacts in his participation in the war with France. "[H]e risked his life a thousand times. ... Danger was clearly his pleasure ... he flushed with joy when the clash of arms began, and it was only then that the weight on his heart lifted, allowing him to breathe easily. ... [H]e felt less guilty for being so close to dying" ("[I]l exposa mille fois sa vie ...; On remarquait que le danger était un plaisir pour lui; ... il rougissait de joie, quand le tumulte des armes commençait, et c'était dans ce moment seul qu'un poids qu'il avait sur le cœur se soulevait et le laissait respirer à l'aise; ... il se croyait moins coupable, en étant si près de périr"; pp. 384–5; pp. 391–2). Thus his military exploits in the name of England are exposed as suicidal and self-indulgent rather than heroic.

If, as Staël suggests in her early work on the passions, Romantic melancholy is socio-political in origin, a wound to the collective psyche inflicted by the Revolution's betrayal of its ideals, first in its disintegration into barbaric violence and then in its acceptance of tyranny and militarism, Corinne herself symbolically reopens this wound rather than healing it. Indeed, by succumbing to her passion for vengeance, she reiterates the power dynamic that she herself, as well as feminist historians such as Wollstonecraft and Helen Maria Williams, believed had doomed the Revolution to failure. And if, as Doris Kadish suggests, Oswald's obsessive guilt over the death of his father allegorizes France's guilt over the execution of Louis XVI, then Corinne's ultimate choice to take on the role of substitute father-king in search of vengeance/retribution has profoundly reactionary political as well as psychic implications.[35] Thus, from a feminist perspective, it is this relinquishment of – indeed betrayal of – her brilliant political, spiritual, and aesthetic vision to the power of masculinist Romantic melancholy that makes Corinne such a tragic and disturbing figure. Yet it is also precisely in opposing melancholy to a model of female genius and transcendence that the radical import of *Corinne* lies. For Staël's novel renders explicit the ineluctable ties between Romantic melancholy and a patriarchal moral and social order at the same time that it announces Staël's model of self-transcendence and abandonment as feminist and emancipatory. Undoubtedly influenced by Kant and Schiller's ideal of aesthetic detachment and disinterest, Staël lays bare, from a woman's perspective, the ideologically liberating potential of this supposedly apolitical theory of art, prefiguring, from a feminist perspective, the analyses of such twentieth-century critics as Adorno, Marcuse, and Eagleton.

Furthermore, Corinne's defeat and self-betrayal is also a mark of Staël's honesty and courage as a novelist, her willingness to face the realities of the social position of the early nineteenth-century woman artist. As Simone Balayé asserts, Staël's theoretical works and her fiction serve complementary and mutually corrective functions: "In short, the critical and political work of Mme de Staël proposes, constructs, and comforts while the novels are destructive in their expression of the anguish of the writer. Reassuring perfectibility is vanquished by fear. Corinne symbolizes inevitable defeat" (p. 168; my translation). Indeed, toward the end of her life, Staël herself did surmount her fear of the judgments leveled at her as a free-spirited, politically influential, renowned woman writer.

In 1814, three years before her death, she wrote a second Preface to her first published work, her *Letters on Rousseau,* a Preface that serves as a powerful summation of her entire literary career. Once again the themes of perfectibility through intellectual effort and detachment from self appear, but with a new sense of strength and confidence in her own potential and that of all women:

> The study of literature has brought me more joy than sorrow. Anybody who is more hurt by criticism than pleased by praise must be violently affected by love of self. Moreover, the process of developing and perfecting one's own mind provides a continual activity – hope springing eternal – which the ordinary course of life simply cannot offer.
>
> (p. 40)

In pleading for women's education and "literary cultivation," Staël launches a wonderful tongue in cheek attack against those who would wish women to remain devoted to "household cares" by reminding them that "distinguished women are few and far between ... so that men who do not want them will always have plenty of other choices available" (p. 41). Furthermore, there can, of course, be no question of the "domestic slavery" of women since "Christian society requires nothing but justice in human relationships" (p. 40) and enlightened women would clearly be more attuned to morality than uneducated ones! In a plea that could have come from Mary Wollstonecraft, she exhorts her fellow women to seek "a distinguished education: "[If] you do not find a sense of the natural in spiritual exhilaration, and sincerity in a knowledge of the truth – if you do not finally breathe easy in some wider realm, you are nothing but a doll who has learned her lesson well ... " (p. 41). Fame and literary accomplishment are no longer as they are for Corinne, "a brilliant way to bury the happiness of a woman" (p. 318).

Talents may have their drawbacks, like all the other good things of this world, but I prefer such drawbacks to the boredom of a limited mind belittling things it cannot achieve or laying claim to things it cannot feel. Finally, if we consider only our relationship to ourselves, a greater intensity of life is always an increase of happiness. Unhappiness does penetrate deeper into more energetic minds; but … all in all, there is no one who should not be thankful to God for giving him some talent extra.

(p. 41)

In the end, she calmly acknowledges gratitude for her own genius.

"The vast tableau of destinies": Corinne, Lucile, and Juliette

The historical import of Staël's commitment to women's education is powerfully and problematically figured in the conclusion of the novel by the relationships among its heroine, her half-sister Lucile, and niece Juliette. For a feminist reader, the conclusion is both memorable and troubling in its emphasis upon the strong relationships that develop among these women. Lucile, for instance, though jealous of Corinne's pre-eminence in Oswald's affections, is "dissatisfied with Oswald for his cruelty to a woman who loved him so much; and it seemed to her that for the sake of her own happiness, she should fear a man who had thus sacrificed another woman's happiness" ("mécontente d'Oswald, qui avait pu se montrer si cruel envers une femme dont il était tant aimé, et il lui semblait qu'elle devrait craindre, pour son propre bonheur, un homme qui avait ainsi sacrifié le bonheur d'une autre"; p. 384; p. 391). Thus she turns to her sister and her daughter, not to her husband, for guidance and comfort at the end of the novel. In focusing on the legacy, aesthetic and moral, that unites Corinne, Lucile, and Juliette, Staël is opposing a tradition of Romantic novels like Chateaubriand's *René* (1802) and Constant's *Adolphe* (1816) (written at least in part as a *roman à clef* about his relationship with Staël) which conclude, as Margaret Waller has shown, with the triumph of homo-social bonding through the hero's empowering confession of a secret crime to an audience of sympathetic males such as Chactas and Père Souel in *René*.[36] Nelvil, on the other hand, though he has repeatedly acknowledged the primacy of his love for his father ("I have never loved anything more deeply than my father" ("Je n'ai jamais rien aimé plus profondément que mon père"; p. 208; p. 213)), receives no comfort or empowerment from sympathetic father substitutes. In fact, Prince Castel-Forte pronounces Nelvil guilty in a sincere and straightforward response to Nelvil's confession. Unlike the hollow rhetoric of Père Souel's final lecture to René, Castel-Forte answers Oswald's plea for sympathy with an assessment of the murderous potential of the power imbalance inherent in male–female relations: "there is no risk to us when we hurt [women], and yet that hurt is dreadful. A dagger thrust is punished by law, and breaking a sensitive heart simply occasions a joke, so we would do better to choose the dagger thrust" ("Aucun inconvénient ne résulte pour nous de leur faire du mal; et cependant ce mal est affreux. Un coup de poignard est puni par les lois; et le déchirement d'un cœur sensible n'est l'objet que d'une plaisanterie: il vaudrait mieux se permettre le coup de poignard"; p. 404; p. 410).

Furthermore, Corinne herself takes charge of the education of both Lucile and Juliette. Her advice to Lucile objectifies her as a means to male pleasure and satisfaction, suggesting Corinne's ultimate complicity with masculinist domination of the female body: "You will have to be you and me at the same time; your virtues must never sanction the slightest neglect of your attractions, and you must never use them to authorize pride or coldness" ("Il faut que vous soyez vous et moi tout-à-la-fois; que vos vertus ne vous autorisent jamais à la plus légère négligence pour vos agréments, et que vous ne vous fassiez point un titre de ces vertus, pour vous permettre l'orgueil et la froideur"; p. 413; p. 420). While ostensibly training her to please Oswald, she is perhaps also encouraging her to challenge restrictive conceptions of female character and comportment. She makes it clear in her words to Lucile that her own qualities and those of Lucile are not mutually exclusive, that sensuousness need not destroy virtue in a woman, as prejudice and stereotype would have it. Even more portentous is the fact that because Lucile's imagination had been absorbed with thoughts of her sister during pregnancy, Juliette eerily resembles Corinne. The two sisters, Madonna and Sibyl, are one, and need not be fragmented and divided in the next generation of women:

> She was holding a lyre-shaped harp made for her size, in the same way that Corinne held it, and her little arms and pretty expression imitated Corinne perfectly. It was like seeing a beautiful painting in miniature, with a child's grace tinging everything with innocent charm.
>
> (p. 411)

> Elle tenait une harpe en forme de lyre, proportionnée à sa taille, de la même manière que Corinne; et ses petits bras et ses jolis regards l'imitaient parfaitement. On croyait voir la miniature d'un beau tableau, avec la grâce de l'enfance de plus, qui mêle à tout un charme innocent.
>
> (p. 418)

Yet, once again, even as she is passing on her artistry to the next generation and remaining true to a Staëlean vision of the perfectibility of history, Corinne is also betraying the aesthetic of collectivity, multiplicity, and dialogue embodied in her improvisatory art, replacing it with a mimetic reification of her own selfhood. The cult of free genius has become the cult of personality. We see prefigured in the dying Corinne the Germaine de Staël who defined herself in *On Germany* as exceptional woman and victimized artist against that other great personality of the age, Napoleon Bonaparte. As John Isbell acutely observes, "tyrant and victim share a symbiotic relationship in Staël's pages" as "two individuals placed above the masses."[37] Mary Shelley, Bettine von Arnim and George Sand will all seek to free their artist heroines from this stultifying symbiosis. Indeed it is no exaggeration to suggest that, for the next hundred years, American and European women writers, in a kind of collective repetition compulsion, sought to free themselves from Corinne even as they obsessively paid tribute to her.[38] Thus, the troubling image of Juliette prefigures Staël's incomparable power of influence and inspiration for the "vast tableau of destinies" that constituted the history of European women's writing in the nineteenth century.

2 "The sweet reward of all our toil"

Content of mind in Mary Shelley's *Valperga*

Mary Shelley's intellectual and literary career is eloquent testimony to the unique power of influence Germaine de Staël's writings held over the future development of nineteenth-century women's literature. Indeed, Staël's influence for Shelley as a literary ancestor is second only to that of her biological parents, Mary Wollstonecraft and William Godwin. From the incorporation of *On Germany's* discussions of German scientific and illuminist communities into her first novel *Frankenstein* (1818) to her biography of Staël written in 1839 for the *Cabinet Cyclopaedia of Eminent Literary and Scientific Men of France* [sic], Shelley's works give witness to Staël's vital presence in the writings of her literary descendants. As Shelley herself asserted in her intellectual biography of Staël, no other writer of her epoch "left such luminous ideas on her route."[1]

Mary Shelley's second novel *Valperga: or, The Life and Adventures of Castruccio, Prince of Lucca* (1823), in fact, constitutes her response to the fascination of Staël's *Corinne*. In three remarkable and extravagantly named female characters, Euthanasia, Beatrice, and Mandragola, Shelley defines her own vision of the possibilities of female response to the psychological and social strictures that disfigure women's lives in patriarchal culture and answers what she sees as a failure of "moral courage" in Staël's celebrated artist heroine.[2] Furthermore, *Valperga*, in its presentation of Castruccio, extends, deepens, and makes explicit the critique of militarism and Napoleonic tyranny implicit in *Corinne*. And finally, at the conclusion of *Valperga*, Euthanasia defines a climactic vision of female transcendence that she sustains until her death. This chapter is not, however, intended primarily as a comparison of *Valperga* and *Corinne*.[3] Rather, my aim is to show a congruence of aesthetic, philosophical, and spiritual preoccupations in the two novels and their authors, preoccupations that form the heart of a cosmopolitan European Romanticism in which these women writers played a central – and critical – role.

Corinne portrays the defeat of its heroine by the oppressive power of the psycho-social structures embodied in Romantic melancholy. As Chapter 1 argued, the novel celebrates Corinne's capacity for aesthetic transcendence in her first appearance in the novel, and then records her loss of this capacity as she internalizes an obsessive desire for psychic punishment and revenge that destroys her when, in witchlike fashion, she turns it against both her lover and herself.

The trajectory of *Valperga* is precisely the opposite. As a *Bildungsroman* contained within the form of a historical novel, *Valperga* follows the development of its fourteenth-century heroine Euthanasia, Countess of Valperga, as she develops from youth to maturity. Along the way she loses her family, her property, and her considerable political power, as well as her illusions about romantic love and human capacity for kindness and justice. Nevertheless, she develops a moral strength and vision at the conclusion of the novel that Shelley presents as an exemplary spiritual triumph. Her attainment of wisdom and serenity as the novel progresses makes a powerful contrast with Castruccio's development as a character from young adventurer to feared and hated tyrant, just as the novel's title sets up the alternative *Valperga: or, The Life and Adventures of Castruccio, Prince of Lucca* (my emphasis). For Castruccio sacrifices the generosity and sensitivity that characterize him as a youth to his overwhelming ambition and will to power so that at the end of the novel he is described as a cruel and evil tyrant who seeks "the empire of the world" and who is "forever deprived" of "peace, sympathy and happiness."[4]

If *Corinne* demonstrates the treacherous seductiveness of Romantic melancholy, then *Valperga* provides an analogous, though even more direct, critique of Byronic will to power and obsessive, passionate love. *Valperga* opens with an account of the historical Castruccio's life and rise to political power culled from sources such as Machiavelli, Moreri, and Staël's close friend Simonde de Sismondi and then relates a fictionalized record of his childhood and early adulthood in the first of its three volumes.[5] As the daughter of English "Jacobins," Shelley witnessed the betrayal of the French Revolution and the French republic by Napoleon's imperial policies. Accordingly, through its glorification of Florentine republican politics, her *Valperga* implicitly condemns Napoleon and places itself firmly in the civic humanist tradition that J.G.A. Pocock, in *The Machiavellian Moment*, traces so magisterially from Aristotle, through republican Rome and Renaissance Florence, down to eighteenth-century France, England, and America.[6] In Volumes II and III, however, Shelley shifts the focus to the three female characters who are connected by their relation to and fascination with Castruccio and thus concludes the novel with a response to civic humanism that is explicitly modern, idealist, and feminist. In depicting the devastating effects of Castruccio's egotistical drive for socio-political power on these three women, Shelley clearly asks the reader to reject this will to power utterly and thus opens the way for Euthanasia's alternative and potentially healing vision of political leadership and spiritual transcendence that concludes the novel. *Valperga*, then, is a meditation on political, psychological, and sexual power, a meditation that formulates a vision of oppositional spirituality meant to enable women to resist and to transform existing masculinist structures of church and state. The conclusion of the novel interiorizes the struggles for power and the historical contingencies that civic humanist and Machiavellian thought labeled *fortuna*, in a sense prefiguring and responding to the anti-humanist vision of modern descendants of Byron like Nietzsche, Freud, and Foucault. For the ultimate fates of its characters render evident Shelley's proto-Nietzschean, even Foucauldian, understanding of all human relationships as rooted in a struggle for power and demonstrate her belief – so distinct from theirs – that only through spiritual or meditative practice can such struggles be turned to positive ends.

Accordingly, if my analysis of *Corinne* proceeded from an elucidation of Corinne's emancipatory ethical and aesthetic visions to their silencing in masculinist guilt and melancholy, this chapter will first examine Castruccio as an embodiment of Byronic glorification of the ego and power of the superior individual in order to demonstrate Shelley's subsequent celebration of an alternative set of socio-political and moral values in her heroine Euthanasia. In asserting that Shelley sets her heroine in opposition to the excesses of Byronic Romanticism, I am not suggesting that she rejects Byron's or Percy Shelley's influence as altogether repressive or destructive. For, as critics from Betty Bennett (1978) to Tilottama Rajan (1994) have argued, the influence of Percy Shelley's Romantic philosophy of imagination, universal love, and egalitarianism is strikingly evident in the character of Euthanasia.[7] Shelley had a close and deep friendship with Byron. Staël also valued his friendship highly and Arnim considered dedicating the diary section of *Goethe's Correspondence with a Child* to him. All three clearly were wise enough to distinguish between the man and his heroes.

And indeed as we shall see, Mary Shelley's critique of Castruccio has much in common with Byron's own presentation of the flaws of his heroes. Rather I wish to emphasize that in *Valperga* Shelley, like the other women writers of Romanticism who are the subject of this book, seeks to reshape the philosophical and literary production of her age which we now label Romantic to include a heightened sensitivity to the psychological, material, and historical realities of gendered subjectivity.[8] Rather than creating a distinct women's Romanticism, Shelley seeks to enrich and reconfigure the aesthetic and intellectual concerns she shared with Wollstonecraft, Godwin, Percy Shelley, and Lord Byron to reflect more directly a woman's perspective. Just as Staël knew first hand the egotism of Constant and Chateaubriand's *mal du siècle* and its blindness to the psychological and social needs of woman, so *Valperga* is evidence that Shelley was inclined to read *Manfred* from the perspective of Astarte and *The Giaour* from the point of view of the murdered beloved.

Castruccio Castracani and the "arched palace of eternal fame"

Readers of Shelley's day tended to conflate Byron with his heroes, and Castruccio possesses traits of the man Shelley knew, admired, and even loved as well as attributes typical of his poetic creations.[9] He has the fiery eyes and lofty, "aspiring spirit" (p. 83) of Byron's heroes as well as their Satanic defiance of heaven. Setting out from home as a young man, Castruccio, like Childe Harold, experiences nature as a stage, a backdrop for a spectacular personal drama. Rather than being in awe of nature or respecting it, however, as does the narrative voice of Childe Harold, Castruccio, perhaps more akin to Manfred, experiences nature as a "tributary to his will" (*Manfred*, Act II, Scene iv, ll.159–60):

> He experienced a peculiar sensation of pleasure, as he descended from the
> mountains into Tuscany. Alone on the bare Apennines, over which the fierce
> wind swept, he felt free ... his own will guided his progress, swift or slow, as
> the various thoughts that arose in his mind impelled him. He felt as if the air
> that quickly glided over him, was a part of his own nature, and bore his soul
> along with it; ... he suffered his imagination to dwell upon the period when
> he might be recalled from exile, and to luxuriate in dreams of power and
> distinction.
>
> (pp. 65–6)

Later, his "exuberant vanity" pictures his future life as "transcendent with glory
and success" in an explicit challenge to heaven:

> Thus, in solitude, ... he would throw his arms to the north, the south, the
> east, and the west, crying, – "There–there–there, and there, shall my fame
> reach!" – and then, in gay defiance, casting his eager glance towards heaven:
> – "and even there, if man may climb the slippery sides of the arched palace
> of eternal fame, there also will I be recorded."
>
> (p. 76)[10]

Transcendence, then, for Castruccio, is equivalent to the renown of the
individual ego. "Is it not fame that makes men gods?" (p. 81) he exclaims,
exhibiting the pride that will later lead Shelley to compare him with Satan, "the
fallen arch-angel," when Euthanasia permanently breaks with him because of his
political ruthlessness. Byron himself, of course, had a much more sophisticated,
detached, and ironic perception of his own fame. Nevertheless, it would be naïve
to suggest that his own unequalled renown among Romantic authors did not
contribute to a sense of self that Byron transmuted into much more than mortal
heroes as Prometheus, Manfred, and the Giaour. Furthermore, like Byron,
Castruccio's life is marked by exile; as a passionate Ghibeline, his family is forced
from their home in Lucca when it is conquered by Guelphs. Like Byron also, he
possesses a remarkable beauty that appeals to both men and women as his close
relationship with Edward II and Gavaston suggests:

> His beauty took a more manly cast; and somewhat of pride, and more of
> self-confidence, and much of sensibility, were seen in his upturned lip; his
> eyes, dark as a raven's wing, were full of fire and imagination; his open
> forehead was shaded by the hyacinthine curls of his chestnut-coloured hair.
>
> (p. 131)

Though Shelley is careful to emphasize the "manly" nature of his beauty, the
adjective "hyacinthine" – referring to the youth beloved by Apollo – complicates
that assertion as does the mention of the feminizing trait of sensibility.

Most significant for the plot and the ideological import of the novel is the
parallel between Castruccio and Napoleon. Byron of course was known in his

day for his admiration, shocking to his English countrymen, of the French general and ruler, though this admiration was anything but unequivocal, as the address to Napoleon's fiery, Romantic spirit in Canto Three of *Childe Harold's Pilgrimage* attests:

> But Quiet to quick bosoms is a hell,
> And *there* hath been thy bane; there is a fire
> And motion of the Soul which will not dwell
> In its own narrow being, but aspire
> Beyond the fitting medium of desire;
> And, but once kindled, quenchless evermore,
> Preys upon high adventure, nor can tire
> Of aught but rest; a fever at the core,
> Fatal to him who bears, to all who ever bore.
>   (III, 42)[11]

One such breast "laid open," Byron writes, "were a school/Which would unteach Mankind the lust to shine or rule" (III, 43), a lesson which is one of the ultimate aims of *Valperga*.

In transforming Castruccio into a fourteenth-century Napoleon, Shelley also has a specifically political and historical aim, for as Pamela Clemit asserts in *The Godwinian Novel: The Rational Fictions of Godwin, Brockden Brown, Mary Shelley*, Shelley "had learned from [Godwin's] *St. Leon* and *Mandeville* that a historically distanced setting gave unusual scope for a displaced treatment of contemporary social pressures on the individual."[12] Hence the great importance of the work of Staël's friend and colleague Sismondi. His *History of the Italian Republics* (1807–17) was written, as Clemit asserts, "as a protest against Napoleon's campaign to gain control of Italy" and "sought to present fourteenth-century republican Florence as a living inspiration for liberal thinkers" (p. 177).

Like Sismondi, Shelley implicitly charges Napoleon with a betrayal of the French Revolution's republican and egalitarian ideals that become associated in the novel with Euthanasia and her beloved Florence. These doctrines are elucidated first in utopian fashion by the character Guinigi, a former soldier and knight to whom Castruccio's father entrusts the care and education of his son after his death.[13] Guinigi, who has "turned his sword to a ploughshare" (p. 77), "thought only of the duty of man to man, laying aside the distinctions of society, and with lovely humility recognized the affinity of the meanest peasant to his own noble mind" (pp. 78–9). A "strange enthusiast" (p. 79), he expresses the highest potential of the Romantic imagination: "Exercising the most exalted virtues, he also cultivated a taste and imagination that dignified what the vulgar would term ignoble, as the common clouds of day become fields of purple and gold, painted by the sun at eve" (p. 79). His imagination refuses, however, to lend an aura of glory to agents of war and destruction, the "privileged murderers of the earth," or "to adorn with beauty vice, death and misery, when disguised by a kingly robe, by the trappings of a victorious army, or the false halo of glory spread over the smoking ruins of a ravaged town" (p. 79). The narrator sets up an explicit contrast between Guinigi and conquering spirits such as those of Napoleon and Castruccio: "Men, like Alexander and other conquerors, have indulged the hope of subduing the world, and spreading by their triumphs refinement into its barbarous recesses. Guinigi hoped, how futilely! to lay a foundation-stone for the temple of peace among the Euganean hills" (p. 79).

If Guinigi's hopes are presented as utopian, Florence nevertheless offers the possibility of a realization of these ideals as the narrative commentary on a treaty between Pisa and Florence suggests:

> If this treaty had been fulfilled, the hopes of the Ghibelines would have been crushed forever, nor would Castruccio ever have returned to his country; the scenes of blood and misery which followed would have been spared; and Florence, raising its benign influence over the other Tuscan states, would have been the peace-maker of Italy.
>
> (p. 130)

The fear inspired in the Ghibeline supporters by republican Florence is described in terms that explicitly mirror monarchist reactions to the French Revolution, thus rendering evident Shelley's association of Napoleon with counter-revolution and her character Guinigi's "strange" enthusiasm with the Revolution's republican and egalitarian ideals. The character who most strongly voices these fears is Benedetto Pepi, a mean-spirited, hideous creature whose life Castruccio saves as he is returning to Italy from his victorious campaigns with Alberto Scoto, agent of Philip le Bel, king of France, campaigns which earn Castruccio renown for his military prowess and personal valor. Pepi speaks of Florentine democracy and liberty as a "contagion" in danger of spreading over Lombardy, a "monster" that must be chained, precisely the metaphors, as Ronald Paulson has shown, employed by conservatives to characterize the French Revolution.[14] Similarly, Pepi advocates the alliance of the Italian states with the forces of Imperial power against Florence, just as the European monarchies banded together against revolutionary France: "[If] the few princes that there need exist in the world, would league in amity, instead of quarrelling, such a state as that of Florence would not subsist a year" (p. 114).

Pepi functions as a double or shadow figure for Castruccio, embodying his most selfish, destructive impulses and beliefs. It is entirely fitting that Castruccio saves the terrified Pepi from falling to his death from an Alpine precipice, that quintessential locus of Romantic sublimity. As she had in her first novel *Frankenstein*, Shelley once again reveals fear and cowardice to be the double of that will to power implicit in the Alpine obsessions of masculine romanticism; this will is represented by Victor's face-to-face encounter with his creature in the shadow of Mont Blanc and by Castruccio's triumphant return to Italy through the Alps. For Pepi, the ideal government is an aristocracy of wealth built upon the enslavement of the "vile multitude":

My friend, the world, trust me, will never go well, until the rich rule, and the vulgar sink to their right station as slaves of the soil. . . . Such is the order, which, if I were a prince, I would establish, and every town, such as Florence, where all is noise and talk, should be reduced to silence and peace; about two thousand rich men should possess all the rest of the inhabitants, who, like sheep, would flock to their folds, and receive their pittances with thankfulness and humility.

(pp. 113–14)

Pepi's tree of tyranny is a grotesque parody of Edmund Burke's English oak, suggesting an iconoclastic reading of this venerable British symbol: "tyranny is a healthy tree, it strikes a deep root, and each year its branches grow larger and larger, and its shade spreads wider and wider" (p. 114). Though as a young man, Castruccio responds with amused horror at Pepi's crude political philosophy, it eventually becomes his own, so that after a few years of experience, "[he] now fully subscribed to all the articles of Pepi's political creed, and thought fraud and secret murder fair play, when it thinned the ranks of the enemy" (p. 280). Once Euthanasia understands the extent of Castruccio's corruption, she breaks with him forever, even though they have been betrothed in heart and mind since childhood, rather than be bound to the enemy of republican Florence. By this time, Castruccio's Napoleonic desire for the "empire of the world" (p. 397) has "deluged the country in blood" (p. 268). And like the early nineteenth-century emperor, Castruccio disdains "the name of consul" (p. 282) and has himself named prince of Lucca for life. Eventually, Euthanasia participates in a failed plot to oust him from power, believing that she can thus free Florence and prevent his assassination. Before the failure of the conspiracy, she even imagines for him an exile à la Bonaparte on a Mediterranean island, with this difference – that he learns to "love obscurity" (p. 412) through the lessons of her Stoic philosophers. No longer the fiery, Vesuvian Romantic hero, he would be "an extinguished volcano" wise and beautiful with the "vivifying heat of mighty and subdued passions" (p. 413). Instead, however, the plot leads to *her* own sentence of exile to Sicily and ultimate death.

One is left then, in *Valperga*, above all else, with a sense of Castruccio's destructive effect on all around him, and on the three female characters, Beatrice, Euthanasia, and Mandragola, in particular, who together form a kind of archetypal nexus of Maiden, Mother, and Crone and thus represent three stages or possibilities of female response to masculinist power. These three characters are distinguished among Shelley's novelistic heroines and perhaps among early nineteenth-century British heroines in general for their strength and rich historical and ideological import. There is no doubt that Shelley emphasizes in this novel the mutualities of interest that bind these women with the lower classes whom Castruccio, like Pepi, considers pawns in his war games. As his chosen mentor Alberto Scoto asserts, making clear the assumptions about class and gender that he shares with Castruccio:

A chief in Italy ought to pay strict attention to the discipline and equipment of his followers, and to the spreading the terror of his name among his enemies. This must be his first step; and without that the foundations of his power are as sand; for to have many cities subject to his command is as nothing in the hour of danger, since if he control them not with iron, gold will ever find its way into the councils of the citizens; and woe and defeat are to that chief, who reigns only by the choice of the people; a choice more fickle and deceitful than the famed faithlessness of woman.

(p. 100)

It is, of course, Castruccio who is deceitful and faithless, not Euthanasia or Beatrice.

Because the last two volumes of *Valperga* focus upon Castruccio's power to annihilate these fascinating characters, the effect of the novel is very different from that of Byron's poetry, for example, which is ultimately sympathetic to the unbending will of Prometheus and Manfred, the murderous desire and despair of the Giaour, and even the will to power of Bonaparte. Witness the perspective of knowledge through identification from which Byron writes the famed concluding lines of his portrait of Napoleonic sublimity in *Childe Harold*:

He who ascends to mountain-tops, shall find
The loftiest peaks most wrapt in clouds and snow;
He who surpasses or subdues mankind,
Must look down on the hate of those below.
Though high *above* the Sun of glory glow,
And far *beneath* the Earth and Ocean spread,
Round him are icy rocks, and loudly blow
Contending tempests on his naked head,
And thus reward the toils which to those summits led.

(III, 45)

In contrast, Shelley writes of Castruccio that "[he] became all in all to himself," and "every new act of cruelty hardened his heart for those to come" (p. 268). And as we shall see, Shelley's Euthanasia has a radically different vision of transcendence, as she terms it, "the sweet reward of all our toil" (p. 366).

Witchcraft, heresy, and "the love of power"

Beatrice and Mandragola demand our attention as more forceful, even melodramatic, responses to the realities of female oppression and to the vision of power that Castruccio represents before we turn to Euthanasia as a kind of ideal, climactic presence in the novel. In the responses of these three allegorically named fictional female characters to a historical figure whom Shelley transforms into an embodiment, both seductive and repellent, of Napoleonic tyranny, imperialism, and militarism, Shelley represents three stages of female resistance to a masculinist politics of domination: witchcraft, heresy, and carefully reasoned political action rooted in a meditative spiritual consciousness. Furthermore, each of these three characters corresponds to what might be termed an archetypal stage in female psychic development: Beatrice, the maiden-child; Mandragola, the crone; and Euthanasia, the mature woman. (By archetypal I do not mean Jungian but rather inevitably repeated in the historical succession of women's full lives.) Shelley's (perhaps unconscious) choice to experiment with the archetypal mold of Maiden, Mother, and Crone suggests that she is emphasizing the multiplicity of female personality just as Staël did in representing Corinne and Lucile as doubles of each other. Thus, more than simply being three distinct characters, these women represent three closely related and intertwined possibilities of oppositional religious response to a world of ubiquitous male domination epitomized by Castruccio. And in the interrelations of these women, Shelley is, in a sense, depicting the psychic as well as the historical development of women both as individuals and as a collectivity into spiritual and political maturity.

At the center of the uncanny web of relationships that bind the characters of *Valperga*, spider-like in her manipulations, is the witch Mandragola. In this character, who at first seems contrived and almost peripheral, and who has been virtually ignored by previous criticism, we find the essence of Mary Shelley's understanding of the dynamics of power at the heart of all human relationships. Shelley is careful to be explicit, through narrative commentary on female attraction to black magic and witchcraft as symbols of destructive spiritual practice, that desire for power is more basic and all-pervasive in human nature than the desire for any material advantage:

> What made these women pretend to powers they did not possess, incur the greatest perils for the sake of being believed to be what they were not, without any apparent advantage accruing to themselves from this belief? I believe we may find the answer in our own hearts: the love of power is inherent in human nature; and, in evil natures, to be feared is a kind of power.
>
> (p. 325)

For Shelley, then, men like Castruccio have no monopoly on the will to power; it is essential to all human natures, male and female. Indeed, Mandragola seems a kind of mythic manifestation of the urge to power, outside of time and social history: "[S]he was very old; none knew how old: men, verging on decrepitude, remembered their childish fears of her; and they all agreed that formerly she appeared more aged and decrepid than now" (p. 323). At the same time, however, Shelley makes it clear that her compulsive search for power has its origin in a lack, in a form of socially constructed powerlessness: "It was believed, that the witch loved evil as her daily bread, and that she had sold her soul to the devil to do ill alone; *she* knew how powerless she was; but she desired to fill in every part the character attributed to her" (p. 373). Indeed, Mandragola stands as an emblem of victimized and vengeful womanhood; the history of crimes against her is so old and so relentless that it has transformed her into myth:

She had been young once; and her nature, never mild, had been turned to ferocity by wrongs which had been received so long ago, that the authors of them were all dead, and she, the victim, alone survived. Calumny had blasted her name; her dearest affections had been blighted; her children torn from her; and she remained to execrate and avenge.

(pp. 372–3)

Her vengeance takes the form of a plot to destroy Castruccio, Beatrice, and Euthanasia; "she thought she saw one mighty ruin envelop three master-spirits of the human kind, plotted by her alone" (p. 373). Her plan is irrational, and anarchic, purely malicious and destructive in that she has no clear sense of any real benefit that it will bring her. That this witch, in her obsession with Castruccio in particular, formulates the proto-Nietzschean notion of the master-spirit reveals Shelley's strikingly modern understanding of the abject sources of such conceptions and their glorification of the superior individual, as well as highlighting the Romantic/Byronic roots of Nietzsche's work.[15]

Like Mandragola, named for the phallic mandrake root thought to spring from a hanged man's sperm, *Valperga*'s Beatrice is also particularly rich with historical and cultural resonance. Recalling Dante's ideal woman, she is also explicitly compared with the historical Beatrice Cenci, incest victim and patricidal heroine of Percy's tragedy *The Cenci*; perhaps Mary Shelley is suggesting the frightening proximity of these two objects of male desire. In any case, as James Rieger has pointed out, *Valperga* was both an analogue and a source for *The Cenci* – Mary's favorite of Percy's works.[16] A young prophetess or *Ancilla Dei* who believes in her own divine inspiration, Beatrice is also Shelley's rewriting of the character Corinne, a rewriting which allows Shelley the opportunity to clarify her own vision of the imbrication of Romantic love, Romantic imagination, and socio-political power.[17] Beatrice's entrance into *Valperga* replicates the first spectacular appearance of Staël's heroine in the chapter "Corinne at the Capitol." Like Corinne, she is capable of extemporaneous eloquence and ecstasy, as the bishop who raised her explains: "As she grew older, her imagination developed; she would sing extempore hymns with wild, sweet melody, and she seemed to dwell with all her soul on the mysteries of our religion" (p. 211). And just as Corinne in her triumphal procession and subsequent improvisational performance is compared with a "goddess amid the clouds," a "priestess of Apollo making her way toward the Temple of the Sun," so Beatrice shines in "the light of her divine beauty" (p. 202). Similarly, according to her female companion and follower, the Viscountess di Malvezzi, Beatrice is a "sacred maiden, who by her more than human beauty, … by her wisdom beyond that of woman, and her prophecies which have ever been fulfilled, demonstrates, … that she is inspired by the grace and favour of the blessed Virgin" (p. 203).

Beatrice's association with the Virgin Mary and with a female spiritual tradition is essential to an understanding of her role in *Valperga*, for Shelley is clearly seeking in the three central female characters of this novel to define a spiritual power that will allow women to stand up to the masculinist Church and state. Beatrice is the daughter of Wilhelmina of Bohemia, a historical figure recorded in Ludovico Antonio Muratori's *Antichità Italiane* (1738), who believed herself, in Shelley's explicitly feminist rendering of her, to be "the Holy Ghost incarnate upon earth for the salvation of the female sex" (p. 204) and who claimed that the angel Raphael had announced to her Beatrice's divine conception as (again) the "incarnation of the Holy Spirit in favor of the female sex" (p. 204). And as Emily Sunstein emphasizes, Shelley had another contemporary model besides Corinne for Wilhelmina and Beatrice in the millenarian Joanna Southcott, who claimed to be the New Savior sent to raise women and redeem humanity; she attracted thousands of followers during Mary Godwin's girlhood until her death in 1814, following a hysterical pregnancy that was supposed to deliver Shiloh, the second Christ (p. 53). Descendant of this extraordinary lineage, Beatrice is, however, like Corinne, doomed by her remarkable gifts; because she is convinced that heaven has decreed the eternal union of their souls, she gives herself to Castruccio, who is attracted to her "prophetic fire," her "rich and persuasive eloquence" (p. 212) and her "enthusiasm" (p. 213). "She prayed to the Virgin to inspire her; and, again giving herself up to reverie, she wove a subtle web, whose materials she believed heavenly, but which were indeed stolen from the glowing wings of love" (p. 227). Like Byron, who accepted Claire Clairmont's offer of herself to him but never intended to sustain any relationship to her, so Castruccio abandons Beatrice when his political ambitions call and he returns to Euthanasia. Ultimately Beatrice falls into complete despair and depression and is "for ever lost" (p. 231) when she realizes the truth that she has mistaken "for the inspirations of Heaven the wild reveries of youth and love" (p. 223).

As an avatar of Corinne, Beatrice is clearly a figure for the female artist. Indeed both Jane Blumberg and Barbara Jane O'Sullivan interpret Beatrice as an embodiment of Shelley's anxieties about her own female creativity.[18] O'Sullivan, in a fascinating article that places Beatrice in the tradition of Western female spiritual and imaginative power typified by the figure of Cassandra, even charges Shelley, in her "depiction of Beatrice's awkward and vulnerable state" (p. 150), with "complicity in the repression and discrediting of the [strong, female] voices she herself has created" (p. 151). This is certainly a plausible reading of the character of Beatrice. We have seen that Staël was to a certain extent complicit in the seduction and betrayal of her female artist by the judgmental, masculinist strictures of Romantic melancholy and that only at the end of her life did Staël finally permit herself unequivocal gratitude for her artistic gifts. What of Mary Shelley?

If we take Beatrice as a sympathetic critique of the figure of Corinne reflecting Mary Shelley's disappointment in that character, then another reading of the prophetess is possible, particularly if we place her next to Euthanasia, who also asks to be read as a figure for the female intellectual, philosopher, and artist. Beatrice's fate then represents submission to the dangers to which faith in the imagination exposes any artist, but particularly the female artist, and Euthanasia's the successful negotiation of these dangers and the resultant possibilities of self-assertion and self-expression.

The key to understanding Shelley's central characters in *Valperga* is the recognition of her almost Foucauldian and proto-Freudian perception of the inextricability of power struggles from human relationships. Rather than being a critique of the Romantic imagination per se, *Valperga* is an attack on the perversion of the imagination that results when this faculty is bound to the service of the individual human ego and its desire for power. Thus Shelley is wary of that deification of passionate love which we now term Romantic love both because she sees it as a reflection of blind egotism and because she recognizes its culturally determined destructiveness to women. Describing the "delusive sanctity" of Beatrice's "entrancing dream of love" Shelley writes:

> It is said, that in love we idolize the object; and, placing him apart and selecting him from his fellows, look on him as superior in nature to all others. We do so; but, even as we idolize the object of our affections, do we idolize ourselves: if we separate him from his fellow mortals, so do we separate ourselves, and, glorying in belonging to him alone, feel lifted above all other sensations, all other joys and griefs, to one hallowed circle from which all but his idea is banished; we walk as if a mist or some more potent charm divided us from all but him; a sanctified victim which none but the priest set apart for that office could touch and not pollute. . . .
>
> (p. 231)

Romantic love, then, for Shelley, represents a delusive effort at deification of self and beloved that ends with the victimization and sacrifice of the woman on the altar of passion. This is certainly true for Beatrice, for she, like Corinne who sacrifices her artistic expression to Oswald, symbolically gives up her own power to Castruccio when she removes the silver plate inscribed with the words *Ancilla Dei* from her brow because it seems an obstacle to her union with him. Her fate replicates that of Corinne precisely; as Beatrice confesses to Euthanasia, "I . . . met him at the full height of my glory, when I was burning with triumph and joy" (p. 352), but when he left, "[my] very powers of speech deserted me, and I could not articulate a syllable" (p. 354). As with Corinne, passionate love silences Beatrice's exceptional voice; abandonment calls forth debilitating depression.

Despite Castruccio's cruel irresponsibility, Beatrice never ceases her obsession with him. When she learns from Euthanasia that she has rejected Castruccio, has chosen her own beliefs and ideals over him, she answers Euthanasia with a distinctly Byronic vision of passionate love, one worthy of Manfred or the Giaour:

> *He* remained, and was not that everything? Methinks, it would please me, that my lover should cast off all humanity, and be a reprobate, and an outcast of his species. Oh! then how deeply and tenderly I should love him; soiled with crimes, his hands dripping blood, I would shade him as the flowering shrub invests the ruin; I would cover him with a spotless veil; – my intensity of love would annihilate his wickedness; – every one would hate

him; – but, if all adored him, it would not come near the sum of my single affection.

(p. 350)

Predictably, however, it is not Beatrice who protects and saves Castruccio by pouring out "large draughts of love" until he, "drunk with it," grows "good and kind" (p. 350). Rather it is Castruccio who destroys Beatrice, for as Euthanasia ironically asserts, in answering Beatrice, Castruccio loves domination and death more than other human beings:

> Glory and conquest are his mistresses, and he is a successful lover; already he has deluged our vallies in blood, and turned our habitations into black and formless ruins; he has torn down the banners of the Florentines, and planted his own upon the towers of noble cities; I believe him to be happy.

(pp. 350–1)

After her abandonment by Castruccio, Beatrice's demise and death may seem rather far-fetched and sensationalistic when measured by the demands of the realistic plot; her fate is, however, brilliantly apt in terms of its symbolic significance, for through the bizarre connections it lays bare, Shelley reveals a sado-masochistic death wish at the core of Castruccio's Byronic will to power. When Beatrice recognizes the truth of her encounter with Castruccio, she undertakes a pilgrimage of atonement to Rome. Significantly, she never reaches this destination. Along the way she stops for a brief visit at Euthanasia's castle of Valperga, but will not stay and eventually ends up mysteriously imprisoned in a gothic chamber of horrors most likely suggested to Shelley by the works of Matthew Lewis or the Marquis de Sade.[19]

Shelley's presentation of Beatrice's prophetic powers, ambiguous from the outset, shifts in this episode to an unequivocal assertion of her ability to foresee the future, for she dreams repeatedly of this gothic torture chamber before coming upon it in reality: "a dreary, large, ruinous house, half like a castle, yet without a tower, dilapidated, and overgrown with moss, ... islanded by the flood on which it cast a night-black shade" (p. 358). This scene of torture, though it exists objectively, is also, significantly, a part, perhaps the essence, as Beatrice claims, of her psyche: "I was haunted as by a prophecy, or rather a sense of evil, which I could neither define nor understand. ... Again and again I have dreamed this dream, and always on the eve of some great misfortune. It is my genius, my daemon" (p. 358). The "fiendlike" owner of this castle is an embodiment of pure power and transgression, translated into sadistic sexual dominion over others:

> There was something about him that might be called beautiful; but it was the beauty of the tiger, of lightning, of the cataract that destroys. Obedience waited on his slightest motion; for he made none, that did not command; his followers worshipped him, but it was as a savage might worship the god of

evil. His slaves dared not murmur; – his eyes beamed with irresistible fire, his smile was as death.

(p. 360)

Readers of James Miller's *The Passion of Michel Foucault* which emphasizes the links between Foucault's analytic of power and his fascination with sado-masochism will find an eerie consonance in Mary Shelley's gothic imagery of raw human power as Beatrice comes face-to-face with it.[20] She "alone among his many victims was not quelled to submission" but "changed his detested love into less dreadful, less injurious hate" (p. 360). When he is finally defeated at the hands of the Pope's agents and the local peasantry who "flocked as to a crusade to destroy their oppressor," (p. 361) – again the connection between sexual and class conflict is rendered evident – Beatrice watches him die, like a Byronic hero, "calm, courageous and unrepenting" (p. 361).

This experience transforms Beatrice into a Paterin, a member of a heretical, Manichean sect about which the Shelleys read in Sismondi's *History*. Beatrice's Paterin beliefs, like her deification of Castruccio and her love for him, enable Shelley to illustrate another example of the perversion of the faculty of imagination, for Beatrice comes to believe that God and his gift to humanity, the creative imagination, are evil. After Beatrice is abandoned by Castruccio, she loses all faith in her imagination; as Rieger writes, "when the imagination is denied, it has a nasty trick of returning as terror" (p. 127). This terror that manifests itself in her daemon, her gothic nightmare, causes her to curse God and his gift of the imagination in one of the most remarkable passages of the novel:

> And the imagination, that masterpiece of his malice; that spreads honey on the cup that you may drink poison; that strews roses over thorns, thorns sharp and big as spears; . . . that diadem of nettles; that spear, broken in the heart! He, the damned and triumphant one, sat meditating many thousand years for the conclusion, the consummation, the final crown, the seal of all misery, which he might set on man's brain and heart to doom him to endless torment; and he created the Imagination.
>
> (p. 343)

Even after Beatrice has been soothed by the friendship and counseling of Euthanasia, she still refuses to see any positive potential in the faculty of imagination, reiterating the imagery of phallic wounding that she repeatedly associates with it: "if imagination live, it is as a tyrant, armed with fire, and venomed darts, to drive me to despair" (p. 367).

It is no accident that Beatrice terms imagination a tyrant, the term consistently used in the novel to describe Castruccio. For it is ultimately Castruccio's connection to her gothic nightmare – to Beatrice's daemon – that makes it clear that his seduction of her was a psychic rape and that renders him the agent of her death. Late one night when he is in the company of Tripalda, "the evil genius of her life" (p. 390), a consort of her former mysterious, sadistic persecutor, she seeks Castruccio out, only to come face-to-face with Tripalda. Mandragola's tool for manipulating Beatrice and bringing about the desired confrontation with Castruccio is the character Bindo, Euthanasia's albino servant, who, in the service of the witch, brings Beatrice to her. Bindo, who calls himself a "dwarf, a blight, a stunt" (p. 377), is, once again, an embodiment of frustrated powerlessness, revealing yet again in stark fashion as does Mandragola the abject roots of the will to superhuman power. "He felt his defects in bodily prowess; perhaps also he felt the weakness of his reason; and therefore he sought for powers of art, which might overcome strength, and powers of mind, which were denied to the majority of the human species" (p. 325). In the end, then, Beatrice herself succumbs to her desire to see Castruccio once more, a desire that is framed in terms of a struggle for domination. "She would have risked her soul, to gain a moment's power over Castruccio" (p. 381). Indeed, she desires to see him "divested of the ceremonial of power" (p. 383) and is seduced by Mandragola's vow that Castruccio "will obey my voice, . . . not by magic art, but by that innate power, which, by the order of the universe, one spirit possesses over another" (p. 382). Instead of gaining control over Castruccio, however, Beatrice is confronted with the image of Tripalda which intervenes between her and the object of her desire. She soon dies, though not without having been soothed into serenity by Euthanasia. After Tripalda makes sure that Mandragola is captured, she is tried by the Inquisition and put to death as a witch.

In the figures of Beatrice and Mandragola, Shelley gives us examples of a female will to controvert, appropriate, and usurp male power that is ineffectual and self-destructive. Despite their associations with exclusively female realms of witchcraft and of feminist spirituality, neither of these women is able to envisage an alternative to power struggles ending in dominance or submission. The crone, spiritually disfigured by centuries of abuse, dreams of power manifested in malice and vengeance. The maiden-child deludes herself with visions of self-aggrandizement or vicarious power gained through romantic love or through the blind rebellion of Paterin heresy. Shelley is careful to make it clear that Beatrice never matures, that her psychic development is truncated because she has suffered "evils tremendous and irremediable" (p. 349). Thus she is termed a "divine girl" (p. 201), a "sacred maiden" (p. 221), when she first enters the novel and she dies "peacefully, and calmly as a child" (p. 393) with Euthanasia by her side as mother figure to sooth, and comfort her.

Euthanasia, Countess of Valperga: "A new and mightier power"

Euthanasia's bond with Beatrice is, in fact, as Rajan asserts, "the most compelling part of the novel" (p. 63), "the affective core" (p. 64) of *Valperga*. And if, as I have asserted, the two women represent two parts of one self, then it makes sense as Rajan suggests that "Euthanasia . . . finds her vocation and her own cure in caring for Beatrice" (p. 64). In Euthanasia Mary Shelley figures the mature woman who has the capacity to nurture herself as well as others. Thus *Valperga* moves beyond the glimpse of the curative potential of female relationship offered at the conclusion of *Corinne* to make the relationship between Euthanasia and Beatrice the emotional heart of the novel. Euthanasia is never jealous of this woman who becomes the lover of her betrothed; she feels only concern and compassion: "she felt that they were bound together, by their love for one who loved only himself" (pp. 345–6). Indeed she surmounts her grief over her loss of faith in Castruccio – the predominant emotion in her life after their break – once Beatrice enters her life: "the feelings of her heart were so completely absorbed in pity and love for Beatrice, that the painful ideas of many years' growth seemed rooted out by a new and mightier power" (p. 349). In Euthanasia's case, love for another woman – characterized by that all important word in this novel – power – is more than able to compensate for the loss even of a man as charismatic as Castruccio.

Euthanasia, then, is Mary Shelley's answer to the doomed Beatrice, mirror of Staël's Corinne. In fact, the similarity in the narrative structure of the two novels highlights the parallels among all three female characters. In *Corinne* individual chapters in the third person narrative are devoted to the first person narration of "Lord Nelvil's Story" and "Corinne's Story"; in *Valperga* it is "Euthanasia's Narrative" and "Beatrice's Narrative." Significantly, unlike Oswald, Castruccio is not allowed to speak for himself, for as Clemit asserts, Shelley wishes to undercut his history through the use of first person female narratives: "In a strategy which recalls the narrative complexity of *Frankenstein*, she opens up her apparently uncompromisingly historical account into a more dialogic form reminiscent of earlier Godwinian novels. But, more markedly than in *Frankenstein*, the novel's alternative points of view are voiced by women" (p. 179).

As an alternative to masculinist visions of power, Euthanasia's world view has much in common with Staël's emancipatory model of transcendence embodied in Corinne before her demise. Like Corinne, she is distinguished by a more than earthly eloquence, imagination, and enthusiasm that make her the center of the cultivated and refined society in which she lives. However, as Daniel Schierenbeck has emphasized, whereas Beatrice's enthusiasm inspires the threatening worship of the masses, associated in Britain with religious fanaticism and the Civil Wars, the aristocratic Euthanasia is the leader of a little band of elite Florentines.[21]

> Her beauty, her accomplishments, and the gift of flowing yet mild eloquence that she possessed, the glowing brilliancy of her ardent yet tempered imagination, made her the leader of the little [Florentine] band to which she belonged. It is said, that as Dante sighed for Beatrice, so several of the distinguished youths of Florence fed on the graceful motions and sweet words of this celestial girl, who, walking among them, passionless, yet full of enthusiasm, seemed as a link to bind their earthly thoughts to heaven.
>
> (pp. 133–4)

Shelley, like Staël, defines enthusiasm here by its opposition to personal emotion and passion. Yet Euthanasia's enthusiasm is theorized against a much more explicitly political backdrop than is Corinne's vision of aesthetic transcendence, for Shelley did not have to battle Napoleonic stricture and censorship daily as did Staël who was constantly threatened with exile or worse. The concluding meditation on enthusiasm was the chapter Shelley most admired from Staël's *On Germany*, a text that was pulped by Napoleon's agents and survived only because August Wilhelm Schlegel smuggled it safely out of France. And, of course, Shelley is writing a historical novel, indeed a feminist historical novel. Shelley's challenge thus becomes the perhaps utopian one of envisaging a mode of power based in a spiritual awareness that subverts and transcends the sado-masochistic dynamic of domination and submission that she, in Foucauldian fashion, has shown to be at the heart of existent political structures. In order to emphasize Euthanasia's detachment from the imperial political ambitions that define Castruccio, Shelley defines her enthusiasm explicitly and repeatedly as a "love of liberty" (p. 142), an enthusiasm for freedom: "Euthanasia had this foible, if indeed it might be called one in her, to love the very shadow of freedom with unbounded enthusiasm" (p. 142). This "enthusiasm for the liberties of [her] country" (p. 146) takes the form of support for the Florentine republic, a support nurtured by her readings, with her father, of authors from the Greek and Roman republics. Euthanasia's father is clearly, as numerous critics have noted, an idealized Godwin figure, a transposition of the emancipatory potential in Mary and Percy's lives of Godwin's influence into her fictional fourteenth-century world. It is the art of the Greeks and the Romans and of the Florentine Dante that compels her irresistibly "to connect wisdom and liberty together; and, as I worshipped wisdom as the pure emanation of the Deity, the divine light of the world, so did I adore liberty as its parent, its sister, the half of its being" (p. 147).

In politicizing the concept of enthusiasm as she does, Shelley runs the risk of enmeshing her heroine in the partisan politics that will indeed eventually destroy her. In order to reinforce Euthanasia's significance as a symbol of oppositional power, Shelley repeatedly emphasizes her independence and detachment from the Guelph–Ghibeline strife. Her castle of Valperga is midway between the respective Guelph and Ghibeline strongholds of Florence and Lucca. Whereas her mother, from whom she inherited the castle and villages of Valperga, was a "violent partisan" (p. 148) of the Guelph cause, Euthanasia seeks to maintain distance from perpetual quarrels and "glories in her independence and solitude" (p. 137). Her mother's partisanship is defined explicitly as a lack of perspective, an obsessive absorption in petty political intrigues. In contrast, Euthanasia above all else hates war and longs for peace: "I am more attached to concord and the alliance of parties, than to any of the factions which distract our poor Italy" (p. 138) she asserts to one of Castruccio's allies. In fact, her favorite contemporary Italian author Dante is a Ghibeline, a member of the opposite faction.

Crucial to Euthanasia's effort of detachment and distance from the political strife of her day is her historical perspective; the lessons of "the great and good of past ages" (p. 267) are her Bible. Not only does she see past examples of human wisdom as her guide, but she also strives to make her life an example for future generations. In a passage from her first person narrative which constitutes her own "Defence of Poetry," Euthanasia expresses her faith in art as a symbol of human potential, a distillation of human accomplishments both transcendent and historical. She assumes, in the artist, the capacity to fly as well as to walk:

> If time had not shaken the light of poetry and of genius from [man's] wings, all the past would be dark and trackless: now we have a track – the glorious foot-marks of the children of liberty; let us imitate them, and like them we may serve as marks in the desert, to attract future passengers to the fountains of life.
>
> (p. 147)

One cannot help but think here of Shelley's reference, in her intellectual biography of her predecessor, to the "luminous ideas" left by Staël along her route through life. Indeed, by rewriting the concluding sentence of Staël's *On Germany*, an attack on Napoleon that Staël believed was found to be particularly offensive by his police censors, these lines strongly suggest that Shelley here defines herself and her character Euthanasia as "children of liberty" in the ongoing struggle in the name of enthusiasm and freedom defined by Staël. Here is Staël's conclusion:

> Oh, France! . . . If one day enthusiasm were extinguished on your soil, if self-interest decided everything, . . . what would be the use of your beautiful sky, your brilliant minds, your fertile nature? An active intelligence, a clever impetuosity would make you the masters of the world; but you would leave in it nothing but the trace of torrents of sand, flood-like in their terror, and arid as the desert![22]

If for Staël, Napoleon's mastery of the world finally represents nothing but arid torrents of sand, Euthanasia's artists of genius, "children of liberty," provide pathways in this desert, "to attract future passengers to the fountains of life."

Clearly, then, like Staël, Shelley's Euthanasia has a strong sense of her own potential role in the "vast tableau of destinies" that is European history. And, if republican Florence represents the possibility of contemporary freedom for Euthanasia, it is Rome which in her narrative she terms "this city of my soul" (p. 151), that provides the inspiration for a perspective that unites the historical and the eternal. Among the Roman ruins, "rather a wandering shade of the ancient times, than a modern Italian," Euthanasia describes herself in a dialogue with spirits of the past who can teach and guide her in her efforts to free Italy from imperial domination: "In my wild enthusiasm I called on the shadows of the departed to converse with me, and to prophesy the fortunes of awakening Italy" (p. 150). In a visit to the Pantheon by moonlight that replicates Staël's extended meditations in *Corinne* on the significance of the Roman landscape,

Euthanasia experiences the union of her spirit with those of the past and future: "[N]ever had I before so felt the universal graspings of my own mind, or the sure tokens of other spiritual existences, as at that moment" (p. 150).[23]

In Rome to nurse her dying brother, Euthanasia finds comfort in this sense of communion with the disembodied; her recogition of the limitations of the individual's power and accomplishment and the inevitability of death and decline becomes an awareness, akin to that of Staël, of a connection with and absorption into the collective history of humanity. This is the inverse of Castruccio's sense of self; as a head of state, he asserts that he is "no longer a private man" (p. 262). Instead of being subsumed by the history of humanity, Castruccio seeks to absorb the humanity under him into himself and his desires. As the narrator of *Valperga* observes, in truly Godwinian fashion:

> [H]owever cruel an individual may be, no one is so remorseless as a ruler; for he loses even within himself the idea of his own individuality, and fancies that, in pampering his inclinations, and revenging his injuries, he is supporting the state; the state, a fiction, which sacrifices that which constitutes it, to the support of its mere name.
>
> (p. 261)

One must certainly acknowledge, as does Joseph Lew, that Euthanasia's Roman heroes – Virgil, the Scipios, and Cato the Elder – were associated with empire, slavery, and colonialism, and that her regret at not living among their wisdom and eloquence is perhaps ideologically contradictory.[24] More importantly, however, as Rajan's notes to the Broadview edition of *Valperga* indicate, the Scipios were known above all else for their moral rectitude, and Shelley may in fact be referring to Cato the Younger, who was "a committed Republican who sided with Pompey, and then took his life rather than yield to Julius Caesar after his defeat" (p. 452). Furthermore, Euthanasia's final recognition is of the inevitability of the death of empire:

> Beautiful city, thy towers were illuminated by the orange tints of the fast-departing sunset, and the ghosts of lovely memories floated with the night breeze, among thy ruins; I became calm; amidst a dead race, and an extinguished empire, what individual sorrow would dare raise its voice?
>
> (p. 151)

Perhaps, as historian and politician, Euthanasia is more sophisticated than Lew gives her credit for being.[25] After all, she makes it clear that Dante's art breathes a spirit of freedom despite his Ghibeline and imperial politics; she seems to be expressing a belief, akin to Percy Shelley's in *A Defence of Poetry*, that in moments of inspiration, writers and orators are capable of moving beyond their own individual moral and political codes.

Finally, in her meditation on Dante, the first to arouse her "enthusiasm for the liberties of my country, and the political welfare of Italy" (p. 146) despite his adherence to the Ghibeline faction, she defines freedom itself as productive, regenerative self-conflict:

> the essence of freedom is that clash and struggle which awaken the energies of our nature, and that operation of the elements of our mind, which as it were gives us the force and power that hinder us from degenerating, as they say all things earthly do when not regenerated by change.
>
> (p. 147)

Such a conception of freedom privileges multiplicity of perspective over fixedness of opinion and suggests a non-rational, creative element in the exercise of freedom. Thus, like Corinne, whose complex character presents a disturbing enigma to Oswald, Euthanasia's enthusiasm is associated with a depth of mystery and seeming self-contradiction well worth exploring for its suggestion of something beyond the limitations of the cultural and moral codes of a specific historical moment and place:

> [T]here was in her countenance, beyond all of kind and good that you could there discover, an expression that seemed to require ages to read and understand: a wisdom exalted by enthusiasm, a wildness tempered by self-command, that filled every look and every motion with eternal change.
>
> (p. 142)

Euthanasia's wildness and wisdom find their source and their expression in her capacity for a universal love that, as Betty Bennett (1978) asserts, owes much to Percy Shelley's "Promethean ideal, in which love becomes a means of developing a viable alternative to the existing social structure."[26] Indeed, Rajan states that "in *Valperga* [Mary] figures Percy as herself, as Euthanasia" (64). It is this love, then, that Mary Shelley sets in opposition to the sado-masochistic struggles for dominion embodied in Castruccio and his shadowy double Tripalda. This love, though not the consuming, Byronic sort, is quintessentially Romantic in linking love of nature and love of humankind:

> [W]hen ... the sublime feeling of universal love penetrated her, she found no voice that replied so well to hers as the gentle singing of the pines under the air of noon, and the soft murmurs of the breeze that scattered her hair and freshened her cheek, and the dashing of the waters that has no beginning or end.
>
> (p. 144)

Indeed, *Valperga* renders palpable Shelley's deep love for and exquisite sensitivity to the Italian landscape in haunting descriptions of great beauty and sensuousness markedly different from the abstract Alpine and Arctic scenery of *Frankenstein*.

Though temporarily displaced by her passionate and idolatrous love for Castruccio, Euthanasia's capacity for universal, unconditional love returns in her appreciation of nature and her feelings for Beatrice when Euthanasia learns the folly of making "a god of him she loved" (p. 143) and breaks with Castruccio, feeling "solace in the contemplation of nature alone" (p. 267). Finally, then, this love which Euthanasia terms "the ruling principle of my mind" (p. 300) is the heart of her experience of transcendence which she pictures to Beatrice in her mystical response to music, for her, as for Staël's Corinne, the highest art: "[M]usic seems to me to reveal to us some of the profoundest secrets of the universe; and the spirit, freed from prison by its charms, can then soar, and gaze with eagle eyes on the eternal sun of this all-beauteous world" (p. 348). This god-like, transcendent, and mystical perspective allows both distance from and intense appreciation of natural, earthly beauties without any of the violence associated with Castruccio's fiery eagle eyes.

A parable of the cave

If this were the extent of Euthanasia's vision of transcendence, despite its eloquence and beauty, there would be little original in it nor would it reflect a specifically female perspective. But Euthanasia elucidates to Beatrice – and it is important to see this as a scene of female instruction – her own vision of the human mind, her parable of the cave that revises both Plato's parable and the vision of the cave dwelling of Prometheus and Asia in the last acts of Percy's *Prometheus Unbound* (1820). Significantly, Shelley terms the mental faculties "powers" which one must learn to "regulate," thus internalizing the power struggles which are the narrative and thematic key to *Valperga*. "The human soul, dear girl, is a vast cave, in which many powers sit and live" (p. 365).

Unlike Plato's cave which is a realm of illusion and untruth, the deeper one ventures into Euthanasia's cave, the nearer one comes to truth and virtue. The farther one proceeds away from consciousness, the more precious, dangerous, and powerful are one's mental and spiritual faculties.[27] Consciousness is merely a "centinal" at the entrance of this cave, allowing such emotions as Joy, Sorrow, Love, and Hate to enter our hearts. Proceeding farther, one comes to the vestibule where one finds Memory, Judgment, Reason, Hope, and Fear as well as Religion and Charity and their "counterfeits" Hypocrisy, Avarice, and Cruelty. Interestingly Shelley thus presents reason and religion as related faculties that possess only a limited power in her mental hierarchy, incorporating this enlightenment dichotomy into her schema of the mind and then moving beyond it to a Romantic realm similar to E.T.A. Hoffmann's mystical Kingdom of Dreams in *Ritter Gluck*. Before entering this inner cave, one meets Conscience who occupies a middle realm between the vestibule and the inner cave, a realm "excluded from the light of day" so that Conscience – clearly figured as masculine – must and can see like an owl in the dark. Unlike the deluded inhabitants of Plato's cave, Conscience does not need light for clarity of moral vision. Conscience means pain, suffering, and punishment, however; he wears a "diadem of thorns and … bears a whip" (p. 366) and is thus symbolically associated not only with Christianity but also with the sado-masochistic struggles for domination that Shelley critiques in Castruccio and his shadow double Tripalda.

Ultimately, however, the Conscience has "no authority" over the "strongest and most wondrous" mental faculties that dwell in the inner cave, beyond God the Father and the Son. Like Staël's Corinne, then, Euthanasia grants power and authority to an aesthetic and a spiritual realm beyond morality, for this inner sanctum holds Poetry, Imagination, and the highest virtues, as well as Madness, Heresy, and Evil. Euthanasia's parable is schematic and cryptic in its description of how to negotiate these dangers. She tells Beatrice that she will learn to regulate [the mind's] various powers, but gives her only clues as to how to do so. In order to exercise and express the Poetry and Imagination of the self, one must possess and cultivate an "inborn light" (p. 366). Though Euthanasia does not explicitly indicate how one develops such an inner light, her example throughout the novel suggests that it results from the searching meditation and introspection that she repeatedly practices, for example, in her decisions to break with Castruccio and to defend her castle Valperga against his attack and in the devastating emotional aftermath of these momentous decisions.

> Euthanasia was so self-examining, that she never allowed a night to elapse without recalling her feelings and actions of the past day; she endeavoured to be simply just to herself, and her soul had so long been accustomed to this discipline, that it easily laid open its dearest secrets. . . . She now searched her soul to find what were the feelings which still remained to her concerning Castruccio. . . . She felt neither hatred, nor revenge, nor contempt colder than either; she felt grief alone, and that sentiment was deeply engraven on her soul.
>
> (p. 351)

This symbolism of inner enlightenment also resonates with her praise of Dante, whom she had previously termed a proponent of wisdom and liberty, "pure emanation[s] of the Deity, the divine light of the world" (p. 147). If Euthanasia's meditative visions must first be read as evoking a Protestant "inner light," Michael Schiefelbein observes that they also correspond to Dante's God of Eternal Light in the *Paradiso* where "the soul's greatest joy is to contemplate that light, indeed to merge with it."[28] If one succeeds in illuminating this inner spiritual realm, one ultimately reaches, beyond emotion, Euthanasia asserts, "the sweet reward of all our toil, Content of Mind, who crowned with roses, and bearing a flower-wreathed sceptre, rules, instead of Conscience, those admitted to her happy dominion" (p. 366). This Content of Mind is clearly female, akin to a meditative Eastern goddess; in her association with beauty and with nature, she rules without force. Unlike the cave of Prometheus and Asia, in Percy Shelley's *Prometheus Unbound* (1820), this realm is solitary; Mary Shelley seems to suggest either that self-knowledge and self-respect are necessary preconditions for positive relations with others or, more somberly, that finally one can only rely on oneself; as Euthanasia exclaims in a moment of sorrow over her loss of

Castruccio: "We can alone call that ours which lives in our own bosoms" (p. 275).

Thus it is that Euthanasia is able to remain strong and calm even after learning of the failure of the plot against Castruccio and realizing that she is doomed by his misunderstanding of her part in it. As the narrator asserts approvingly, her source of courage is "the inner sanctuary of her heart, which throned self-approbation as its deity, and cared not for the false gods that usurp the pleasant groves and high places of the world" (p. 423). Clearly, then, *Valperga* is the record, as William D. Brewer asserts, of "the triumph of Euthanasia's mind" in its suggestion that "even when events are out of control, mental serenity is possible – historical chaos can be transcended by those who turn inward and master their passions" (p. 144). And beyond this control of passion, is the meditative, mystical "Content of Mind" that Euthanasia enthrones as the ultimate and transcendent reward of spiritual effort.

The prominent presence in *Valperga* of "historical chaos" and the conflicts of powers and passions that Machiavelli and civic humanists would term *fortuna* also renders this goal of peace of mind a clearly political one as well. Euthanasia's interiorization of these conflicts in her parable of the cave can be seen as a projection back into history of Shelley's post-revolutionary and quintessentially modern sense that these tensions were unresolvable on an empirical or material plane. Pocock suggests that Rousseau, in his understanding of the chasm that separated the individual and society, virtue and passion, value and history, was "the Machiavelli of the eighteenth century" (p. 504) who "exposed the theme of the alienation of personality with such completeness that, it can be argued, no recourse was left short of the adoption of an idealist mode of discourse in which the personality was seen articulating in itself, and seeking to unite, the contradictions of history" (p. 505). In this light, Euthanasia's parable can certainly be seen as a brilliantly original and proto-feminist contribution to this post-eighteenth-century idealist mode of discourse.

Euthanasia is intended, then, as a spiritual guide not just for Beatrice but also for her female reader. She teaches, as Shelley would have had Corinne, "for the dignity of womanhood," how to rise wiser and better from the trials of one's life. An exemplary figure, she is, for Castruccio, "the saint of my life" (p. 425). Euthanasia terms herself a hermitess and her castle is described as "cloister-like" (p. 170) at the same time that her fierce independence, her "wild eyes," and her face, "fair as the moon encircled by the night" (p. 178), link her to the virgin nature goddess Diana. As countess of Valperga, Euthanasia lives up to the example of her namesake, Saint Valperga (or Walpurga), who, according to canonical legend, was an English abbess of the eighth-century convent-monastery in Heidenheim, Germany and a protectress against witchcraft.[29] That her saint's day is May Eve or Walpurgisnacht, date of the pagan festival of spring, suggests that she represents Christianity's attempt to incorporate these pagan rituals into itself while claiming to transcend them. Just as the oil which exuded from the cave in which the saint's bones lay was said to have miraculous healing power, so Euthanasia's parable of the cave has curative potential still today in its assertion of women's claim to the consolations of a sisterhood and a realm beyond the negative pleasures of vengeance, a realm that transfigures the immanence of nature into a meditative deity.

Staël, Shelley, and the footprints of the "children of liberty"

Shelley does not choose, however, to conclude her novel with a vision of Euthanasia's triumphant spirituality. Instead, she pulls her heroine back into the whirlwind of power struggles surrounding Castruccio and compels her to choose between her pacifist, utopian ideals and participation in a conspiracy against Castruccio in the hopes that she can thereby prevent his assassination. This turn of the plot is completely consistent with civic humanist values that assert the necessity of balancing the politically active life and the contemplative life in the virtuous existence.[30] Furthermore, Euthanasia's choice to enter the political fray suggests Shelley's recognition, akin to that of feminist Foucauldians today, that despite exclusion from positions of power, no woman can remain truly outside of or above masculinist struggles for domination.[31] What Shelley furthermore demonstrates is that Euthanasia's perspective is radically different from that of men like Castruccio and Tripalda, who are unable to comprehend the integrity and sense of duty that compel her to join the republican plot. She responds as Biddy Martin suggests feminists must do, by seeing her "position within existing power structures but [responding] from somewhere else."[32] In Euthanasia's case, it is her spirituality that provides for her this "somewhere else" from which to gather strength and serenity in her ultimately futile battle against the cruelty and ruthlessness of Castruccio and Tripalda. In dooming the conspiracy in which Euthanasia participates by Tripalda's support and ultimate betrayal of it, Shelley is acknowledging, in a subtle and sophisticated fashion, Euthanasia's implication in the sado-masochistic power struggles that underlie the political structures as they are constituted in her day. Indeed Euthanasia knows that the plot is doomed as soon as she learns that Tripalda is involved. Nevertheless, she does not regret her choice, considering it the best possible in an impossible world, taking full responsibility for her actions, and even recognizing her culpability in the deaths of those who may have been persuaded to join in the "plot for liberty" because of her participation in it.

Exiled to Sicily by Castruccio, Euthanasia is lost in a shipwreck off the coast of Italy. Before her death, however, she is granted a climactic experience of the meditative "Content of Mind" that she values above all else:

> The eternal spirit of the universe seemed to descend upon her, and she drank in breathlessly the sensation, which the silent night, the starry heavens, and the sleeping earth bestowed upon her. All seemed so peaceful, that no unwelcome sensation in her own heart could disturb the scene of which she felt herself a part. She looked up, and exclaimed in her own beautiful Italian, whose soft accents and expressive phrases then so much transcended all

other European languages – "What a brave canopy has this earth, and how graciously does the supreme empyrean smile upon its nursling!"

(p. 435)

Like a child united with her mother, earth is united with sky; Euthanasia drinks in the sensation of the nature surrounding her, and with it, the "eternal spirit of the universe" which is matched by the peace in her heart and the transcendent beauty of her language.

Given the explicit maternal imagery in this climactic scene, it is particularly troubling then, that Euthanasia dies as the result of a storm at sea which prompts the following narrative commentary on the cruelty of mother nature: "[T]he spirits of the deep wondered that the earth had trusted so lovely a creature to the barren bosom of the sea, which, as an evil step-mother deceives and betrays all committed to her care" (p. 438). Perhaps Shelley is reinforcing here Euthanasia's all important realization that "[we] can alone call that ours which lives in our own bosoms" (p. 275). Still, it is nature alone who mourns her; the "piteous skies" and the sea-birds weep and moan for her and "the muttering thunder alone tolled her passing bell" (p. 438). Furthermore, and most importantly, that Euthanasia's parable of the cave and her pantheistic state of mind at death represent ultimate spiritual goals for Mary Shelley herself is rendered explicit in the following journal entry, written less than two months after she completed the fair copy of *Valperga* in December 1821:

[L]et me love the trees, the skies and the ocean, and that all encompassing spirit of which I may soon become a part ... above all, let me fearlessly descend into the remotest caverns of my own mind, carry the torch of self-knowledge into its dimmest recesses: but too happy if I dislodge any evil spirit or enshrine a new deity in some hitherto uninhabited nook.[33]

Significantly, as both Clemit and Rajan have emphasized, Euthanasia's disappearence is not exactly a death.[34] "She slept in the oozy cavern of the ocean" (pp. 437–8), entrusted to the care of the sea. As Rajan points out, this conclusion "resonates with echoes of the Poet's death in *Alastor* and also with anticipations of Byron's last poem *The Island* (1823)," echoes that "acknowledge Romanticism as the psycho-intellectual complex that gave Shelley the space to develop her feminism" (p. 65). Even more significant are the symbolic associations between the "ocean-cave" in which Euthanasia lies and the underwater cavern of the Cumaean Sibyl that opens Shelley's next novel *The Last Man*. (*Valperga* was finished in the fall of 1821 and published in 1823; Shelley began work on *The Last Man* in the spring of 1824.) In the introduction to this novel, Shelley presents a fictionalized account of tours she and Percy took around Naples in 1818 before she had begun *Valperga* in 1820.

This exploration of the cave of the Cumaean Sibyl is clearly an elaboration of the parable of the cave with which Euthanasia seeks to enlighten Beatrice. And the Bay holding the cave which the author-narrator of *The Last Man* visits with her companion, is a pre-eminently female realm; "the blue and pellucid element was such as Galatea might have skimmed in her car of mother of pearl; or Cleopatra, more fitly than the Nile, have chosen as the path of her magic ship."[35] In fact, Sandra Gilbert and Susan Gubar, though they do not mention *Valperga*, represent this opening scene of *The Last Man* as the *locus classicus* of female transcendence and artistic inspiration.[36] The leaves scattered on the floor are "Sibylline leaves," records of female prophecy, as "all the leaves, bark, and other substances were traced with written characters" (p. 3). Just as Euthanasia's Content of Mind holds a scepter adorned with roses, the female artist writes on and through the book of nature. Most importantly and remarkably, the inscriptions on the leaves are in many languages, from ancient Chaldee and mysterious unknown dialects to modern English and Italian, thus suggesting a collective, underground female tradition beyond national and temporal boundaries. "Slight," "scattered and unconnected," "obscure and chaotic" (p. 4) as the leaves of the Sibyl are, Shelley expresses no doubt that these "poetic rhapsodies" contain truths and intuitions whose source is divine.

It is the task of the literary daughter, the female artist and her companion, Shelley asserts, to decipher them and make these verses available to the public. In fact it is the author's companion (Percy Shelley, in a biographical reading) who first discovers the writing on the leaves, thus suggesting Mary Shelley's acknowledgment, as Rajan writes, that "Romanticism gave her the space to develop her feminism." Yet her companion is now dead and the solitary woman continues her work of translation, restoration, and recreation, finding in it the consolation and inspiration of sublimity: the "meaning, [of the sacred remains] wondrous and eloquent, has often repaid my toil, soothing me in sorrow, and exciting my imagination to daring flights, through the immensity of nature and the mind of man" (p. 3).

As a continuation of the parable of Euthanasia's spiritual development, the Author's Introduction to *The Last Man* provides an invaluable tool for interpreting her exemplary life within the context of a feminist literary and political history. Thus Mary Shelley herself provides a corrective to the numerous readings of *Valperga* that emphasize the futility of Euthanasia's political efforts and idealism.[37] For in her introduction to her subsequent novel, Shelley suggests that the words and the deeds of women like Euthanasia and Beatrice are never completely lost, but are kept alive in a kind of cultural unconscious from which they eventually resurface "glowing with *imagination* and *power*" (p. 4; emphasis added). Just as the author of *The Last Man* suggests that she finds "solace in the narration of misery and woeful change" because real sorrows are "clothed in that ideality, which takes the mortal sting from pain" (p. 4), so the extremism and ideality of Beatrice and Euthanasia fascinates, soothes, and impels to future action. As Betty Bennett writes, "Mary Shelley ends Euthanasia's story not with her death but rather as a segment of the cyclical view of history earlier articulated by Euthanasia herself. . . . The formulation of historical cycles was critical to both Shelleys, who saw in the concept of renewal the possibility of another wave of political reform that could establish governments dedicated to freedom and republicanism" (p. 145). Further, Castruccio's death, following that of Euthanasia by only a few years, and contrasted sharply with hers in the pomp of his funeral and the hypocrisy of his official epitaph, highlights the futility of masculinist effort at domination in the light of history.[38] As a novelistic character, then, Euthanasia does indeed fulfill her self-professed poetic and historical goal of following "the glorious foot-marks of the children of liberty" and serving as a marker "in the desert, to attract future passengers to the fountains of life" (p. 147). And, as Euthanasia's creator, Shelley answers Staël's panegyric on enthusiasm in *On Germany* with a woman who embodies precisely that quality, maintained in the face of "the world's masters" and defying their "torrents of sand, flood-like in their terror, arid as the desert." Euthanasia's life may not immediately change the course of history, but, as Rajan emphasizes, "it is precisely this measurement of history in terms of events that the novel questions."[39]

Finally, Mary Shelley's pantheism and faith in historical process suggest the possibility of an ironic reading of the powerful line that opens the novel's concluding paragraph: "Earth felt no change when she died and men forgot her" (p. 438). Certainly, however, no happy ending is possible for *Valperga* because, as Bennett asserts, it depicts a process of historical struggle that is clearly unfinished.[40] This struggle for a world that encourages the self-respect and self-expression of women in the realms of art, spirituality, and politics continues in the life and work of Bettine von Arnim to whom we now turn. Her *Die Günderode* records the correspondence of two female artists who seek to fashion a vision of psychic development that will free them from the pains of unrequited love and from the limitations of the cultural standard of *Bildung* bequeathed to them by Goethe and Schiller.

3 Beyond impossibility

Bettine von Arnim's *Die Günderode*, "an ideal relation realized"

In its conclusion, *Corinne* gives the reader a glimpse of the transformative potential contained within the relationship of Corinne and her half-sister Lucile: a poetic, cultural, and historical potential that is embodied in Juliette, their symbolic daughter. In *Valperga*, the relationship between Euthanasia and Beatrice becomes the emotional and spiritual heart of the novel as it is set against the emptiness and cruelty of Castruccio, who dominates the opening and closing of the novel. *Die Günderode* (1840), Bettine von Arnim's poetic reworking of her youthful correspondence with the writer Karoline von Günderode, is devoted from beginning to end to their love for each other and to their mutual efforts at the creation of visionary conceptions of poetry, history, education, and religion that will enable each of them to transcend the social strictures that bind them as nineteenth-century German women.

If *Corinne* conflates the figures of the abandoned woman and the female artist and *Valperga* interrogates that conflation through the opposition and mirroring of Beatrice and Euthanasia, *Die Günderode* confronts the theme of abandonment with the power of language which for Arnim is the suprapersonal power of the spirit.[1] Written and published more than three decades after Karoline von Günderode's suicide in 1806, this lyrical novel represents Bettine von Arnim's attempt to overcome that loss through a discursive resuscitation of her beloved friend. Marjanne Goozé's (1987) astute assessment of the implications of Arnim's use of language in *Goethe's Correspondence with a Child* holds true for *Die Günderode* as well. Goozé suggests that Arnim practices "a feminist writing that goes beyond the limits of representation and that challenges the conception of writing as absence, restoring to language its magical power to invoke presence."[2] As Patricia Anne Simpson similarly asserts, Arnim "suspends Günderode's death sentence textually."[3] Indeed, as the appearance of *Die Günderode* was the stimulus to the first edition of Günderode's collected works published in 1857, it is quite literally true that Arnim's tribute brought her friend back from near oblivion to life again as an author.[4]

Whereas Staël and Shelley focus upon women's responses to betrayal by men, Arnim seeks to come to terms with a doubly cruel abandonment and betrayal by Karoline von Günderode who, at the urging of classics professor Friedrich Creuzer, abruptly broke off her relationship with Arnim and then a few months later in July of 1806 walked down to the Rhine and stabbed herself in the heart.[5] The immediate impetus for her suicide was the refusal of Creuzer to leave his wife despite a feeling for Günderode that bordered on adoration. Yet love for Creuzer or for any other man is never explicitly addressed in *Die Günderode*, despite the fact that Karoline's desire to die young is an important theme in the work and the source of frequently expressed anxiety on Bettine's part.[6] It is as if Arnim chooses to honor her own relationship with Günderode and the memory of her friend by focusing on their shared vision of spiritual courage, intellectual effort, and poetic accomplishment rather than risk portrayal of Günderode as a stereotypically self-destructive and lovelorn female. Instead, Arnim chooses to portray Karoline's melancholy as occasioned by the psychic perils that face all Romantic artists and by what Karoline herself terms the narrow limits of her life. In her last letter to Bettine in *Die Günderode*, for example, while expressing admiration for her friend's remarkable energy, Karoline writes, "Not by circumstances alone, but by nature also, narrower confines are drawn for my sphere of action" ("[M]ir sind nicht allein durch meine Verhältnisse, sondern auch durch meine Natur engere Grenzen in meiner Handlungsweise gezogen...").[7]

The distance here between Arnim and Staël's respective novelistic treatments of suicide is vast and can perhaps best be measured by Bettine's response to her friend Moritz Bethmann's reading out loud from *Delphine*, a novel she describes as "the most absurd thing I could listen to" ("das Absurdeste, was ich hören kann"; p. 230; p. 604), despite her acknowledgment that it is written by the foremost "authoress" in Europe.[8] Arnim turns away from her friends' collective enjoyment of Staël's novel to play games with her family's children, an action that earns her charges of arrogance and conceit from those friends and relatives. In rejecting Staël's suicidal heroine, Arnim is also implicitly and obliquely passing judgment on her own friend's suicide, turning her attention away from melancholy and *Liebestod* to the life embodied in children.[9] Similarly, in the Goethe correspondence, Bettine suggests that if the author of *The Sorrows of Young Werther* had only had the sense to create a heroine like herself instead of the insipid Charlotte, his hero would never have shot himself (p. 244).

The reader, then, haunted by the knowledge of Karoline von Günderode's violent and shocking suicide, is met, in the text itself, not with the tale of her unhappy love affair(s) but rather with Bettine's own fear of abandonment and more importantly with the compensatory presence of their mutually created socio-cultural, aesthetic, and religious vision. Bettine variously describes this utopian vision as a "Weltumwälzung" or "Weltumstürzen" (p. 449; p. 376), a "turning the world on its head," an overthrowing of the present order of things. Thus, the novel answers Günderode's suicide with a spiritual vision meant to eliminate the need or desire for such an action and to bring Karoline von Günderode back to life in all her power, her suffering, and her brilliance. In this fictionalized epistolary exchange, then, Arnim exploits the distance between auto/biography and novel, between historical document and literary artifact, to imbue Karoline von Günderode's tragic life and their unfulfilled friendship with a utopian significance that she herself has consciously created. Finally and even more fundamentally, the novel itself embodies a life-affirming aesthetic response to Günderode's melancholy, self-destructive relation to art, thus implicitly replacing Günderode with Bettine as the central artistic figure it celebrates. Rather than internalizing the repressive aspects of German idealism, as does her Karoline, Arnim's younger fictional self maintains a liberating, ironic distance from cultural authority not unlike the young Friedrich Schlegel's stance. As Ursula Liebertz-Grün has suggested, the novel, as an anti-Werther discourse, moves beyond the glorification of melancholy to become the narrative of Bettine's own future oriented development as an artist.[10]

Turning the world upside down

If *Die Günderode* represents Bettine von Arnim's effort to define and express herself as an artist, this process is made possible for her through a radical and ironic revisioning of the aesthetic and cultural norms of German intellectual tradition in dialogue with another woman. This mutual project of "Weltumwälzung" forms the subject of this chapter, a turning the world upside down or world revolution that is explicitly represented as a product of female intimacy.[11] At the risk of imposing a restrictive structure on the fluidity and freedom of Arnim's text, I demonstrate here that "turning the world on its head" involves, for these Romantic women writers, first, a feminist redefinition of history, second, a radical critique of reified and masculinist concepts of philosophy and *Bildung*, and finally, the creation, in place of these theoretical constructs, of a new religion of art and action, termed a Schwebe-Religion, "a floating religion," by Bettine. Karoline summarizes their religion with the epigram "to think is to pray" ("*Denken* ist Beten"; p. 120; p. 449); faith does not conflict with reason but makes it possible; intellect and spirit, mind and action, are and should be one; thought, through the power of the spirit, can move the world.

While *Corinne* challenges the moral and aesthetic authority of Romantic melancholy with the emancipatory potential of poetic enthusiasm, and *Valperga* attacks Napoleonic/Byronic/Nietzschean self-will with self-knowledge and self-respect, *Die Günderode* offers a critique of the unconsciously masculinist and hierarchical concepts of history and *Bildung* developed by Kant, Schiller, Goethe, and the German Romantics. By choosing women, Jews, and other disenfranchised members of nineteenth-century German society as exemplary embodiments of self-realization and enlightenment, *Die Günderode* takes the concept of *Bildung* out of the realm of theory and places it into the realm of praxis, applying it in egalitarian fashion, and thus radically transforming it, effecting the "Weltumstürzen" that Bettine proclaims.[12] As a female *Bildungsroman*, both lyrical and utopian, this novel questions the limits of the possible for nineteenth-century German women. Arnim clearly takes pleasure in the prospect of challenging and shocking her audience, just as her fictional Bettine, in outlining to an aged professor friend a cosmic vision of botany as the basis for a textbook she will some day write, revels in his astonished response: "That goes even beyond the impossible" ("[D]as geht über alle Unmöglichkeit hinaus"; p. 271; p. 656). The novel, then, is dedicated to the realization of the ideal through relationship and in the everyday. As Arnim writes in her epigraph to Part II, "He who denies the Ideal in himself, can never understand it in others, even if it were perfectly expressed. In him who recognizes the Ideal in others it will even unfold unconsciously" ("Wer das Ideal leugnet in sich, der könnte es auch nicht verstehen in Andern, selbst wenn es vollkommen ausgesprochen wär. – Wer das Ideal erkannte in Andern, dem blüht es auf, selbst wenn jener es nicht in sich ahnt"; p. 200; p. 563).

As Elke Frederiksen and Monika Shafi argue in their analysis of *Die Günderode* as a feminist utopia, the novel suspends the purely theoretical tendencies of utopian fiction by embodying its vision of the transformation of society in the most common and everyday situations. *Die Günderode* denies any distinction between theory and praxis, thus undermining the central distinction advocated in Kant's "What is Enlightenment?" between public contestation of established laws and private obedience to them, disagreement in theory, and obedience in practice.[13] Indeed, Arnim's insistence that words and deeds are and should be one may well constitute her central challenge and contribution to German Romanticism, a challenge embodied in the aesthetic praxis of this lyrical novel.

As many critics have emphasized, the epistolary form of the novel, its poeticization of actual correspondence, breaks down the boundaries between life and art, fact and fiction, chaos and form, practice and theory.[14] And, of course, genres (novel, poem, Socratic dialogue, letter) mix in seemingly indiscriminate fashion. The text constantly challenges reader and critic to conceptualize the relations between these traditionally dichotomized realms in new ways that acknowledge their interpenetration.[15] Thus, of course, the characters Karoline and Bettine cannot be separated and are indeed creations of Bettine von Arnim.[16] This interdependence of their development and education both correspondents acknowledge; Karoline calls it their "organic taking hold of one another" ("organische[s] Ineinandergreifen"; p. 20; p. 325) in expressing her gratitude to Bettine for all she has learned from her. And one of her early letters to Bettine opens, "It seems to me sometimes quite absurd, dear Bettine, that you should, with such solemnity, declare yourself my student, when I might as well hold myself yours; yet it gives me much pleasure, and there is, also, a truth in it, if the teacher feels himself stimulated by the student" ("Es kömmt mir bald zu närrisch vor, liebe Bettine, daß Du Dich so feierlich für meinen Schüler erklärst, eben so könnte ich mich für den Deinen halten wollen; doch macht es mir viele Freude, und es ist auch etwas Wahres daran, wenn ein Lehrer durch den Schüler angeregt wird, so kann ich mit Fug mich den Deinen nennen"; p. 9; p. 309).

Thus the teacher/student dichotomy collapses as well. Nevertheless, in relation to the cultural construct of *Bildung* their roles are quite clearly defined, providing one of the central narrative threads that organizes the text. Bettine is the child of nature, the naïf, the wild child, whereas the older, more sedate and serious Karoline serves as mediator between her rebellious friend and the judgmental Philistinism of friends and family most clearly embodied in the older brother Clemens who insists (often through Karoline) that Bettine study history and Latin and contain her self-expression in acceptable forms such as the traditional autobiography or the poem.[17] In the opening letters, for example, Bettine responds spontaneously and unequivocally to Karoline's fascination with German philosophy: "Your Schellings and Fichtes and Kants are to me quite inconceivable beings" ("Dein Schelling und Dein Fichte und Dein Kant sind mir ganz unmögliche Kerle"; p. 7; p. 307).

Yet this categorical rejection of Romantic philosophy is only a part of the picture, for the reader must of course also take into account not only Karoline's differing perspective, but also the ever-changing synthesis of their two points of view as it develops throughout the novel. And, as both Gisela Dischner and Edith Waldstein argue, this mode of communication and self-expression owes much to conceptions of "Romantische Geselligkeit" developed by Romantic theorists such as Friedrich Schlegel and Schleiermacher and embodied in such paradigmatic Romantic texts as Schlegel's *Dialogue on Poetry* (1799) and *Lucinde* (1799). Waldstein asserts that among Arnim's four epistolary novels, *Die Günderode* is "the only successful portrayal of free and open communication" (p. 58).[18] In fact Margaret Fuller, who, through her articles in *The Dial* and her translation of the novel, brought it to American Transcendentalism, describes the letters, in her Preface to the translation, as "an ideal relation realized."[19]

History as fossil

Romantic *Geschichtsphilosophie*, *Bildung*, and aesthetics, despite their avowedly emancipatory and open-ended goals, on the other hand, represent for the two young women authorities that in reality allow little give and take or conversation. Thus, in a sense, *Die Günderode*, from the perspective of 40 years hence, takes German Romanticism to task for its masculinist limitations and for its refusal/inability to transform into artistic and social reality its own cultural ideals. Indeed, Arnim's work might be said to embody the feminist potential implied but unrealized by the theorizing of male Romantics; Liebertz-Grün even boldly asserts that Arnim's work both fulfills the maxims of Romantic poetics *and* marks the beginnings of a post-patriarchal literature in the German language (p. 138). As critics have frequently noted, Bettine von Arnim was one of the few German Romantics who did not disappear into suicide, madness, untimely death, or political conservatism.[20] The prominent role played by the tragedy of Hölderlin's descent into madness that concludes Part I of the novel suggests just how significant the fates of other Romantic artists were for Arnim's own sense of self.

History, as her brother Clemens would compel her to study it, is a dead and barren narrative. Karoline, nevertheless, also insists that knowledge of history is necessary as grounding for Bettine's imaginative flights. Yet for Bettine, history as it is taught by Arenswald her tutor is cold, lifeless, and skeletal – abysmal, in fact: "When the tutor opens his mouth, I look into it as an impenetrable gulf which spews forth the mammoth-bones of the past and all sorts of fossil-stuff that never buds or blooms to pay back sun and rain" ("Tut der Lehrer den Mund auf, so sehe ich hinein wie in einen unabsehbaren Schlund, der die Mammutsknochen der Vergangenheit ausspeit, und allerlei versteinert Zeug, das nicht keimen, nicht blühen mehr will, wo Sonn und Regen nicht lohnt"; p. 84; pp. 405–6). She rebels against mechanistic academic history "that [is] already stuck fast in the history-mud of weariness" ("das im Geschichtskot der Langenweil immer stecken bleibt"; p. 76; p. 396). Bettine's objection to reified collections of historical "facts" is vehemently political; such studies impede progress and change. At the height of nineteenth-century positivist understandings of history as an "innocent process of discovery" of pre-existing facts and truths, Arnim, with remarkable clarity, recognizes the ideological nature of all knowledge as "active production rather than passive recognition."[21] She sees that, even more dangerously, the focus in traditional histories on domination and war poisons the present and perpetuates itself, contributing to the spread of death and destruction; "I think of all nations, who were fighting, horned and cloven-footed, spitting fire and breathing out pestilential vapor, which the past blows over me" ("[D]a denk ich mir gleich alle Völker, … gehörnt, mit Bocksfüßen, feuerspeiend und pestilenzialischen Gestank verbreitend, den mir die Vergangenheit herüberweht"; p. 85; p. 407). Arnim thus clearly belongs to that nineteenth-century democratizing tendency in historical writing, typified by Jules Michelet and Augustin Thierry, and analyzed by Ann Rigney in *Imperfect Histories*, to acknowledge the significance of the everyday and to seek ways to recover and record cultural as well as political history.[22]

Furthermore, like Catherine Morland of Jane Austen's *Northanger Abbey*, though more mordant and less naïve, Bettine objects not only to historians' preoccupations with political power struggles, but also to their lack of respect for the cultural significance of women: "Over the story of Semiramis the past has let grow such a thick mould, that through the blue eye of immortality only her name looks out; otherwise we would know nothing" ("Über der Geschichte der Semiramis hat die Vergangenheit so dicken Schimmel wachsen lassen, daß sie noch eben mit dem blauen Aug der Unsterblichkeit ihres Namens davon kommt, sonst wüßten wir gar nichts"; p. 85; p. 408). The vehemence of Bettine's rejection of history as scholars had written and taught it in the past finds expression in what today must be read as a radical feminist gesture: "I drew a great Medusa's head, with wide open jaws, in my history book. I wish it would devour all of ancient history, – Arenswald and all" ("[D]a hab ich ein groß Medusenhaupt in mein Geschichtbuch gezeichnet mit aufgesperrtem Rachen; fräß es doch die ganze alte Geschichte mit samt dem Arenswald auf"; p. 100; p. 426).

Clearly, Arnim understands that, for her century, as Christina Crosby has written, "'history' is produced as man's truth, the truth of a necessarily historical Humanity, which in turn requires 'women' to be outside history, above, below, or beyond properly historical and political life."[23] Bettine's intellectual exchange with Karoline, nevertheless, compels her to move beyond her initial emotional and simplistic rejection of history, a gesture which would in fact reinforce masculinist stereotypes of the ahistoricity of the female, to a sophisticated protofeminist formulation of the significance of history in her own life and in the lives of her contemporaries. Thus Bettine's refusal to study history as her tutor teaches it does not mean a refusal to study it at all. Rather she reads it on her own terms, seeking in it political and cultural understanding applicable to her nineteenth-century Europe. She quotes with emphatic approval her friend Voigt's critique of the purely theoretical significance given the great deeds of the Greeks and Romans in the German education system: "The whole fabric of education is mere fiction; all is taught by example, and great deeds are shown like the chimeras in picture-books; each man turns around and leaves them there, without further application" ("[D]as ganze Lehrgebäude ist bloß wie Fabelwerk, alles lehrt man durch Exempel, aber große Taten, die zeigt man nur wie die Chimära aus dem Bilderbuch, da dreht jedermann um und läßt sie stehen ohne weitere Gebrauchsanweisung"; p. 31; pp. 339–40). Furthermore, when Karoline teases her about her diligent study of Suetonius and her careful cataloging of the crimes of all twelve Roman emperors, suggesting that it is motivated by her wish to exonerate Napoleon, we see Bettine truly angry with Karoline for the first and only time. "Your jest infuriates me" ("Dein Scherz erzürnt mich"; p. 256; p. 636), she writes. Her study of Suetonius is instead motivated by the desire to understand the tyrant as character type. And her conclusions are devastatingly accurate, seen from the perspective of the twentieth century; for her, the tyrant such as Napoleon is a "monster of mediocrity": "See ... it is always the same selfish, unjust hypocrite, the same monster of mediocrity, without an impulse of the true spirit, no longing to set up wisdom as the aegis of his actions, no knowledge of the fertile soil of arts and sciences, nor an idea how man develops his mind" ("[I]mmer dasselbe Ungeheuer der Mittelmäßigkeit; kein Trieb zum wahren Geist, keine Sehnsucht, die Weisheit als Ägide seiner Handlungen aufzustellen, keinen Verstand von dem Pflanzenboden der Künste und Wissenschaft, noch wie der Mensch sich erzieht"; pp. 256–7; pp. 637–8).

In no way is Arnim's Napoleon a figure of superior will, intellect, or courage. And like both Staël and Shelley, she opposes art and learning to the exercise of power in the current political realm. Unlike these earlier writers, however, she shows not a glimmer of fascination for the charismatic figure holding that power, instead revealing, in an uncannily prescient vision, its source in arrogance and in the stupidity and unconsciousness of mob mentality:

He rides the raging steed of Presumption, leaping in wild ardor over abysses, flying in proud conceit through the plain, to dash across new ones. On he hurries past the Times that are so altered that they cease to recognize themselves. Men sleep without a thought of awakening, but at the sound of his thundering hoof they tear open their eyes. Dazzled by his glory, they forget what they are about; drowsiness is changed to intoxication, and they rush around him exultingly.

(p. 255)

[D]as Roß des Übermuts tobt unter ihm, es setzt in wildem Feuer über Abgründe und durchfliegt in stolzem Selbstgefühl die Ebne um über neue zu setzen, dahin eilt er, an den Zeiten vorüber, die ungewandelt sich nicht mehr erkennen. Die Menschen schlafen ohne Ahnung vom Erwachen, aber unter seinem brausenden Huf reißen sie plötzlich die Augen auf und seine Glorie blendet sie, daß sie sich selber nicht begreifen, ihr dumpfer Schlaf geht in Taumel über, sie umjauchzen ihn im Gefühl ihrer Trunkenheit.

(pp. 635–6)

Furthermore, for Bettine, opposition to tyranny and identification with the oppressed is equivalent to commitment to her own personal freedom:

> Do you think I could ever desert the sufferers of wrong to side with the wrong that is sanctioned by the world? I feel there is greater freedom in bearing the chains with the oppressed, dying, despised, than in sharing the fate of the oppressor.

(p. 255)

> [M]einst Du, ich könne je dem Unrecht-erliegenden mich lossagen und auch nur in Gedanken übergehen zu dem Unrecht das vor der Welt Recht behält, ich fühle, es liegt größere Freiheit darin mit dem Unterdrückten die Ketten tragen und schmählig vergehen als mit dem Unterdrücker sein Los teilen.

(p. 636)

This commitment never wavered, as Arnim fought, at considerable expense and danger to herself, till the end of her life for causes such as academic freedom, freedom of speech and of the press, better working and living conditions for German laborers, the release of political prisoners, and civil rights for Jews.[24]

History as concourse with spirits

For the activist Bettine, history is alive only in its interpenetration with the present and future. Considered in its meaning for present and future, its interpretive power, the "Geschichtseinöde" (historical desert or wilderness) of empty and predigested facts gives way to a fertile field that nourishes soul and mind. Like Staël and Shelley, Arnim conceives of militarist history as a desert concealing fountains of life to be discovered by future generations of (female) historians. As Bettine's grandmother, the pre-eminent eighteenth-century German woman novelist Sophie von La Roche tells her, meditating on the power of her husband's exemplary political and spiritual life to influence her decades after his death:

> Do you see, my child, that the golden field of the past bears grain, without which many a one would die for want of spiritual nourishment. ... Thus the past belongs to the day of life. ... One past deed, then, is not for its own good, it works on without end; your grandfather said it came from the spirit, and all that was perishable was without spirit.

(p. 226)

[S]iehst Du, mein Kind, so trägt die goldne Au der Vergangenheit die Ähren, ohne welche so mancher an Geistesnahrung Hunger sterben müßte. ... So gehört die Vergangenheit zum Tag des Lebens. ... Eine Vergangenheit is also nicht für das wahre Gute, es wirkt ohne Ende, es kommt aus dem Geist, wie dein Großvater sagte, und alles andre, was vergänglich ist das ist auch geistlos.

(p. 599)

Arnim's maternal grandfather, who wrote a book attacking Monastic institutions and resigned from his position as Chancellor of the city of Trier rather than impose an unjust tax upon the rural population, is for Bettine an embodiment of "die tiefste Philosophie" as yet unreached by those who call themselves philosophers, "namely peace, the union of the profoundest spiritual knowledge with active life" ("nämlich den Frieden, die Vereinigung der tiefsten geistigen Erkenntnis mit dem tätigen Leben"; p. 223; p. 595). Once again, for Bettine, thought and action must be consonant, as she remembers her grandfather espousing a secular and cosmopolitan religion born of Enlightenment humanism:

In a great heart, politics must issue from religion, or rather they must be identical; and an active man who employs his time for the purpose it was given him, has none left to devote to different objects, and his religion must manifest itself in him in an entirely cosmopolitan light.

(p. 222)

In einem großen Herzen müsse die Politik bloß aus der Religion hervorgehen, oder sie müßten vielmehr ganz dasselbe sein, ein tätiger Mensch, der seine Zeit anwende, zu was sie ihm verliehen sei, habe sie nicht übrig, sie in verschiednes zu teilen, so müsse denn Religion als vollkommner Weltbürger in ihm ans Licht treten.

(p. 594)

Through the power of his ideas and his example, this ancestor comes to life before Bettine's eyes. The past, then, is populated with ghosts capable of reanimation, not just skeletal fossils to be excavated and reconstructed. Like her French contemporary Jules Michelet, the true historian, for Arnim, is a medium who, through the power of love and imagination, seeks concourse with the dead – "Geisterumgang" – and brings forth living apparitions, "Geistererscheinung[en]" (p. 597).

In this sense Arnim is herself a historian, for *Die Günderode* is clearly meant as a recreation of her relationship with Karoline, and as I have previously suggested, a poetic resuscitation of this beloved friend. Karoline herself provides the intellectual framework for this vision of history as a vital interchange between harmonious souls, both living and dead, in her very first letter to Bettine. Just as the novel ends with a meditation on the future, so it begins with a philosophic dialogue modeled on the Platonic teacher–student exchange, a discussion of the meaning of the past entitled "Die Manen" ("The Shades"). The prominent positioning of this dialogue suggests its importance for the text as a whole. Significantly, it is thus Karoline, as Socrates to Bettine's Plato, who herself provides Bettine with the mental means to come to terms with lifelong grief over her own suicide, proving through example the truth of the lessons taught in the dialogue.

Tormented by the elusive presence of the historical great in his memory, the student of "Die Manen" experiences his mind painfully as "a deep pit from which the shadows of the past are flitting upwards" ("Grüft, aus der die schwankenden Schatten der Vergangenheit heraufsteigen"; p. 3; p. 302). Here Karoline depicts the student's experience of the historical sublime, prominent in the writings of other nineteenth-century historians according to Rigney, as an experience of mourning over the irretrievability of past existences and realities combined with the painful effort to recapture or reconstruct them.[25] In response, the teacher defines a subtle understanding of the eternity of the spirit based in a sophisticated hermeneutic of historical interpretation. "[N]othing is lost, young Scholar; that can in no wise be; only the eye cannot follow an infinite series of consequences. ... How can you say that is lost which works so powerfully on yourself?" ("Verloren ist nichts, junger Schüler, und in keiner Weise, nur das Auge vermag nicht des Grundes unendliche Folgenkette zu übersehen. ... Du kannst doch nicht verloren nennen ... was so mächtig auf Dich wirkt"; p. 3; p. 302). The spirits of the past do not die, but live on in the minds of the present inhabitants of the earth through an eternal and unfathomable chain of cause and effect, not unlike the "vast tableau of destinies" that, for Staël, gives mysterious collective meaning to the efforts of the individual. Furthermore, historical figures have no fixed, objectively determinable significance; rather they take on a new and different life in each individual consciousness. As the student questions, "The great man then lives not in me after his own law, but after mine?" ("So lebt denn ein großer Mensch nicht nach *seiner* Weise in mir fort, sondern nach der meinen?") and the teacher responds: "Truly, that life alone is continued in you which your mind is fitted to receive, in so far as it is congenial" ("Freilich lebt das nur fort in Dir, was Dein Sinn befähigt ist aufzunehmen, insofern es Gleichartiges mit Dir hat"; p. 4; pp. 302–3).

According to the Teacher in Karoline's dialogue, it is an inner harmony between spirits of the living and the dead that makes possible contact between the two realms, a harmony that awakens the imagination so that barriers between inner and outer, spiritual and sensory, subjective and objective disappear. Past and present speak and are visible to each other as "the inner apparition shall become palpable to the bodily eye, as, on the other hand, the outward apparition is palpable to the spiritual eye" ("die innere Erscheinung vor das körperliche Auge treten kann, wie auch umgekehrt die äußere Erscheinung vor das geistige Auge tritt"; p. 5; p. 304). It is precisely in this heightened state of memory that Arnim, clearly still haunted decades after the fact by the image of her friend's wounded body, wrote *Die Günderode*, as she indicates in a moving evocation of its composition process from a letter to Julius Döring. If Karoline is figured as a resurrected Christ, the idealist Bettine refuses the role of doubting Thomas:

The past has become so vivid to me that I could not say like Thomas, "Let me put my fingers in your wound so that I may believe it is really you." Günderode stands before me, and she often calls me away from my place when the light burns in the evening. [She stands] there in the corner where the tall green pines have stood since Christmas, reaching the ceiling in front of my sofa, and then I wrap myself in my coat because I cannot resist going to meet her in my thoughts, and then sleep overcomes me. ... But in the daytime, I feel so close to everything in the past that I am absolutely convinced of the enduring presence of everything which we have truly experienced.[26]

This awakened state of imagination also makes historical prophecy possible, a capacity which Arnim, through Karoline, explains not as a supernatural capacity, but rather as a sensitivity, undeveloped by most people, to perceivable causes and effects:

Out of this power to discern connections, too subtle for the perception of those whose inner eye is still closed, arises the gift of prophecy; that is, of binding together the past and future, and following out causes to their inevitable results. Prophecy is a perception of the future.

(p. 5)

Aus dieser Sinnenfähigkeit, Verbindungen wahrzunehmen, die andere, deren Geistesauge verschlossen ist, nicht fassen, entsteht die prophetische Gabe, Gegenwart und Vergangenheit mit der Zukunft zu verbinden, den notwendigen Zusammenhang der Ursachen und Wirkungen zu sehen, Prophezeiung ist Sinn für die Zukunft.

(pp. 304–5)

Thus it is that Bettine von Arnim had a "prophetic" sense of the importance of Jews for German cultural history, a sense of their wisdom, embodied in the idealized scholar Ephraim, whom she elevates in proportion to her mockery of the Germanic Arenswald. Born of persecution and ostracism, this wisdom, Bettine suggests, is glaringly lacking in the philistinism and the hierarchical thinking that surround her. Indeed, the courage of Arnim's pro-Jewish stance becomes even clearer when one remembers the vituperative anti-semitism of her brother, Clemens Brentano, as well as the profound prejudice of her husband, Achim von Arnim.[27] In *Die Günderode* Bettine makes clear her distance from Clemens's anti-semitism in the concluding lines of the first letter of Volume Two, highlighting the significance, both ideal and uncanny, that she attributes to German Jews throughout that Volume:

Yesterday we strolled through the Judengasse, ... many strange figures came and vanished, so that one might have taken them for ghosts. It was twilight already and I begged to go home; but Clemens would call, see here! and see there how he looks! till I thought they were all running after me, and I was glad enough to get home.

(p. 205)

Gestern wanderten [Clemens und ich] durch die Judengasse, es liefen so veil sonderbare Gestalten herum und verschwanden wieder daß man an Geister glauben muß, es ward schon dämmerig, und ich bat daß wir nach Haus gehen wollten, der Clemens rief immer seh den, seh da, seh dort wie der aussieht, und es war als liefen sie mir alle nach, ich war froh als wir zu Haus waren.

(pp. 572–3)

Though of course Bettine does not "predict" the Holocaust, she clearly illustrates here the psychic process through which her brother's hostile projections transform the Jewish ghetto into a realm of the shadowy, threatening, and despised other. This "other" is the ghostlike and guilty Ahasverus or Ewige Jude, the essential anti-Jewish stereotype from the late middle ages to the present day.[28]

In rejecting her Teutonic history teacher Arenswald and choosing the Jewish peddlar–scholar Ephraim as her mentor, Bettine ultimately places him alongside her beloved grandmother, the novelist and salonnière Sophie von La Roche, as a figure of cultural wisdom whose legacy she will accept and pass on to the future. This legacy is exquisitely figured in the metaphor of the rosebush with which Arnim opens and closes this novel. In her first letter, Bettine compares herself with a wild rose that will not survive unless it can take root – be grounded – in her beloved friend Karoline: "You have said that your desire is to be free; but I do not desire to be free, but to take root in you, – a wood-rose refreshing itself, in its own fragrance, it opens its bosom to the sun, but then, if the earth crumbles from its roots, all is over" ("Frei sein willst Du, hast Du gesagt? – ich will nicht frei sein, ich will Wurzel fassen in Dir – eine Waldrose, die im eignen Duft sich erquicke, will die der Sonne sich schon öffnen und der Boden löst sich von ihrer Wurzel, dann ists aus"; p. 2; p. 300). This wildflower becomes, after the process of self-development figured in the novel, a cultivated rose bush that Bettine receives from her mentor Ephraim, scholar of Hebrew and mathematics, and then gives back to him in the text's last letter. In the second volume of the novel, the figure of Ephraim as teacher takes his place alongside Günderode as she begins to recede from Bettine into her fears that she will never realize her dreams. She writes, in her last letter, "The impossibilities of fulfilling what I desire in my mind increase, and not knowing how to overcome them, I must allow myself to be carried on as accident wills" ("[D]ie Unmöglichkeiten dem nachzukommen was ich in Gedanken möchte, häufen sich, ich weiß sie nicht zu überwinden und muß mich dahin treiben lassen, wie der Zufall es will"; p. 324; p. 724).

The idealized Ephraim, on the other hand, is an exemplary figure of realized enlightenment. Returning the rosebush to him when he is near death, Bettine thus unites herself in a symbolic marriage with his wisdom:

O Ephraim! You please me infinitely . . . the roses have opened much more; how beautiful they looked contrasted with his white beard. I said to him, that his beard and the roses belonged together, and I was glad not to have broken any of them, for you are wedded to the roses, they are your bride.

(p. 337)

O Ephraim Du gefällst mir unendlich wohl . . . die Rosen sind viel mehr aufgeblüht, wie schön standen sie bei der hellen Lampe zu seinem schneeweißen Bart. Ich sagte die Rosen und Euer Bart gehören zusammen, und es ist mir lieb daß ich keine abgebrochen habe, denn Ihr seid vermählt zusammen mit den Rosen, sie sind Eure Braut.

(p. 740)

Furthermore, though her idealization of Ephraim is in one sense merely the other side of demonization, her sensitivity to the material realities of his life – the limitations placed upon him in earning money to support his orphaned grandchildren, the cleverness required of him in the face of potential persecution, the recognition of her own arrogance in allowing herself the use of the disrespectful familiar form of address with him because of his Jewish identity – take this portrait beyond stereotype as she pays tribute to his moral accomplishment in the face of a contemptuous world:

You must acknowledge that if, under this oppression, these most degrading outward conditions, the nobility of mind asserts itself freely and irreproachably, not even feeling itself bowed by the lowest occupation, it proves an elevated soul, that has a greater claim to our solemn respect, because it is all the more exposed to misconception and contempt.

(p. 297)

Du wirst mir recht geben, daß unter solchem Druck unter so erniedrigenden Bedingungen der Adel des Lebens so frei und untadelhaft bewahrt, daß sie nicht einmal durch das niedrigste Geschäft sich gebeugt fühlt, für eine hohe Seele spricht; daß sie um so mehr Recht hat auf unsere feierliche Achtung als sie vielleicht dem Äußeren nach, der Mißdeutung der Verachtung ausgesetzt ist.

(p. 689)

Finally, she sees the only possibility for her own freedom in the effort to liberate herself, through the honest recognition of spiritual value, from the stultifying prejudice that surrounds her: "Oh, for shame! Who would regulate their social relations according to outward rank, boasting with the fetters prejudice places upon us. The only pride I have is to be free from them; and whoever seeks advantages anywhere, except in the sacred conviction of his conscience, is not my companion" ("Oh pfui, wer seinen Umgang wollte richten nach dem aüßeren Rang, von Vorurteilen sich wollte Fesseln lassen anlegen; und mit denen prangen!

– der einzige Stolz den ich habe, der ist frei sein von ihnen"; p. 298; p. 690). When her family expresses concern that learning Hebrew from a Jew will alienate future suitors, because she will be tainted and unappetizing, Bettine makes it clear that she has chosen this tutor to save her from the boredom of marriage and from "the moth-eaten joys of domestic bliss" ("Mottenfraß der Häuslichkeit"; p. 293; p. 684), thus explicitly forging a connection between the woman outside of bourgeois marriage and domesticity and the Jew as outsider in Germanic culture.

It is no accident that Arnim's last published novel *Gespräche mit Dämonen* constituted, as Claire Baldwin asserts, an outspoken plea and a carefully sustained argument for the emancipation of Jews.[29] (The reactionary christlich-deutsche Tischgesellschaft founded earlier in the century by her brother and husband had, of course, already made this connection between Jews and women as "outsiders" explicit in its exclusion of "Frauen, Franzosen, Philister und Juden.") That Arnim made a point of finding a Jewish publisher – Wilhelm Levysohn – for this autobiographical novel suggests the importance that the parallels between the social positions and spiritual aspirations of German Jews and German women held for her.[30] The significance and courage of this publication decision is brought into sharp relief when one considers the cultural climate in which this novel appeared. According to Paul Lawrence Rose, the year 1840 constituted a major turning point in the intensification of modern anti-semitism, as the Blood Libel Trials in which Damascas Jews were accused of murdering a Christian friar to obtain blood for their Passover rituals were widely and sensationally reported throughout Europe.[31]

Bildung as blossoming of the spirit

This bond between young German woman and elderly Jewish man, figured in the image of the red rose and the white beard that concludes the text as an exemplar of *Bildung*, can be read as a rewriting of the relationship between Mignon and the Harper in Goethe's prototypical *Bildungsroman*, *Wilhelm Meisters Lehrjahre* (1795–6). Indeed, in what I believe is an ironic jab at Goethe's novel, she explicitly refers to Ephraim as her "Meister." Arnim, in her first and best-known *Briefroman*, *Goethe's Correspondence with a Child*, had styled herself famously as Mignon in relation to Goethe at the same time that she referred to *all* of the female characters in that novel as "disgusting" (p. 244).[32] Subsequently, in *Die Günderode*, however, she emphasizes that she has now accompanied Mignon into death and come back to life again (p. 680). Not only does she resurrect Mignon's spirit of poetry in herself through an Orphic effort, she also completely transforms the vision of old age presented in Goethe's supremely cynical and subtly anti-semitic novel.[33] Whereas the Harper, who, though Catholic, is repeatedly and explicitly associated with stigmatized Jewry through reference to his long white beard and the strangeness of his appearance, incarnates the profoundest guilt in his associations with incest, madness, and suicide, Arnim's Ephraim reveals wisdom and serenity to be the attributes of an old age metaphorized as a perfect blossom: "[W]hen the soul pierces the accumulated misery of Philistinedom, ... to heavenly freedom, ...

then age is but a vigorous sign of eternity ... Ephraim seems to me a perfect spirit-blossom, now standing in the spring rain" ("[Wo] der Geist durch alles gehäufte Elend des Philistertums, ... durchdringt zur Himmelsfreiheit, ... da ist Alter nur das kräftigste Lebenszeichen der Ewigkeit. ... Ephraim deucht mir eine vollkommne Geistesblüte, die jetzt im Frühlingsregen steht"; p. 306; p. 700).

And whereas the symbolic relations in *Wilhelm Meister* demand that the Harper's guilt doom Mignon, the product of his incestuous love, to an early death, Ephraim, above all else, in tragically prophetic irony, nurtures future generations in his grandchildren, his students, and in Bettine herself. Indeed, Bettine's references to her resurrection in relation to Mignon may be explicit echoes of Ludwig Börne's reading of *Goethe's Correspondence with a Child* as a devastating critique of Goethe: "Goethe beat Mignon to death with his lyre and buried her deep, and honored her memory with the most beautiful songs. ... After 40 years, she reappeared and called herself Bettine. ... Bettine is not Goethe's angel, she is his avenging fury" (my translation).[34]

Furthermore, Bettine replaces the counselings of the elite *Turmgesellschaft* who seem to guide and admonish Wilhelm almost against his will with her own visits to a watchtower for meditative, solitary counselings with the stars. Thus Part II of *Die Günderode* transforms the dialogue of Part I between Karoline and Bettine into a triangulated structure whose three points are either Bettine, Karoline, and Ephraim or Bettine, Karoline, and the stars. These three establish a kind of communion with oppositional significance that Ruth-Ellen Joeres, with reference to women, has termed "a sign of elected difference" (p. 44).[35] Bettine writes frequently that the stars speak to Karoline through her: "[T]he stars have told me this for you" ("Die Sterne haben mirs gesagt für Dich"; p. 307; p. 702). Similarly Karoline communicates to Ephraim through Bettine; in the concluding paragraphs of her last letter she writes: "Farewell, and many thanks for your love; you can also greet good Ephraim in my name, and write to me about him, and speak to him also about me" ("Lebe wohl und habe Dank für alle Liebe und auch den guten Ephraim grüße in meinem Namen, und schreib mir von ihm, und sprich auch mit ihm von mir"; p. 328; p. 729). And Ephraim is clearly aligned with the spiritual knowledge of the stars as Bettine frequently climbs her tower directly upon his departure: "Evenings when I go to my tower on the days he has been with me, the thoughts that come from the stars coincide with his words, so that I sometimes think they must have suggested them" ("Wenn ich abends auf den Turm geh, an Tagen wo er da war, sind die Gedanken, die mir da oben von den Sternen kommen, immer so übereinstimmend mit seinen Reden daß ich manchmal meinen muß sie hättens ihm eingegeben für mich"; p. 302; p. 695). Indeed, Bettine explicitly and heretically refers to this triangular relationship as a trinity in which the stars/Ephraim play the role of the spirit: "Ah, if the trinity could but continue to exist between you and me and the Spirit, ... I would be satisfied forever" ("Ach wenn nur diese Dreieinigkeit fortbesteht zwischen Dir und mir und dem Geist, ... so bin ich befriedigt für immer"; p. 274; p. 660). Here we find, in Arnim's emphasis upon the realization of the trinity and the incarnation of spirit in a contemporary Jew, a literalization of Hegel's focus in

The Philosophy of History on the incarnation of spirit in Christ as the legacy and ultimate purpose of Judaism.[36] Hegel suggests that through the self-conscious understanding of God as spirit, in the concept of the Trinity, "we see the world-historical importance and significance of the Jewish people; for from it has sprung the higher development by which the spirit arrived at absolute self-consciousness" (p. 86). In appearing to take Hegel at his word, Arnim, true to her iconoclastic aims, ultimately challenges the hegemony of the Christian religion at the heart of Hegel's philosophy of history. For she represents Judaism not as a superannuated ghostlike religion of the past that must inevitably die or dissolve into the ashes of history, but as a key element – indeed a model of – future spiritual and cultural progress. She thus undermines a key theoretical pillar of what Paul Lawrence Rose terms German revolutionary anti-semitism – the belief that the Jews had fulfilled their historical purpose in antiquity and that, as a guilty Ahasverian people, their redemption would come through disappearance either by assimilation or extinction.

In the place of the dehumanized and instrumentalized letter carrier who makes possible communication between Karoline and Bettina in Part I and is objectified as "The Jew," Ephraim becomes an equal partner, in fact, an inspiration to their dialogue. Here spiritual transcendence, elevation, and freedom are inseparable from ostracism by a corrupt, prejudiced, and uncomprehending social world: "Inwardly victorious, soaring above all; outwardly unacknowledged, misunderstood. Indeed, rather be despised than let them dream how it is, this heavenly trinity between you and me and the stars" ("Innerlich siegend wegfliegen über Alles; äußerlich nicht erkannt, nicht verstanden; ja lieber verachtet als nur ahnen lassen wie es ist. Diese göttliche Dreieinigkeit zwischen mir und Dir und den Sternen"; p. 274; p. 659). This harmonious poetic trinity replaces the destructive triangles composed of Karoline, Creuzer, and his wife or of herself, Karoline, and Creuzer that most likely played a role in her friend's suicide when he pressured Karoline to disassociate herself from Bettine and the Brentano family, only to abandon her shortly thereafter. Here Arnim is in a sense rewriting the past to suggest that things might have turned out differently had Karoline been truly open to plots other than the traditional heterosexual plot that ends for the woman in marriage or death.

This triangulated relationship furthermore allows Arnim to create an identification among these three outsiders to middle-class German values as well as to place the exemplary fulfillment of Ephraim's life alongside the specter of Karoline's truncated existence. Repeated discussions of Karoline's wish to die young bring forth in Bettine a conception of *Bildung* that unites youth and old age as mirrors that complete each other in their reflections of an ineffable and infinite self. Through her remarkable grandmother Sophie von La Roche, Bettine articulates her conception of the circular or spiral-like pattern of human development that brings together youth and old age and owes much to Schiller's *Naïve and Sentimental Poetry*. Watching her grandmother admiring the glow of ruby-red blossoms held up to the light, Bettine remarks that she is like a child seeing everything for the first time. Her grandmother's response embodies a romantic organicism in which the natural and the human, the body and the spirit are one. Like Ephraim, she is a fully blooming flower, open to the future:

> What then shall I be but a child; are not all the distractions of life now past which stood in the way of the childlike mind? Thus human life describes a circle, and shows even here that it is assigned to eternity ... so many blossoms have faded for me, so many fruits ripened; now that the leaves are falling, the spirit prepares itself for fresh shoots in the next sphere of life.
>
> (p. 129)

> Was soll ich anders als nur ein Kind werden, sind doch alle Lebenszerstreuungen jetzt entschwunden, die dem Kindersinn früher in den Weg traten, so beschreibt das Menschenleben einen Kreis und bezeichnet schon hier daß es auf die Ewigkeit angewiesen ist ... so viel der schönen Blüten sind mir abgeblüht, so viel Früchte gereift, jetzt, wo das Laub abfällt da bereitet sich der Geist vor auf frische Triebe im nächsten Lebenskreislauf.
>
> (pp. 461–2)

Here, then, is the realization of Schiller's ideal of human development in which culture brings the individual human being, now with heightened consciousness, back to childhood and to nature. Describing what he perceives as a nearly universal love of children, flowers, animals, and the beauties of nature in his fellow human beings, Schiller writes:

> We love in them the tacitly creative life, the serene spontaneity of their activity, existence in accordance with their own laws, the inner necessity, the eternal unity with themselves. They are what we were; they are that we should once again become. We were nature just as they, and culture, by means of reason and freedom, should lead us back to nature.
>
> (p. 85)

In Schiller, however, these manifestations of the naïve elicit a response of melancholy and nostalgia rooted in the conviction that such serenity and unity of self is unattainable to the rational adult: "In them, then, we see eternally that which escapes us, but for which we are challenged to strive, and which, even if we never attain to it, we may still hope to approach in endless progress" (p. 85). Bettine, on the other hand, vows to achieve this peace of mind before she dies, as she sees it manifested in her grandmother and in Ephraim, valorizing earthly life and joy over both Karoline's longing for the absolute and Schiller's eternal striving: "Ah, Günderode, I too will become a child again before I die, moving in a circle, and not, as you, desire to die early" ("Ach Günderode, ich will auch erst wieder ein Kind werden eh ich sterb, ich will einen Kreis bilden, nicht wie Du willst, recht früh sterben, nein, das will ich nicht"; p. 129; p. 462). As Katherine Goodman writes, "the child in [Arnim] is not merely a retrospective image, but also a prospective one."[37] The almost ubiquitous disapproval with which "polite" society met Bettine von Arnim in response to her eccentric and spontaneous behavior and conversation suggests that she did indeed endeavor to regain – or maintain – her childlike openness into her old age.[38] It is as if the Italian-German Bettine Brentano von Arnim chose to perform the Romantic myth of opposition between south and north, naïve and sentimental, childhood and maturity, and believed herself capable of uniting them in her life and her art.

Despite her close association with Goethe through the publication of *Goethe's Correspondence with a Child*, the work for which, predictably, she has been best known until very recently, and despite her long preoccupation with her Goethe monument, Bettine von Arnim's intellectual affinities for and debts to Schiller are, in my opinion, much more striking.[39] She seems, to some extent, to have realized this herself, when, in 1850, she imagines the two artists' respective responses to the political upheavals of 1848, had Goethe and Schiller still been alive: "Schiller, in his great humanistic striving, would have joined the battle, whereas Goethe would perhaps have stayed at home."[40] Like Heine, Arnim has little patience with what, in *Die Romantische Schule*, he termed Goethe's political "Indifferentismus."[41] In fact, as I have suggested, critics from Ludwig Börne's time to the present day have read *Goethe's Correspondence with a Child* as an implicit critique of the artist it supposedly enshrined.[42]

The female philosopher: kissed by nature

If Arnim's representation of *Bildung* rewrites Schiller's *Naïve and Sentimental Poetry* through its emphasis upon the (provisional) attainability of one's ideals and its refusal of his melancholy and nostalgia, Arnim's persona Bettine, through her "star-lessons" on the watchtower, replaces Goethe's complex social hierarchy culminating in the *Turmgesellschaft* of *Wilhelm Meister* with a female sublime that also pushes the theoretical limits of Schiller's conception of that crucial term in Romantic aesthetics. The sublime for Schiller represents the possibility of "absolute liberation" from subjection to violence, most especially through a sense of mental freedom from the coercive inevitability of death. Similarly, Bettine writes to Karoline, significantly in the same letter condemning Napoleonic tyranny, that the stars have the potential to free her from her fear of death: "I will tell you how it is to die. I have learnt it on my old tower" ("Ich will Dir sagen wie es ist beim Sterben, ich habs auf der alten Warte gelernt"; p. 257; p. 638). Like Kant and Schiller before her, Arnim figures the sublime as a victory of the spiritual faculties (Geist) over the imagination, though for the former philosophers imagination means sensory perception of reality, whereas Arnim uses the term to mean illusion:

> Man is a slave to his imagination; it denies his inner self, but Divine Truth shines down into his dark, ruinous tower, and with double daring he now mounts the dilapidated ladder that leads him to freedom.
>
> (p. 258)

> Der Mensch ist Sklave der Einbildung die ihm sein Inneres leugnet, aber die göttliche Wahrheit haucht schon in den dunklen, baufälligen Turm zu ihm nieder daß er die morschgewordne Leiter die zur Freiheit führt mit doppelter Kühnheit erschwingt.
>
> (p. 639)

Indeed, Arnim does not claim originality for the sublime revelations of her persona, asserting that they are "nichts Neues." What she does claim is the authority of firsthand experience, the importance of which, for a young nineteenth-century German girl, is not to be underestimated in this previously and implicitly masculinist realm of the sublime: "Indeed it was nothing new to me either, but derives its value from being an experience not understood by the senses alone. The starry heavens taught it me" ("[A]ber doch ists was anderes, weil ichs erlebt hab, und nicht bloß mit den äußeren Sinnen erfaßt, der freie Sternenhimmel hat michs gelehrt"; p. 258; p. 639).

Even more significantly, Arnim's sublime challenges Schiller's conception of aesthetic semblance (Schein) according to which the virtual reality of art represents "an inoculation against inevitable destiny" (p. 209) which allows the mind, through repeated experience of "imaginary and artificial misfortune," to practice asserting its absolute independence in preparation for a real misfortune, actual danger, or impending death. Bettine's "star lessons," on the other hand, are learned through the trial of actual danger, so much so, that Karoline repeatedly expresses her fears that her friend will fall and seriously injure herself as she climbs her tower. Once again Arnim's text questions the possibility of a clear distinction between theory and practice, between art and life. In fact, Karoline suggests that, in her near absolute opposition to bourgeois culture, Bettine cannot write a poem or a fairy tale as Clemens wishes her to do because she has turned her life into a sublime work of art and a dangerous one at that: "Icarus was a careful, considerate, searching youth compared to you" ("Da war der Icarus ein vorsichtiger, überlegter, prüfender Knabe gegen Dich"; p. 108; p. 436). Karoline then retreats into a traditional reading – complicit with masculinist appropriations of the feminine – of Bettine as incapable of writing poetry because she herself embodies poetry, an interpretation that denies Bettine agency and subjectivity. The lyricism of *Die Günderode*, however, renders any such reading glaringly inadequate, troubling, with romantic irony, Schiller's distinction between the artist and the work of art as "object of free contemplation" (p. 212).

Finally Bettine's visits to the watchtower are recorded in a playful tone in keeping with their intimate, epistolary format that contrasts sharply with the painful and solitary solemnity of Schiller's "On the Sublime":

> There is an old tower here at the end of the hilly garden, with a broken ladder inside that no one dares to mount; but I can get up with a few scientific leaps, and find myself quite alone, looking over the land, who knows how far? But I do not see. I carry myself out into the distance where it is lost in mist, not drawing my eye to account for its impressions, glad to be

alone, and that all is mine as far as I can feel. Up there I am with you, and bless the earth in your name.

(pp. 243–4)

Es ist eine alte Warte hier am Ende des Berggartens, eine zerbrochne Leiter inwendig die keiner zu ersteigen wagt führt da hinauf, ich kann mich aber hinauf schwingen mit einigen Kunstsprüngen, da bin ich also ganz allein and sehe wie weit? – aber ich sehe nicht, ich trage mich hin, wos in der Ferne nur nebelt und schwimmt, und fordere nicht Rechenschaft vom Auge, froh, daß ich allein bin, and daß mein gehört so weit ich mich fühle da oben bin ich mit Dir, da segne ich die Erde in Deinem Namen.

(p. 622)

Arnim hints here at the desire for dominion and self-aggrandizement that so often accompanies poetic evocation of sublime vistas only to compel those desires to disappear, replaced by an even more sublime obscurity and a dialectical movement between spiritual self-possession, love for another human being, and a sense of the sacredness of the earth itself. Transcendence, for Bettine, implies dialogue and relationship: "But to be understood, that seems to me to be the sole metamorphosis, the true ascension" ("Aber ganz verstanden sein, das deucht mir die wahre alleinige Metamorphose, die einzige Himmelfahrt"; p. 113; pp. 441–2).

In fact, despite Arnim's affinities for Schiller's thought, when a friend of her grandmother's gives her Schiller's *On the Aesthetic Education of Man* to read in order to "form her mind," Bettine throws it away in mock horror, reacting violently against programmatic learning and exclaiming: "To form my mind – I have no mind – I want no mind of my own. In the end I will not be able any more to understand the Holy Ghost. Who can form me but he? What is all politics against the silvery glance of Nature!" ("[M]einen Geist bilden! – ich hab keinen Geist – ich will keinen eignen Geist; am Ende könnt ich den heiligen Geist nicht mehr verstehen – Wer kann mich bilden außer ihm. Was ist alle Politik gegen den Silberblick der Natur!"; p. 135; p. 468). She seems to understand quite acutely that in Schiller's aesthetic economy, nature (like the minds of young girls) has the status of a threatening object over which man seeks to assert control, just as Schiller gives ultimate priority to his dualistic aesthetic of the sublime over his conception of the beautiful as harmony of sense and spirit. In a brilliantly succinct and psychologically revealing description of the ideology of enlightenment, Schiller writes in his "Twenty-fifth Letter" of this victory over nature that is anathema to Bettine:

From being a slave of Nature, so long as he merely perceives her, Man becomes her lawgiver as soon as she becomes his thought. She who had formerly ruled him only as *force*, now stands as *object* before the judgment of his glance. What is object to him has no longer power over him; for in order to be object it must experience his own power. ... Only where substance holds its ponderous and shapeless sway, and the dim outlines fluctuate between uncertain boundaries, does fear have its abode; Man is superior to every terror of Nature so long as he knows how to give form to it, and to turn it into his object.[43]

(pp. 120–1)

In the light of this ideology of form, the perceived formlessness of Arnim's *Die Günderode* as well as her other *Briefbücher* takes on a clear ideological significance as the manifestation of a (proto) feminist effort to escape male domination. In fact, in contrast to Schiller's conception of form as domination, and the glance as agent of objectification, Bettine represents form as the product within the spirit of an erotic relationship to nature, the fruit of a kiss between the human eye and the natural world:

> To kiss is the form, and to receive within us what we touch is the form, is the kiss; form indeed is born within us. ... I have learnt it of Nature, she is constantly kissing me; ... I am already so accustomed to it that I run to meet her with my eyes, for they are the mouth that Nature kisses.

(p. 185)

> Küssen ist die Form und den Geist der Form in uns aufnehmen die wir berühren, das ist der Kuß; ja die Form wird in uns geboren. ... [I]ch habs von der Natur gelernt, sie küßt mich beständig, ... und ich bin auch schon so ganz dran gewöhnt daß ich ihr gleich mit den Augen entgegenkomme, denn die Augen sind der Mund, den die Natur küßt.

(p. 528)

It is precisely the attitude toward nature delineated above by Schiller that compels Arnim to call for a redefinition of philosophy in an effort to protect nature from the violence of the analytical mind. Her critique of philosophy clearly resembles Mary Shelley's prescient and unendingly troubling portrayal of Victor Frankenstein's scientific efforts to "penetrate the secrets of nature" and to use that knowledge for self-aggrandizement. Bettine contrasts a relation of erotic mutuality to a feminized nature with the destructive exploitation and violation that seems inevitably to follow from philosophical or scientific analysis:

> Is not the philosopher fearfully presumptuous? ... Man must, above all, love nature with true love; then he blooms! Then nature plants intellect in him. But none of these philosophers seem to me like such a one, who leans on her bosom and trusts her, and, with all his powers, is dedicated to her. Rather, he seems on the watch, like a robber, for what he can pilfer from her; what he gets he puts in his private workshop ... he explains to scholars his perpetual motion, all in a sweat, while the scholars stand confounded, and have not a word to say.

(p. 8)

Glaubst Du ein Philosoph sei nicht fürchterlich hoffärtig? . . . Der Mann des Geistes muß die Natur lieben über alles, mit wahrer Lieb, dann blüht er – dann pflanzt die Natur Geist in ihn. Aber ein Philosoph scheint mir so einer nicht, der ihr am Busen liegt, und ihr vertraut und mit allen Kräften ihr geweiht ist. – Mir deucht vielmehr er geht auf Raub, was es ihr abluchsen kann, das vermanscht er in seine geheime Fabrik.

(pp. 307–8)

Like Shelley, Arnim represents the philosopher's desire for god-like superiority over others as egotistical and ultimately demonic:

The Philosopher combines, and transposes, and considers, and writes the processes of thought, not to understand himself, that is not the object of this expense, but to let others know how high he has climbed. He does not wish to impart his wisdom to his low-stationed companions, but only the hocus-pocus of his superlatively excellent machine. . . . Others deceive, misinterpreting nature; they prepare this scaffold on which to climb, out of vanity, and at the top it becomes arrogance, breathing down sulphureous fumes to the men below.

(p. 66)

[S]o verbindet und versetzt, und verändert, und überlegt, und vereinigt der Philosoph also nur sein Denkwerk, nicht um sich selbst zu verstehen, da würde er nicht solchen Aufwand machen, sondern um den andern von oben herab, den ersten Gedanken beizubringen wie hoch er geklettert sei, und er will auch nicht die Weisheit seinen untenstehenden Gefährten mitteilen, er will nur das Hokuspokus seiner Maschine Superlativa vortragen . . . [er] lügt, wenn er die Natur verleugnet und diesem Sparrwerk anhängt und auch hinaufklettert; es ist Eitelkeit, und oben wirds Hoffart, und der haucht Schwefeldampf auf den Geist herab.

(p. 384)

Here Arnim anticipates Foucault, who, in his meditations on her contemporaries Nietzsche, Fichte, and Hegel, reveals cruelty and desire for power to be the source of the will to knowledge: "The historical analysis of this rancorous will to knowledge reveals that all knowledge rests upon injustice . . . and that the instinct for knowledge is malicious (something murderous, opposed to the happiness of mankind)."[44]

Yet whereas Foucault, like Nietzsche before him, seems to take pleasure in resigning himself to acceptance of this cruelty, Arnim posits instinctual love of nature and of fellow human beings as a force even more powerful than the will to knowledge. In response to the arrogance of masculinist philosophy, both Karoline and Bettine proclaim their commitment to a female philosophy of "Unbedeutenheit" (insignificance) sensitive to the "everyday life of nature" ("Alltäglichkeit der Natur"; p. 49; p. 362). And ultimately Bettine claims the name of philosopher for herself and for Karoline even as she pictures their radical speculations as the product of female intimacy and closeness to nature:

> In the castle on the hill, in the night-dew it was good to be with you. Those were the dearest hours of all my life; and, when I return, we will again dwell together there …; we will have our beds close together, and talk all night, and then the wind will rise and make the old roof clatter, and the mice will come and drink the oil from the lamp, while we two philosophers, though now and then interrupted by these pretty interludes, hold grand and profound speculations, enough to make the old world creak on its rusty hinges, if not to turn quite round.
>
> (p. 25)

> Auf der grünen Burg im Graben, im Nachttau, da war es auch schön mit Dir; es sind mir meine liebsten Stunden von meinem ganzen Leben, und sowie ich zurückomm, … da stellen wir unsere Betten dicht neben einander und plaudern die ganze Nacht zusammen, und dann geht als der Wind und klappert in dem rappeligen Dach, und dann kommen die Mäuschen und saufen uns das Öl aus der Lampe, und wir beiden Philosophen halten, von diesen Zwischenszenen lieblich unterbrochen, große tiefsinnige Spekulationen, wovon die alte Welt in ihren eingerosteten Angeln kracht, wenn sie nicht gar umdreht davon.
>
> (pp. 331–2)

The radical courage exemplified by Arnim's playful claiming of the title philosopher for her two early nineteenth-century young women becomes even clearer when one considers the effort to remasculinize the realms of philosophy that followed the French Revolution.[45]

A religion of free flight

In the place of the dualisms of canonical German idealism, then, Arnim's female philosophers proclaim a new religion of nature and of love termed a "Schwebe-Religion" (floating/hovering/soaring religion). This new philosophy must partake of the transcendent, the unearthly, and the utopian because, as Bettine unequivocally asserts, in her response to attending a society ball, worldly wisdom and accomplishment mean nothing to her but restriction and limitation. Her vision must be otherworldly because, as a woman, she is forbidden the freedom to control her earthly fate. "No earthly destiny interests me, because I have yet no freedom to guide it" ("Mich geht kein Erdenschicksal was an, weil ich doch nicht Freiheit es zu lenken hab"; p. 37; p. 348). Transcendence is thus rendered explicitly political and feminist. At the same time, however, theirs must also be a religion of nature and of immanence. In order to transform the restrictive social world, this new religion seeks to break down distinctions between nature and humanity, spirit and matter, human and divine, control and instinct, masculine and feminine, intellect and feeling through movement, flight and hovering between opposites.[46] The image of the tightrope walker comes to her mind. Asserting that complete and uninhibited self-expression might lead to a healthy and revolutionary balance of freedom and control, Bettine asks "if this unrestrained exercise among the allurements of nature, this exercise of our powers … does not also strengthen our inmost soul, … not enduring but overthrowing the unworthy" ("ob überhaupt dies freie Bewegen in der Natur, dies Üben aller Kräfte in ihren Reizungen, … nicht auch die inneren Seelenkräfte stärkt, … daß sie das kleinliche nicht mehr ertragen sondern übern Haufen stürzen"; pp. 238–9; p. 615). In this emphasis upon full expression of the self, the new religion meets her critique of scholarly *Bildung* as she articulates her belief that "True culture is produced by using the powers within us" ("[e]chte Bildung geht hervor aus Übung der Kräfte, die in uns liegen"; p. 135; p. 468):

> Truly it shall be a chief principle of our Hovering-religion to permit no formation of the mind, that is no trained formation; each one shall eagerly look upon and bring himself to light from the depth, like a rich ore, or a hidden spring; all culture shall tend towards bringing the spirit to light.
>
> (p. 135)

> [D]as soll auch ein Hauptprinzip der schwebenden Religion sein, daß wir keine Bildung gestatten – das heißt kein angebildet Wesen, jeder soll neugierig sein auf sich selber und soll sich zu Tage fördern wie aus der Teife ein Stück Erz oder ein Quell, die ganze Bildung soll darauf ausgehen daß wir den Geist ans Licht hervorlassen.
>
> (p. 468)

The exuberant and playful endorsement of psychic exploration expressed through Arnim's mining metaphor contrasts sharply with the darkly troubled tone of Ludwig Tieck's *Der Runenberg* (1801) and E.T.A. Hoffmann's *The Mines of Falun* (1819), earlier Romantic narratives that employ mining metaphors to represent the psyche as a dangerous, uncanny, and female realm.

Of their intellectual contemporaries, it is the Romantic theologian Friedrich Schleiermacher with whom these female philosophers feel the greatest affinity, as Bettine reminds Karoline, quoting her friend's assessment of his significance: "Had he said but these words: 'Man shall bring to light all that dwells in the soul within, so that he may learn to know himself,' Schleiermacher would be divine, and the first great mind" ("Und wenn er auch nur das einzige Wort gesagt hätte: der Mensch solle alles Innerliche ans Taglicht fördern was ihm im Geist innewohne, damit er sich selber kennen lerne, so wär Schleiermacher ewig göttlich und der erste größste Geist"; p. 148; p. 485). Indeed, it is likely, as Elisabeth Moltmann-Wendel points out, that the name "Schwebe-Religion" was inspired by Schleiermacher's meditative visions, in *Talks On Religion* (1799), of floating in the infinite between the self and the universal.[47]

The ultimate aim of this movement between the self and the universal in Bettine's *Schwebe-Religion* is the divinization of the self, the full expression of human nature ("alles Innerliche") leading to a union with universal nature, the divine. As Bettine playfully writes, adding a touch of irony with her emphasis upon "Inkonsequenz," to weighty idealist deliberations on the meaning of Geist: "Soul is really flight … inconsistency is spirit; to hover hither and thither on the wing, to unite with everything it comes in contact with, that is Spirit" ("Geist ist ja eigentlich Fliegen. … Inkonsequenz ist Geist – im Flug hin und her schweben alles was er berührt, gleich mit ihm zusammenfließen, das ist Geist"; p. 186; p. 530). This psychic process makes possible a self-abandonment that is a self-fulfillment rather than self-sacrifice.[48] Bettine's acceptance of inconsistency and movement as the essence of spirit is reminiscent of Corinne's understanding of multiplicity and Euthanasia's belief in contradiction as fundamental to human freedom. Furthermore, the philosopher's desire for control and his rapacity are replaced in Arnim's vision of understanding with an attitude of receptivity that calls into play what we today call the unconscious, at the same time that it privileges feeling: "I feel there is an unconscious consciousness, that is, feeling and that the soul is unconsciously made living" ("[D]a fühl ich, daß es eine bewußtlose Bewußtheit gebe, das ist Gefühl, und daß der Geist bewußtlos erregt wird"; p. 9; p. 309).

Engagement for the welfare of others cannot be separated from the well-being of the self, if, as Schleiermacher advocates, in his critique of bourgeois individualism, the sharp outlines of the individual should gradually dissolve into the universal as spirituality develops.[49] In fact, the origins of the political and social activism that distinguished Arnim's entire later life can be traced to her first years of acquaintance with Schleiermacher as she sought to intercede with King Friedrich Wilhelm III on his behalf when he was threatened with removal from his post for his progressive theological writings, critical of the monarch's religious positions.[50] And in 1831, when cholera broke out in the slums of Berlin, Schleiermacher delegated some of his overwhelming duties of caring for the poor to Arnim, thus opening up in her a sense of concern and responsibility for their welfare that never left her. This sense of social responsibility culminated in her remarkable posthumously published *Das Armenbuch*, an unfinished sociological study of the living and working conditions of the Silesian weavers.

Almost ten years later when Arnim was writing *Die Günderode*, she embodied his belief in social activism into the first principle of Schwebe-Religion, a demand for courage in all that one does: "Man shall always do the greatest deeds, and no others … all actions can and must be great" ("Der Mensch soll immer die größte Handlung tun und nie eine andre … jede Handlung eine größte sein kann und soll"; p. 119; p. 449). She challenges herself and her beloved friend to have the courage to transform their ideals into reality. "[M]an clamors for wisdom, but has not the courage to support it. … Ah, in our religion courage shall stand first … and we will soon prove things in which as yet no one has faith" ("[D]er Mensch will immer die Weisheit, er hat aber *den Mut nicht* sie durchzusetzen. … Ach in unserer Religion soll die Tapferkeit obenan stehen … und wir werden bald Dinge beweisen die kein Mensch noch glaubt"; p. 124; pp. 454–5).

Institutionalized Christianity, on the other hand, like her kindred spirit William Blake, she judges as cowardice and hypocrisy. Expressing her desire to visit the suffering poet Hölderlin, hoping that she can be of help to him, she knows, at the same time, that her desire will be thwarted by her family's concern for propriety and their judgment of her as mentally unstable:

> I want to hear no more about religion and Christendom, they have become Christians only to falsify the teachings of Christ. To throw crumbs to the hungry and rags to the naked, are called works of charity – but to follow Christ into the desert, and learn his wisdom, that no one finds time to do. Patches of learning are hung upon one, which avail nothing, while for the investigation of the depth and power of a human soul, no one has any time.
>
> (p. 103)

> Ich mag gar von Religion und von Christentum nichts mehr hören, sie sind Christen geworden um die Lehre Christi zu verfälschen. – Brocken hinwerfen und den nackten Leib decken, das nennt man Werke der Barmherzigkeit – aber Christus in die Wüste folgen und seine Weisheit lernen, das Weiß keiner anzufangen. – Bildungsflicken hängt man einem auf, mit denen man nichts anzufangen weiß, aber die Tiefe und Gewalt eines einzigen Seelengrunds zu erforschen, da hat kein Mensch Zeit dazu.
>
> (p. 430)

The daring and vertiginous self-exploration that Hölderlin represents Bettine knows to be off limits for young girls, even inconceivable in them by society's standards; thus earlier in the novel she warns Karoline not to communicate anything about their mutual meditations to her brother Clemens. Predictably, he would imagine that she is possessed or in love when in reality she has undertaken a spiritual journey into her own soul: "He would ask other people if I am in love, when I have but retired into the holy orders of my own nature" ("[E]r frägt andre Leut, ob ich verliebt sei, wo ich doch nur im heiligen Orden meiner eignen Natur lebe"; p. 86; p. 408). Like Shelley's Euthanasia, Arnim's Bettine privileges self-knowledge over Romantic passion.

Poetry as "heilende Liebe"

For Bettine, then, Hölderlin, in his poetic pursuit of divinity, is a hero according to the principles of her Schwebe-Religion which is ultimately a religion of art. "Ah, such an one as Hölderlin, passionately carried away in labyrinthine search, we too must meet somewhere, if we follow the Divine with as pure a heroism as he" ("Ach, einem solchen wie Hölderlin, der im labyrinthischen Suchen leidenschaftlich hingerissen ist, dem müssen wir irgendwie begegnen, wenn auch wir das Göttliche verfolgen mit so reinem Heroismus wie er"; p. 197; p. 548). From the very first letters in which Bettine proclaims the goal of their new religion to be union with God – "ein Sein mit Gott" (p. 445) – it is clear that their labyrinthine spiritual search will also be an aesthetic one, for "Gott is Poet" (p. 446) and "All great deeds are poetry, the metamorphosis of the individual into deity" ("Alle große Handlung ist Dichtung, ist Verwandlung der Persönlichkeit in Gottheit"; p. 118; p. 447).

Bettine concludes Part I with Hölderlin's story, seeing in him an exemplar of the age-old tradition of divine poetic frenzy, but emphasizing as well that his daring originality makes him a model to her and to other future poets: "I know now that I must follow him. ... He is an apparition to my senses, and into my thought he infuses light" ("[I]ch werde ihm noch viel müssen nachgehen ... eine Erscheinung ist er in meinen Sinnen, und in mein Denken strömt es Licht"; p. 198; p. 549). Bettine registers a clear sense, rare for her time, of Hölderlin's originary significance for modern European poetry.[51] Defining insanity as solipsism, as that which finds no echo in the spirit of others, she refuses to label Hölderlin mad, instead acknowledging the power of his poetry to echo like thunder in her own spirit. Like her literary daughter, Emily Dickinson, Arnim recognizes that "much madness is divinest sense," and that Hölderlin's fate cannot be separated from the fate of the common man: "that all must be healed by love, in order ourselves to be healed" ("daß alle von der Liebe geheilt müssen werden um uns selber zu heilen"; p. 193; p. 543). Indeed those considered normal are embodiments of a collective unconsciousness that is both ubiquitous and stultifying:

> But we are no longer conscious of our own disease, nor of our ossified senses. That this is a disease we do not feel, nor that we are insane, and more so than he whose genius should illumine his native land, but was extinguished in the turbid pool of commonplaces that slowly collect.
>
> (pp. 193–4)

> Aber wir sind uns der eignen Krankheit nicht mehr bewußt, nicht der erstarrten Sinne; daß das Krankheit ist, das fühlen wir nicht, – und daß wir so wahnsinnig sind und mehr noch als jener, dessen Geistesflamme seinem Vaterland aufleuchten sollte – daß die erlöschen muß im trüben Regenbach zusammengelaufner Alltäglichkeit, der langweilig dahinsickert.
>
> (p. 543)

Arnim holds German Philistinism responsible for quenching the fiery spirit of the artist who instead should have been collectively celebrated as a symbol of the best in German culture. *Die Günderode*, then, constitutes Arnim's effort to counteract German Philistinism with healing love, this "heilende Liebe" (p. 543) being an Eros that is embodied in the poetic form of the text. Unable to approach Hölderlin, Bettine focuses her attention on Karoline who, in Part II of the novel, is increasingly vulnerable and melancholic. As critics have frequently noted, Bettine's efforts to cure Karoline of her Romantic melancholy, her longing for death, are central to the novel's narrative from beginning to end. Indeed Bettine creates her religion specifically as a cure for melancholy.[52]

Unlike Bettine, however, Karoline cannot give herself up to their mutual doctrine of "Inkonsequenz" and "Unbedeutenheit" even though it is she who had proposed it in response to her sense of exclusion from traditional poetic community and canon. Like Staël's Corinne, she cannot escape the power of the cultural nexus of abandoned woman/Romantic melancholy. Furthermore, as Bettine reminds her friend, Karoline had previously written to Clemens, expressing unequivocally her desire to join, in eternity, a community of great artists:

> Ever new and living is the desire in me to express my life in a permanent form; in a shape that may be worthy to advance towards the most excellent, to greet them and claim community with them. Yes, after this community have I constantly longed. This is the church, towards which my spirit constantly makes pilgrimages upon the earth.
>
> (p. 66)

> *[I]mmer neu und lebendig ist die Sehnsucht in mir, mein Leben in einer bleibenden Form auszusprechen, in einer Gestalt, die würdig sei, zu den Vortrefflichsten hinzutreten, sie zu grüßen und Gemeinschaft mit ihnen zu haben. Ja nach dieser Gemeinschaft hat mir stets gelüstet; dies ist die Kirche, nach der mein Geist stets wallfahrtet auf Erden.*
>
> (p. 383)

Instead of the openness of movement, hovering and flight, Karoline seeks permanent form and spiritual community with those poets previously anointed as "den Vortrefflichsten." Seduced by Romantic melancholy and *Todestrieb* as well as obsessed with classical form and canonical presences, her religion is ultimately one of violence and of death to the self, as these double-edged lines from her poem "Die Pilger" suggest: "The cure is bitter, / The journey long, / But I reach for the staff / And heal my wrong" ("Die Heilung ist bitter, / Der Weg ist wohl weit, / Doch greif ich zum Stabe / Und ende mein Leid" p. 538).[53] As with Staël's Corinne and Shelley's Beatrice, internalization of a masculine ethos of repressive violence to the self dooms Arnim's Karoline. The reader's sense of Karoline's impending tragedy is heightened by her own admission, in a brilliant formulation of her experience of cultural hegemony as hydra, that she will fail her friend: "As you know me, have patience, and remember that it is not a single voice I must resist, but a general one, which like the Lernæan Serpent is constantly putting forth new heads" ("Hab Geduld mit mir da Du mich kennst, und denke daß es nicht eine einzelne Stimme ist der ich zu widersprechen habe, aber eine allgemeine die wie die lernaeische Schlange immer neue Köpfe erzeugt"; p. 157; p. 497). Karoline's vulnerability to the devastating power of the hydra, archetype of melancholia since Tasso, suggests her attachment to the cultural prestige of masculinist models of genius as well.[54] Furthermore, the radical political import of this metaphor becomes clear when one remembers that the hydra was a central symbol of "monarchical, aristocratic and clerical tyranny" pitted against the Herculean power of the common people.[55]

Karoline clearly feels herself incapable of this Herculean heroism. Echoing the epigraph of Part II, she admits that in refusing to defend Bettine against her detractors, she is betraying and denying herself: "Your most absurd demonstrations, as your opponents call them, I have never doubted, understanding you like my own faith … at the same time I must commit the sin of denying you" ("Deine absurdesten Demonstrationen wie sie Deine Gegner nennen, habe ich noch nie in Zweifel gezogen, ich hab Dich verstanden wie meinen eignen Glauben, … und doch muß ich in die Sünde verfallen Dich zu verleugnen"; p. 157; p. 497). Contrary to the principles of their mutually declared *Schwebe-Religion*, for Karoline word and deed cannot be one, because, like Peter of the Bible, she feels herself too weak and confined to fight earthly battles for her ideals. "Poetry is balm on the wounds of non-fulfillment in our lives," she writes, suggesting the compensatory, regressive function of a poetry that grows out of a painful wounding of the self: "In time they heal, and from the blood that moistened the soil of the soul, the mind has cultivated beautiful red flowers, that blossom one day, when it is sweet to draw the fragrance of recollection from them" ("Gedichte sind Balsam auf unerfüllbares im Leben; nach und nach verharscht es, und aus der Wunde deren Blut den Seelenboden tränkte hat der Geist schöne rote Blumen gezogen die wieder einen Tag blühen, an dem es süß ist der Erinnerung Duft aus ihnen zu saugen"; p. 191; p. 536). The utopian hovering between spirit and flesh, word and deed, humanity and nature, life and death, eternal and earthly that Bettine believes possible in poetry is countered toward the end of their correspondence by Karoline with a haunting vision of the absolute duality of written word and life: "When I read what I have written some time ago, I think I see myself lying in my coffin, staring at my other self in astonishment" ("[Es] kommt … mir vor wenn ich lese was ich vor einiger Zeit geschreiben habe, als sähe ich mich im Sarg liegen, und meine beiden Ichs starren sich ganz verwundert an"; p. 292; p. 682). And whereas Arnim persistently blurs the boundaries between the masculine and the feminine, Günderode cannot escape the feeling of being a masculine spirit caught in a female body.[56]

Günderode's conception of an absolute opposition between body and spirit, nature and the ideal, life and death, female and male, renders evident both her ultimate distance from Bettine and her affinity with later poets like Baudelaire, Mallarmé, Valéry, and George. Indeed, Bettine's remarkable visual correlative of Günderode's poetry is an exquisite portrait of the legacy of German idealism and classicism in later nineteenth-century European Symbolist and Parnassian poetry, replete with the images and metaphors of vast spaces, pillars, and aesthetic worship central to their poetry:

> In your poems I feel what seems a silent array of pillars across a distant plain; against the far horizon the outlines of mountains swell softly like the waves of the summer-sea, rising and falling … all is lost in silent worship of this sacred symmetry. Passions, poured like libations upon the hearth of the gods by the pure priestesses, gently flame upwards.
>
> (p. 242)

In *deinen* Gedichten weht mich die stille Säulenordnung an, mir deucht eine weite Ebne; an dem fernen Horizont rundum heben sich leise wie Wellen auf dem beruhigten Meer, die Berglinien, … alles ist stille Feier dieses heiligen Ebenmaßes, die Leidenschaften, wie Libationen von der reinen Priesterin den Göttern in die Flammen des Herdes gegossen, und leise lodern sie auf. …

(p. 620)

In this landscape of sublimation and "stille Hieroglyphen," Günderode, the poet, moves as a swan in mysterious dialogue with the reeds on the shore of the lake, inscribing circles around itself, like the poet of Coleridge's "Kubla Khan," as "sacred signs of its isolation from the impure, the unrestrained, the unspiritual" ("heilige Zeichen seiner Absonderung von dem Unreinen, Ungemeßnen, Ungeistigen"; p. 243; p. 621).

This vision fulfills Günderode's desire to see her poetry placed in the canon of great European poetry by demonstrating, in proleptic fashion, precisely where it belongs in the movement from German Romanticism and Classicism to the Symbolism of the later nineteenth century. Here pure poetry consumes personal passion as the poetic dicta of Valéry and Mallarmé demand. Ultimately *Die Günderode* did indeed realize Karoline von Günderode's wish to join a spiritual community of great poets and to enter into dialogue with them. For this lyrical novel, after being translated by Margaret Fuller and celebrated by Ralph Waldo Emerson, played a crucial and hitherto rarely acknowledged role in Emily Dickinson's poetic formation.[57]

At the same time, however, that Bettine recognizes the exquisite beauty of the aesthetic embodied in Günderode's poetry, she senses its origin in pain and longs to transport her friend from this world of death-like ideality into the healing realm of nature. Bettine wants to kidnap her friend and take her into her own world of Romantic nature – a hut deep in the woods surrounded by flowers and cooing doves. In honoring Günderode's poetry, Arnim is also proclaiming her independence from her friend's ethos of violence and her aesthetic of death. As Bettine had asserted early on in their correspondence, "I cannot make poems like you, Günderode, but I can talk with nature, when alone with her" ("Ich kann nicht dichten wie Du Günderode, aber ich kann sprechen mit der Natur, wenn ich allein mit ihr bin"; p. 24; p. 331). In essense, Arnim, in a characteristic gesture of romantic irony, is here redefining poetry as a dialogue with nature. Yet, again paradoxically, this dialogue with nature brings Bettine into correspondence with her beloved friend. In concluding the letter evoking the pure spirituality of Günderode's poetry, Arnim, assuming the reader's knowledge of Günderode's suicide on the banks of the Rhein, creates a scenario for her younger self's dialogue with nature that mirrors the landscape of Günderode's suicide.

Yes, I see you, swan! Holding converse with the whispering sedges by the shore, and the soft wind, you gaze after, as it bears onward your sighs, far, far over the waters, no messenger returning to say if they ever landed. … I know

not, what you are, I am undecided; but where I wander in solitude I am ever
seeking, and where I repose I think of you.

(p. 243)

Ja ich seh Dich Schwan, ruhig Zwiesprache haltend mit den flüsternden
Schilfen am Gestade, and dem lauen Wind Deine ahnungsvolle Seufzer
hingebend, und ihnen nachsehend, wie er hinzieht weit, weit über den
Wassern – und kein Bote kommt züruck, ob er je landete ... ich weiß nicht
was Du bist, es schwankt in mir, aber wo ich einsam gehe in der Natur, da ist
es immer, als suche ich Dich, and wo ich ausruhe, da gedenk ich Deiner.

(pp. 621–2)

Now it is Karoline who, mythic and Lohengrin-like, converses with nature as well
as with Bettine, as Arnim honors her distinctiveness at the same time that she
incorporates her into her own poetic vision.

It is at this moment in the text that Bettine first mentions her solitary visits to
the watchtower and her conversations with the stars, preparing the shift from her
dialogue with Karoline to the three-way conversation of the two young women
and the Jewish peddlar-tutor that concludes the novel. The Apollonian ideals of
Günderode give way to Dionysian openness and diffusion. Earlier in the novel,
when Bettine asserts to Clemens that she cannot write a book because she refuses
to collect her thoughts like dried flowers to be pasted in a book, she defines
Karoline as the proverbial victim of Apollo: "Daphne, pursued by Apollo, is
rooted to the ground in her flight, and transformed into a laurel tree" ("Daphnis
vom Apoll verfolgt, wurzelt fest mit der flüchtigen Sohle und sprießt in Lorbeer
auf"; p. 100; p. 426). Setting her own freedom of movement and expression in
opposition to Günderode's fixity of form, she once again pays tribute to the
poetry of her friend's art and life at the same time that she makes room for the
unconventionality and freedom of her own poetry and destiny.

One could in fact argue that Arnim, in a sense, objectifies her friend in order
to define herself as an artist against the negative example of Günderode. Indeed,
Bettine identifies herself with Theseus, for her the archetypal artist figure braving
the labyrinth of the self, explicitly defining Karoline as her mirror, her muse, her
Ariadne.[58]

You look deeper into my breast, know more of my spiritual fate, than I,
because I need only read in thy soul to find myself ... protected by your
spirit, I have ventured to think and maintain the impossible; nothing was too
rash, and everywhere I felt the thread of your wise understanding leading
me through the labyrinth.

(p. 312)

Du bist tiefer in meiner Brust und weißt mehr von meinem Seelenschicksal
als ich selber, denn ich brauch nur in Deinem Geist zu lesen so find ich
mich selbst. ... [S]o habe ich alles Unmögliche gewagt zu denken und zu

behaupten und nichts war mir zu tollkühn, überall fühlt ich den Faden in Deinem klugen Verstehen, der mich durchs Labyrinth führte.

(p. 709)

If Karoline von Günderode represents, for Arnim, the female poet as Ariadne, as abandoned woman, then Arnim at the same time challenges this stereotype by refusing to abandon her, returning to her in tribute more than 30 years after their separation. Furthermore, Arnim is absolutely explicit in recognizing her debt to her beloved friend, acknowledging that it was through their relationship that she first became conscious of herself.[59] She shows Karoline, early on in their correspondence, bringing order to Bettine's chaotic room during her absence and, in the process, freeing a butterfly that Bettine had put into a box in chrysalis stage. Quite self-consciously, then, Arnim suggests that contact with Karoline von Günderode's sense of order and form was necessary to her development and freedom as a spirit and as an artist.

That *Die Günderode* is meant as a *model* of mutual development and education is made clear by its opening dedication to the current generation of German students, a generation radicalized by the reactionary decade of the 1830s and widespread attacks on academic freedom and freedoms of speech and of the press. When *Die Günderode* appeared, these same students gave Arnim a torchlight parade, an event that heightened her status as a cultural hero for Junges Deutschland writers like Ludwig Börne and Karl Gutzkow and Young Hegelians David Strauß, Edgar and Bruno Bauer. As Christa Wolf emphasizes in her eloquent tribute, "Your Next Life Begins Today: A Letter about Bettine," *Die Günderode* represents a telescoping of the youthful intellectual exchange of Arnim's Romantic past and the intense political awareness and activism of her maturity. For Wolf, it is apparent that Arnim applied the insights she had gained early in the century in her later political struggles, her role in the 1848 Revolution, and her progressive salon, and that "she intended, with the Günderode book, to pass on the legacy of her own youth to her grandchildren's generation" (p. 202). Thus Ephraim's promise to distribute the roses, as exemplary emblems of *Bildung*, among his students means that Bettine herself, Dionysian figure that she is, will be dispersed among the students of the next generation, to whom she, in a striking shift from third to second person narration, directly addresses the concluding lines of the book: "Only wait, . . . and then the best among you may wear my roses in your button-holes" ("Wartet nur, . . . und dann werden die Artigsten unter Euch meine Rosen in der Weste tragen dürfen"; p. 338; p. 742). As Ephraim says goodbye to Bettine, he lays his hand on her head in a gesture of blessing and pronounces these words, now full of deep and bitter irony to the twentieth-century reader; "All existence is developed for the future" ("Alles Werden is für die Zukunft"; p. 338; p. 741). Meditating on his last message, Bettine adds, complicating our notions of chronology and linearity, "Yes, we live upon the Future, it inspires us" ("Ja wir nähren uns von der Zukunft, sie begeistert uns"; p. 338; p. 741), making clear that, in some sense, the future already exists and that for Bettine it means the life and spirit of the coming generations of German students.

Arnim, then, concludes her novel with a historical vision of Karoline von Günderode's place in the European poetic canon as well as an evocation of her own vital, activist legacy embodied in the next generation of artists and intellectuals. Significantly, it is an older man, a father figure, who mediates Bettine's own connection with future political ferment just as the university students to whom she passes on her idealism are exclusively male. Similarly, Arnim's years of intensified political activism leading up to and following the 1848 Revolution give little evidence of direct involvement with the burgeoning German feminist movement.[60] Perhaps her abandonment by Günderode caused her to shy away from close female allegiances.[61] Whatever the reason for her distance from the women's movement of her time, her life and works, as Ulrike Landfester has demonstrated, have exerted a uniquely powerful influence on future German women writers and feminists.[62] This influence cannot be separated from her belief, embodied in such a lively fashion in *Die Günderode*, in the potential of each woman, for courageous and heroic actions, however ordinary or everyday they might seem in the light of masculinist history and values. In her religion of "Unbedeutenheit" (insignificance), then, Arnim moves beyond the cult of genius that underlies *Corinne* and the concept of master spirit that dominates *Valperga* to acknowledge the potential of every individual to influence history. And like Shelley in *The Last Man* and Staël in her non-fiction works, Arnim figures her own cultural legacy, as well as that of her dear friend, as meditative, impersonal, and collective. We will see that George Sand, in *Consuelo*, continues this process of radicalizing and democratizing the concepts of heroism and genius.

4 Rewriting Romanticism

George Sand's *Consuelo* and revolutionary history

George Sand's monumental *Consuelo* and its sequel *La Comtesse de Rudolstadt*, written from 1842 to 1844 and serialized in *La Revue Indépendante*, constitute a kind of compendium of the separate critiques of previous models of Romantic genius and of masculinist history and *Bildung* engaged in by Staël, Shelley, and Arnim. A historical novel set in the decades prior to the French Revolution of 1789, *Consuelo* provides a panoramic view of European culture and politics during the pre-revolutionary era, as it takes its eponymous heroine from her triumphs on the Venetian opera stage through a series of Gothic trials in a Bohemian castle, to a picaresque journey with the composer Joseph Haydn, and into the courts of Maria Theresa and Frederick the Great. The novel concludes with an initiation into a secret society called "Les Invisibles" from which Consuelo emerges to become a wandering musician who devotes herself to an art of the people, an art explicitly in the service of "Liberté, Egalité, and Fraternité."

As a female *Bildungsroman* as well as a feminist historical novel, *Consuelo* provides a portrait of the heroine's development into an exemplary artist who is also potentially an agent of revolutionary change. In the 1,600 pages that comprise *Consuelo* and its sequel, George Sand rewrites pre-revolutionary European history as well as the Romantic response to the French Revolution in order to suggest an alternative political, spiritual, and aesthetic vision that, she believed, might actually realize the emancipatory and egalitarian ideals of that revolutionary moment. Indeed, more than simply a historical novel whose pages bring to life a fascinating array of eighteenth-century cultural and political figures, from Voltaire and Frederick the Great to Cagliostro and Saint Germain, *Consuelo* takes history itself as its subject as it seeks to illuminate the ideal role of the artist as an agent of historical process and progress. Just as Sand brings its hero Albert Rudolstadt back to life in *La Comtesse de Rudolstadt* after he is dead and buried at the end of *Consuelo*, so she resuscitates key eighteenth-century historical figures in an effort to reveal their political and cultural meaning for a collective, ongoing effort to transform Europe into a socialist utopia.

Sand thus clearly shares the profoundly historical consciousness already strikingly in evidence in Staël, Shelley, and Arnim in their presentations of the intergenerational significance of the individual woman artist. She fills in with rich detail that section of "the vast tableau" of human destinies that was Europe in the 1750s and 1760s and delineates the role of the female artist – herself and her heroine – in creating that tableau. Furthermore, the program of political action to which her heroine, in the novel's conclusion, dedicates herself, instantiates the idealist vision with which Shelley subtends *Valperga* and prefaces *The Last Man* and Arnim concludes *Die Günderode*. The promise of a revolutionary female creativity suggested but provisionally defeated in *Corinne* is fulfilled in Sand's heroine Consuelo.

From the perspective of the 1840s, then, George Sand looks back on the last century of European political and cultural history and forward to a utopian future. Thus Sand's portrait of Consuelo as ideal artist is set against the backdrop of her critique of previous models of Romantic genius, both male and female. In this chapter, I analyze Sand's critique of three of these models of the Romantic artist, now more than familiar to us from Staël, Shelley, and Arnim, models that had become reified and superannuated by the time that Sand wrote: the poetess or abandoned woman, the self-absorbed and self-destructive melancholiac, and the Byronic, Napoleonic, or Promethean titan. In place of these rigidly gendered and hierarchical models of the Romantic artist, Sand concludes her novel with a vision of the artist – and of the historical and cultural development of that artist – that incorporates socialist and proto-feminist elements of the early nineteenth-century utopian movements of Saint-Simon, Fourier, and Leroux, a vision that applies equally to Consuelo, daughter of an itinerant street musician, and to her aristocratic husband, Albert, the former Count Rudolstadt. The cornerstone of Sand's feminism in *Consuelo* is her unrelenting critique of bourgeois marriage as an institution. Sand does indeed envisage a fulfilling heterosexual union at the end of this novel, but Albert must literally die and be resurrected before it can take place, just as his original Catholic and civil marriage with Consuelo must be dissolved by divorce before the sacred ceremony performed by Les Invisibles can occur. Finally, in the novel's epilogue, Consuelo, accompanied by Albert and their children, returns to her wandering life as an anonymous gypsy artist, an artist ministering to the people, and helping them to create the profound social change to come. She embodies the folk ballad "The Good Goddess of Poverty," that her son sings to her accompaniment in the novel's epilogue. Paradoxically, then, for Consuelo, transcendence, both aesthetic and spiritual, means devotion of the self to an egalitarian ideal.

Liberty: the necessary condition of the true artist

Like all nineteenth-century European women writers of both poetry and fiction, George Sand, in her attempt to reconceptualize the female artist, had to contend with Staël's Corinne – the suicidal, abandoned woman – as reigning model of female genius. Indeed, the legacy of Corinne weighed perhaps more heavily on Sand, as French woman writer and celebrated cultural presence in her own right, than on any other nineteenth-century writer. As Madelyn Gutwirth has shown, Sand "could never altogether escape the vise of this comparison with her too illustrious predecessor."[1] It is hardly surprising, then, that like her fellow novelists, Shelley and Arnim, Sand rejected this cultural stereotype – the myth of Corinne, Ariadne, or Sappho – quite vehemently and pointedly.

That both Corinne and Consuelo are created as explicitly female artists is evident from their lack of patronymic. Corinne rejects her father's name and calls herself by the name of Pindar's legendary mentor, while Consuelo, the daughter of a wandering musician, never knew a father. Her origin seems explicitly parthenogenetic, like that of Shelley's Beatrice. Responding to Staël, Sand makes the question of abandonment crucial to Consuelo's love relationships – both with her fellow opera singer Anzoleto and with Count Albert Rudolstadt. Thus, Sand prepares us to view Consuelo through the lens of Corinne's fate when her most significant early triumph in the opening Venetian episodes of the novel comes in the Jomelli opera *Didone abbandonata*:

> Never had she felt in so great a degree the necessity of breathing forth her sadness; she was sublime in pathos, in simplicity, in grandeur, and her features and expression were even more beautiful than they had been at church. Her complexion was flushed with a feverish glow; her eyes shot forth lurid lightnings; she was no longer a saint, she was even more – she was a woman consumed by love.[2]

> [J]amais elle n'avait mieux senti le besoin d'exhaler sa tristesse; elle fut sublime de pathétique, de simplicité, de grandeur, et belle de visage plus encore qu'elle ne l'avait été à l'église. Son teint s'était animé d'un peu de fièvre, ses yeux lançaient de sombres éclairs; ce n'était plus une sainte, c'était mieux encore, c'était une femme dévorée d'amour.[3]

Yet ultimately Consuelo is betrayed and abandoned by her fiancé Anzoleto, not because he has a "higher" calling than her love, nor because she is somehow unworthy of him, as Corinne fears in her relationship with the judgmental Oswald, but because he is *her* moral and artistic inferior. Sand makes it absolutely clear that it is professional jealousy and weakness of character that impel him into a clandestine love affair with Consuelo's vain and superficial rival Corilla. (The resonance of her name with Staël's heroine, as Gutwirth has pointed out, is certainly *not* accidental.)[4] As Consuelo's mentor and substitute father, the composer Niccola Porpora explains to her when she is unable to accept the fact that "a lover can be displeased with the success of his beloved." "You will learn that a man can be jealous of the superiority of a woman, when this man is an ambitious artist; and that a lover can loathe the success of his beloved when the theater is the arena of their efforts" ("Un amant peut-il haïr le succès de son amante? Tu sauras qu'un homme peut être jaloux des avantages d'une femme, quand cet homme est un artiste vaniteux; et qu'un amant peut haïr les succès de son amante, quand le théâtre est le milieu où ils vivent"; *Romance*, p. 110; trans. modified; *Consuelo* vol. I, p. 145). Anzoleto, in fact, steps back to encourage a love affair between the innocent Consuelo and the corrupt theater owner Count Zustiniani, in the hopes that it will benefit his career. Understanding this at the same time that she learns of his affair with Corilla, Consuelo cries out to him, "[a]nd this is the time you have taken to abandon me?" ("et c'est le moment que tu as choisi pour m'abandonner?"; *Romance*, p. 117; *Consuelo* vol. I, p. 151). Sand thus compels the reader to compare her Consuelo with the long line of Ariadnes, Sapphos, and Corinnes before her and to expect a tragic outcome.

Nevertheless, though Consuelo suffers profoundly in her disillusionment with her first love, she responds to her suffering not by indulging in a self-destructive performance of the role of the abandoned woman, as does Corinne. Instead, she finds the strength to pursue a free and independent life of devotion to art so that, when she meets up with Anzoleto again at the conclusion of the novel, she feels nothing but consummate detachment and a mild friendship for him, recognizing in him only a mediocre musician who has grown fat and vain. Corilla, in the meantime, pregnant and forsaken by Anzoleto, leaves the theater only long enough to deliver and abandon her baby, moving on to other lovers and leaving the reader in no doubt about the theatricality of her passions.

In the heart of the novel, the romance between the Spanish Consuelo, a metaphorical Zingarella or gypsy, and the Bohemian Albert, Sand replicates the contrast between Staël's freedom-loving half-Italian Corinne and the melancholiac northern European Oswald, a contrast that perpetuates the typology established in Schiller's *Naïve and Sentimental Poetry* and Staël's *On Literature*. As Juliet Sychrava has shown in *Schiller to Derrida: Idealism in Aesthetics*, it is the general tendency of this line of thought to privilege the northern/sentimental over the southern/ naïve. In both *Corinne* and *Consuelo* the north/south dichotomy corresponds to a gender dichotomy, as it does in Schiller, who associates the naïve with materiality/sensuality and with children, animals, and women. Sand, like Staël and Arnim before her, struggles with this opposition and recognizes its fatality for the woman artist. Ultimately Sand preserves her heroine from the trap of this binary by keeping her sexually pure throughout a good portion of her narrative before devoting *La Comtesse* to challenging/questioning the spirit/body split implicit in this idealist line of thought.[5] Furthermore, whereas Oswald, Lord Nelvil ultimately leaves Corinne for her virginal and domestic half-sister, judging Corinne's sexual experience, poetic gifts, and artistic renown unacceptable in a wife, the unworldly Albert – something of a feminist's dream – is remarkably free of such patriarchal prejudices, loving Consuelo unconditionally, as the narrator comments:[6]

> He would have accepted everything, permitted everything, . . . so that she should be happy and free – in retirement, in the world, or in the theater – at her pleasure. His complete absence of prejudice or selfishness produced a total want of foresight, even regarding the most simple matters. It never occurred to him that Consuelo should think of submitting to sacrifices which he did not wish to impose.
>
> (*Romance*, p. 401)

Il êut tout accepté, tout permis, tout exigé même pour qu'elle fût heureuse et libre dans la retraite, dans le monde ou au théâtre, à son choix. Son absence de préjugés et d'égoïsme allait jusqu'à l'imprévoyance des cas les plus simples. Il ne lui vint donc pas à l'esprit que Consuelo pût songer à s'imposer des sacrifices pour lui qui n'en voulait aucun.

(*Consuelo* vol. II, p. 77)

Unlike Oswald, Albert is open to learning from Consuelo, indeed being transformed by her so that, in the end, his union with her effaces and transcends the south/north, naïve/sentimental, material/spiritual dichotomy. Albert, in fact, recognizes her profession as "sacred," as "the loftiest a woman can embrace" ("la plus sublime qu'une femme puisse embrasser") since "in the dawn of religion, the theater and the temple were one and the same sanctuary" ("A l'aurore des religions ... le théâtre et le temple sont un même sanctuaire"; *Romance*, p. 335; *Consuelo* vol. I, p. 384). It is the corruption of the theater world, its intrigues and jealousies, its failure to live up to this spiritual ideal, that ultimately tempts Consuelo to leave it, not her fear of a soiled reputation or of moral censure.

More practical than Albert, Consuelo realizes that a career as prima donna would not be compatible with a new social identity as Countess Rudolstadt. She thus does recognize a conflict in herself between artistic career and personal love, effecting a separation from Albert in order to pursue her art and to give herself time to choose between devotion to him and devotion to her music. She defines this conflict in terms of her desire for freedom, so necessary to the artist, to her confidant Joseph Haydn:

Heaven has gifted me with talents, a soul for art, a love of liberty, and of a proud and lofty independence; but, at the same time, ... the same celestial power has implanted in my breast a tender and sensitive heart, which beats only with affectionate emotion. Thus divided between two opposing impulses, my existence is annihilated, and my prospects destroyed.

(*Romance*, p. 599)

Le ciel m'a donné des facultés et une âme pour l'art, des besoins de liberté, l'amour d'une fière et chaste indépendance; mais en même temps, ... cette volonté céleste m'a mis dans la poitrine un cœur tendre et sensible qui ne bat que pour les autres, qui ne vit que d'affection et de dévouement. Ainsi partagée entre deux forces contraires, ma vie s'use, et mon but est toujours manqué.

(*Consuelo* vol. II, p. 314)

Here Sand displaces the conflict between domesticity and public performance, so prominent in *Corinne*, and the cornerstone of the ideology of separate spheres, onto the psyche of her heroine and significantly transforms it into a conflict between love and independence, thus, in a sense, refusing to legitimate the public/private, professional/domestic conflict so central to *Corinne*. Before Consuelo can give herself to love, she must first experience the freedom that, as Sand so eloquently puts it, is essential to artistic development: "[Consuelo] felt the necessity of belonging to herself – that sovereign and legitimate want, the necessary condition of progress and development of the true artist" ("Elle éprouvait le besoin de s'appartenir à elle-même, ce besoin souverain et légitime, veritable condition du progrès et du développement chez l'artiste supérieur"; *Romance*, p. 340; *Consuelo* vol. I p. 389). Though this might seem to place responsibility on the individual for socially constructed tensions, this move in fact bypasses the public/private split so detrimental to the nineteenth-century woman artist and opens the door for Consuelo to practice her art once she finds a way to unite self-determination and freedom with her love for Albert, as she does in the novel's conclusion. Key to the resolution of these conflicts at the end of the novel is, as David Powell asserts, that "Consuelo's devotion [is] to music as an art form rather than a profession."[7] Prior to this utopian moment that dispenses with corrupt theatrical institutions, Consuelo refuses to renounce her art until she has fully experienced what she would be giving up for marriage with Albert. This decision, then, places Albert, not Consuelo, in the position of the abandoned lover who wastes away at the conclusion of *Consuelo* and experiences a symbolic death through an attack of catalepsy brought on by her absence. Meditating on Albert's suffering, Consuelo calls out, "To wait and die! is this then the fate of those who love with passion? And is it the destiny of those who pursue the vain chimera, glory, to make others wait and die?" ("Attendre et mourir! ... est-ce donc là le sort de ceux qui aiment passionnément? Faire attendre et faire mourir, est-ce donc là la destinée de ceux qui poursuivent la chimère de la gloire?"; *Romance*, p. 639; *Consuelo* vol. II, p. 358). This crucial role-reversal allows Sand to hold the gendered nature of the Corinne–Sappho–Ariadne myth up to intense scrutiny.

Albert's identity as abandoned woman, of course, also calls attention to the feminization of the artist prevalent in the late eighteenth and early nineteenth centuries and familiar in Romantic artist figures from Goethe's Werther and Percy Shelley's maniac in *Julian and Maddalo*, to the narrators of Nerval's poetry and fiction. Nearly ten years earlier, in her *Lettres d'un voyageur* (1834–6), written in the narrative persona of an ambiguously male Romantic artist, Sand is quite cognizant of this feminization, as her artist ironically exclaims, figuring revolutionary activity as a kind of Westernized suttee:

> I am a poet, that is to say, a very woman. When there is a revolution your aim will be the freedom of the human race; I shall have no other than to let myself be killed so as to have done with myself and to have been, for the first and only time in my life, of some use, were it only by heightening a barricade by the addition of one more corpse.[8]

Consuelo was clearly written to delineate a more constructive revolutionary role for the Romantic artist, male or female.

The Romantic hero: "gloomy remembrance" and "impious pride"

Indeed, the character of Albert, Count Rudolstadt represents a kind of compendium of Romantic models of male genius – both the melancholy type and the Byronic-Promethean-Satanic type – that he must experience and transcend on his path to union with Consuelo and to their mutual practice of a socially significant and revolutionary art. When Consuelo first encounters Albert at his castle Riesenberg after her flight to Bohemia from Venice, he is the quintessential melancholiac, despairing, tortured by inexplicable grief and excessive sensibility, perpetually threatened by madness. Sand herself, as Isabelle Hoog Naginski demonstrates, in her useful and imaginative delineation of Sand's novelistic output according to four distinct moments, had fully explored Romantic melancholy in her own earlier works before turning to the utopian visions of the third great moment in her artistic development. Following the first two periods, focusing on the *mal du siècle* in the feminine and then on despair and suicide, comes the "antithetical *période blanche*, dominated by the vast *Consuelo* and its sequel *La Comtesse de Rudolstadt*."[9] Indeed, the vituperative critical response occasioned by the earlier *Lélia* was due in large part to Sand's having appropriated the prestige of the *mal du siècle* for herself and her heroine, such that critics felt compelled to attribute Lélia's *ennui* to sexual dysfunction in her author. And Françoise Massardier-Kenney is absolutely correct, I believe, in asserting that, even today, the privileging of male melancholia in the French literary canon plays a significant role in the marginalization of Sand as serious author.[10] Already in *Lettres d'un voyageur*, however, Sand in fact found it difficult to take Romantic melancholy seriously, and her sarcastic allusions to Hamlet provide a refreshing contrast to Staël's reverence for this hallowed emblem of wounded patriarchy:

> There are days when it isn't possible to live with one's kind, when everything inclines one to spleen, everything turns one's thoughts to suicide; and there is nothing sadder in the world than a poor devil procrastinating with his last hour, parleying with it for weeks and years like the man in Shakespeare with his revenge. People make fun of him.
>
> My advice to anyone who might find himself either chronically or accidentally in such a state is to eat frugally so as to avoid the irritation of the brain caused by a difficult digestion.

(p. 74)

If, in *Lettres d'un voyageur*, Sand deflates with grotesque humor the exaggerated sense of self-importance that she sees afflicting the Romantic artist, in *Consuelo* the originality and uniqueness of Sand's portrait of Romantic melancholy consists in her explanation of this affective state through the metaphor of reincarnation. Endowed with a second sight that overwhelms him with memories of his past lives, Albert is tormented by guilt over actions performed in his former existence as fifteenth-century Slavic insurrectionary and Protestant heretic Jean Ziska

(1376–1424). A follower of John Huss, Ziska is described by Sand as a formidable general whose name falls "like a thunderbolt" on the ears of Catholics, for he is said to have murdered twenty Augustinian monks and hung their bodies from an oak tree over a cistern that held the remains of ten previously slaughtered Hussite followers. Incapacitated by guilt, Albert regularly escapes to a secret cavern under this cistern for long periods of solitude and penitential meditation. Described by Albert as an opponent of despotic imperial and religious power, Ziska appeals to nineteenth-century nationalist movements in his embodiment of Slavic resistance to the German oppression represented by his arch-enemy King Sigismund. Ziska also stands as a fifteenth-century analogue to nineteenth-century leaders of democratic and socialist movements, in his Taborite belief that both communion sacraments should be available to all members of the Church regardless of social status and in his advocacy of the breaking up of Church properties so that their land holdings could be distributed among the Bohemian peasants. In an effort to link it to French Revolutionary aims, Sand also terms the Hussite movement explicitly republican in opposition to the monarchical and imperial aims of King Sigismund.

In a remarkably vivid scene, Albert's violin playing of ancient peasant hymns in his subterranean refuge brings forth before the mesmerized eyes of Consuelo "the spectral form of the heroes of old Bohemia" ("les spectres des vieux héros de la Bohême") battling religious persecution and political tyranny (*Romance*, p. 357; *Consuelo* vol. II, p. 27). Consuelo has descended into the realm of the collective historical and political unconscious inhabited by "a new race of beings," the "angels of death" ("de nouveaux êtres ... les anges de la mort"), agents of divine wrath (*Romance*, p. 357; *Consuelo* vol. II, p. 27). Perceiving Albert as Satan, the rebellious angel, "the beautiful one, the sorrowful, the immortal, proudest among the proud" ("le plus beau des immortels après Dieu, le plus triste après Jésus, le plus fier parmi les plus fiers"; *Romance*, p. 358, trans. modified; *Consuelo* vol. II, p. 28), Consuelo witnesses him present "the chalice of forgiveness, of restoration, and of sacred equality" ("le calice du pardon, de la réhabilitation, et de la sainte égalité") to these men of crime, and pledges herself, in a trance, to God *and* to this Angel of Grief forever (*Romance*, p. 358; *Consuelo* vol. II, p. 28). A demonic and Byronic figure akin to Manfred in his guilt and the Giaour in his violence, Albert's avatar Ziska is "[t]he exalted yet abhorred ... chief of the Taborites, a sect which during the war of the Hussites surpassed all other religionists in their energy, their bravery, and their cruelty" ("le nom sublime et abhorré du chef des Taborites, sectaires que renchérirent durant la guerre des Hussites sur l'énergie, la bravoure, et les cruautés des autres"; *Romance*, p. 166; *Consuelo* vol. I, p. 207). Ziska's relentless violence also clearly recalls the bloodbath of the Reign of Terror as it ultimately destroyed the French Revolution and called forth Napoleonic tyranny. The metaphor of past lives, then, for Sand encodes a historical and socio-political analysis of Romantic melancholy.

In her metaphor of soul memory, Sand thus clearly represents the inextricability of Romantic melancholy and Romantic titanism, two states of mind that mire the artist in a vicious cycle of rebellion and guilt and render him culturally and politically ineffectual. As with her ironic rendering of *ennui*, Sand had also already subjected Byronic titanism to a merciless critique in *Lettres d'un voyageur*, akin to those of Shelley and Arnim, though much more personal and vitriolic. Sand clearly has no patience for the aristocratic stance she recognized as essential to the Byronic hero:

> In those days Lord Byron was a shining example of what human presumptuousness can achieve by clothing paltry vanities in purple and setting them in gold like diamonds; that cripple walked on stilts above the heads of those who had two legs of equal length; he was successful because his stilts were sturdy and splendid and he knew how to use them.
>
> (p. 148)

If Chateaubriand, after reading *Lélia*, predicted that Sand would become the Byron of France, Sand herself clearly had other ideas about her artistic destiny. Similarly, Consuelo rejects Byronic self-aggrandizement and deification of self by challenging Albert's desire "to penetrate the secrets of destiny" ("pénétrer les secrets de la destinée") and thus claim a place equal to God by embracing in his view the present and the past (*Romance*, p. 275; *Consuelo* vol. I, p. 321). She demands of him instead "entire abandonment of [his] reflective powers" ("l'abandon entier de votre réflexion") and asks, "Can you descend into your heart, and there concentrate all your existence?" ("Pouvez-vous descendre dans votre cœur, et y concentrer toute votre existence?"; *Romance*, p. 277; *Consuelo* vol. I, p. 323).

Ultimately Consuelo's pledge to Albert, in whom she sees both the Rebellious Angel and Dürer's Angel of Grief, constitutes a vow to free him from the melancholy self-absorption and satanic pride that torment him, just as, in a Herculean effort, she descends into his abysmal subterranean refuge and returns him to life and light. As Naginski has suggested, Consuelo enacts here the mythic descent into hell of Orpheus, with the gender roles significantly reversed so that Albert plays the role of Eurydice.[11] Sand is clearly suggesting here the need for those powers of the heart traditionally labeled feminine to rescue the masculinist intellect, even as she creates a striking example of female heroism and artistic agency, for Consuelo risks death by drowning and by interment in this Orphic journey. The cavern into which Consuelo descends is analogous to the cave of Euthanasia's parable – a realm beyond morality that is the source of both Albert's madness and his imaginative and artistic genius. Seeking to convince herself that this refuge is "the cell of a saint and not the dungeon of a madman" ("la cellule d'un saint, et non le cachot d'un fou"), she does indeed recognize, from Albert's rendering of ancient Slavic hymns on his Stradivarius, that he possesses "the revelation of the true, the grand music" ("la révélation de la vraie, de la grande musique"; *Romance*, p. 272; *Consuelo* vol. I, pp. 317–18). Yet whereas Shelley enshrines a meditative and solitary female deity in this inner self, Sand's inner sanctum resonates with the echoes of repressed collective and historical voices. It is also a space of dialogue and interchange between male and female, with Consuelo ultimately enacting a role akin to that of Asia in Percy Shelley's *Prometheus Unbound*. This dialogue accords well with the discourse of androgyny that recent feminist critics have found to be central to Sand's poetics.[12]

Heretical history

Indeed, once Consuelo and Albert have met, the reader senses that the entire plot of the novel will, of course, hinge on the question of the possibility/impossibility of their union. Yet it is crucial to understand that what the interchange with Albert provides for Consuelo is not a set of reified or essentialized qualities – spirit, mind, will, imagination, etc. – that she, *as Woman* and woman artist, lacks. The fluidity and historicity of Sand's model of selfhood in *Consuelo* avoids any such simplistic, regressive, and heterosexist vision of androgyny. Rather, as a kind of idealized embodiment of historical consciousness, and of the necessarily changing historical role of the artist, what Albert provides for Consuelo is a clearly articulated historical, social, and spiritual context and meaning for her already brilliant and perfected art. As critics have frequently noted, Albert is the character who clearly and repeatedly gives voice to the humanitarian and socialist philosophy of Pierre Leroux, author of *De l'Humanité* (1840) and *De l'Egalité* (1838) that underlies the novel.[13] Indeed, George Sand's words in an 1843 letter to the proletarian poet Charles Poncy, to whom she passes on her version of Leroux's vision of progress through reincarnation, might have been those of Albert to Consuelo: "Humanity is subjected to a long and painful education. Time only appears long to us. In the eyes of God, it does not exist at all. Our centuries do not count in eternity, ... because we die in order to be reborn and to progress."[14]

As erudite and profoundly well-educated aristocrat, Albert possesses knowledge necessarily out of reach to Consuelo, daughter of a wandering and illiterate gypsy whose only formal education has been the music lessons given her by the composer Niccola Porpora. Even more important is Albert's symbolic role as emblem of the collective historical unconscious, as his protest to his Catholic chaplain against official Church histories reveals:

> You have in vain burned the archives of the family, and the records of history, ... in vain have you brought up children in ignorance of the past; in vain imposed silence on the simple by sophistry, on the weak by threats: neither the dread of despotic power, however great, nor even that of hell itself, can stifle the thousand voices of the past which awaken on every side. No, no! they speak too loudly, these terrible voices, for that of a priest to hush them! They speak to our souls in sleep, in the whisperings of spirits from the dead.
> (*Romance*, p. 166)

> Car on a beau brûler les archives des familles et les documents de l'histoire, ... on a beau élever les enfants dans l'ignorance de la vie antérieure; on a beau imposer silence aux simples par le sophisme, et aux faibles par la menace: ni la crainte du despotisme, ni celle de l'enfer, ne peuvent étouffer

les mille voix du passé qui s'élèvent de toutes parts. Non, non, elles parlent trop haut, ces voix terribles, pour que celle d'un prêtre leur impose silence! Elles parlent à nos âmes dans le sommeil, par la bouche des spectres.

(*Consuelo* vol. I, p. 206)

Furthermore, it is initiation into the secret heretical and conspiratorial society, Les Invisibles, that ultimately enables Consuelo to understand and to enact the philosophy of history and art that does justice to her identity as child of the people. As Albert Sonnenfeld writes, Albert's violin playing teaches Consuelo "the lesson of History, that music is not individual passion expressed but passion (in the religious sense) of the peoples. ... [H]e embodies her rejection of the individual psyche, of the individual unconscious with its threatening passions, and her espousal of the collective unconscious of the race, the folk-soul, as Herder called it."[15] Consuelo's relation to Albert, as aristocratic male, facilitates her contact with this fictional society that, like the historical Freemasons, for the most part excluded women and members of the lower orders.[16]

That George Sand intended *Consuelo/La Comtesse de Rudolstadt* as a meditation on women's relation to political and religious history is made absolutely clear in her companion piece to these volumes, *Jean Ziska: Épisode de la guerre des Hussites*, written in between the composition of these two sequential novels. A vital document in the development of nineteenth-century feminist historiography, *Jean Ziska* delineates with great eloquence and clarity the idealist vision of history that underlies *Consuelo*. It resonates powerfully with Shelley's representation of the socio-political significance of witchcraft and heresy in *Valperga* and with the opening dialogue on history – "Die Manen" – of Arnim's *Die Günderode*. Directly addressing her female readers, whom she calls variously "mes patientes lectrices," "mes chères lectrices," or simply "Mesdames," Sand draws explicit parallels between women's history and the history of religious heresy.[17] Neither of these histories has been written, she asserts, because both women and heretics pose too great a threat to intellectual and religious hegemony: "Imagine, Madame, that one half of the intellectual and moral history of humanity was made to disappear by the other half of the human race because it troubled and threatened them" (p. 18). The history of heretical thought and movements has vanished, she suggests, into the abyss created by the conflict between the two mirroring ideologies of "the skeptical hypocrisy of the church" and "the hypocritical skepticism of the university" (p. 17). Moving implicitly beyond the realm of religious history, Sand in fact seems to present a radical challenge to the veracity and objectivity of all prior historiography: "History does not exist, I swear to you; let the pedants think what they like!" (p. 16). Similarly, in an 1843 letter to Leroux, like Bettine in *Die Günderode*, she laments her own sorry education at the hands of "an old pedant," and asserts that history has yet to be made and that a great work could be written "on the *occult* history of humanity."[18] It is precisely this occult history of humanity that Albert incarnates.

In the place of an illusory objectivity and reliance on erudition, Sand emphasizes the importance of acknowledging the role of feeling in the study of history as well as advocating reliance on the ideal, not the factual, in the process of history writing: Because "[n]othing is more obscure and complicated than the certitude of certain past facts," she advocates instead a search for "the ideal fact" (p. 15). And it is women's exclusion from positions of "real" economic, political, and religious power that determines and necessitates their affinities for the heretical and for the great "apostles of the ideal" like John the Baptist and St. Francis of Assisi.

> That is why, poor women, ... the history of heresy must interest you and touch you in particular; because you are all daughters of heresy, you are all heretics; all of you protest in your heart; all of you protest in vain. ... You are all *poor* in the manner of the eternal disciples of evangelical poverty; because, according to the laws of marriage and the family, you possess nothing; and it is to the absence of power and action on behalf of temporal interests that you owe this idealist tendency, this power of sentiment, these impulses of abnegation that make of your souls the last sanctuary of truth.
>
> (p. 19)

Like Staël, Shelley, and Arnim before her, Sand provides a political picture of the genesis of female spirituality and of the revolutionary cultural potential of women's idealism as born of their exclusion from existing power structures.

The oxymoronic concept of "le fait idéal" (the ideal fact) upon which she seeks to base future histories and to create what Naomi Schor has termed a feminist idealism is, for Sand, the truth of the fundamentally good constitution of a divinely created humanity that acts, through Providence and despite all appearances, in the name of truth and justice. The "ideal fact," then, functions for Sand much as the concept of "historical sign" or *Geschichtszeichen* functions for Kant in *The Conflict of the Faculties* or the intellectual idea for Staël in her discourse on the passions, as proof of the innate moral disposition of the human race, the cause of its own advance toward the better. In his discussion of the French Revolution, Kant replaces the word *Schwärmerei*, used in his earlier writings to connote fanaticism, with the word *Enthusiasm*, unusual in the German. As in the novelists discussed here, enthusiasm for Kant becomes associated with divinely instilled human morality. Ultimately, Sand inscribes woman's struggle against patriarchy into a narrative of great clarity, a system of binaries that draws sharp political lines and renders evident the need for concerted action: woman/man, poor/rich, candid/double dealing, oppressed/oppressor, worker/exploiter, free thinker/priest. For Sand, the Hussite rebellion presages the French Revolution and its republican and egalitarian aims, just as that Revolution lives on in the efforts of the followers of Saint-Simon and Fourier and the English Chartists. And it is nineteenth-century socialism that should unite women, workers, students, and intellectuals by fulfilling that spiritual and socio-political function once served by religious heresy. As Sand passionately and inimitably asserts: "The heresy of the past, the communism of today is the cry of starving entrails and ravaged heart that calls out for true knowledge, for the voice of the spirit, for the religious, philosophical and social solution to the monstrous problem suspended over our head for centuries" (p. 25). This monstrous sword of Damocles is of course political and material inequality. In *Jean Žiska*, then, Sand articulates a nineteenth-century idealist version of that "account of the essential mystery of the cultural past," that "single great collective story," that "uninterrupted narrative," that "single vast unfinished plot" that Fredric Jameson in *The Political Unconscious* sees it as the task of the Marxist critic to uncover and articulate.[19]

Les Invisibles: "ardent truth," "implacable reason" and "sublime enthusiasm"

In *Consuelo/LaComtesse de Rudolstadt* it is the secret conspiratorial society of Les Invisibles that keeps alive this story, this "plot" in the eighteenth century, passing on to Consuelo their vision of the political and spiritual function of the artist. Just as Sand asserts the historical necessity of previous titanic and melancholic avatars of the Romantic artist, so she also leaves no doubt that these models of the artist have, in the mid-nineteenth century, long outlived their historical purpose and prepared the way for the female votary of the ideal, Consuelo. As exemplary nineteenth-century artist projected back into the past in an effort to rewrite history, Consuelo is first and foremost a laborer, a worker. Sand makes it clear from the outset that it is hard work and discipline that distinguish Consuelo from the other gifted musicians, like Anzoleto, who surround her. The first time we see her, she is bent over a music lesson, repeating her part in a low voice so as not to disturb anyone. Later, the narrator describes Consuelo's genius as the genius of an indefatigable artistic and spiritual worker:

> Consuelo enjoyed one of those rare and happy temperaments for which labor is an enjoyment, ... a necessary condition, and to which inaction would be an effort, a waste, in short a disease – if inaction indeed to such natures were possible. But they know nothing of the kind; in apparent idleness they still labor, but it is not so much reverie as meditation.
>
> (*Romance*, p. 37)

> Consuelo avait une de ces rares et bienheureuses organisations pour lesquelles le travail est une jouissance ..., un état normal nécessaire, et pour qui l'inaction serait une fatigue, un dépérissement, un état maladif, si l'inaction était possible à de telles natures. Mais elles ne la connaissent pas; dans une oisiveté apparente, elles travaillent encore; leur rêverie n'est point vague, c'est une méditation.
>
> (*Consuelo* vol. I, p. 53)

It is the alienation of this life-sustaining creative labor at the Venetian opera house and in the courts of Maria Theresa or Frederick the Great that renders her so dissatisfied with her career as prima donna and so willing to take up her life at the end of the novel as itinerant musician.

Furthermore, in contrast to her fellow artists who are obsessed with fame and glory, Consuelo's focus is entirely on the art itself: "She was studious and persevering – living in an atmosphere of music as a bird in the air or a fish in the wave ... impelled to combat the obstacles and penetrate the mysteries of art, by an instinct invisible as that which causes the germ to penetrate the soil and seek the air" ("Studieuse et persévérante, vivant dans la musique comme l'oiseau dans l'air et le poisson dans l'eaumais poussée fatalement à combattre les obstacles et à pénétrer les mystères de l'art, par cet invincible instinct qui fait que le germe des plantes cherche à percer le sein de la terre et à se lancer vers le jour"; *Romance*, p. 37; *Consuelo* vol. I, p. 53). This focus allows her to create, in a sense, after the fashion of the true Kantian artist, not in imitation of nature, but as if she were nature itself. And like Corinne under the sway of enthusiasm, Consuelo practices an art that transcends individual emotion in its sublimity: "the ether of heaven seemed to bedew her lofty forehead. ... Her tranquil countenance expressed none of those petty passions which seek, and as it were exact, applause. There was something about her, solemn, mysterious, and elevated. ..." ("Son large front semblait nager dans un fluide céleste. ... Son regard calme n'exprimait aucune de ces petites passions qui cherchent et convoitent les succès ordinaires. Il y avait en elle quelque chose de grave, de mystérieux et de profond"; *Romance*, p. 51, *Consuelo* vol. I, p. 73). It is her utter lack of concern for audience response, her lack of professional vanity, that makes possible this elevation.

This refusal to mold her art to the desires and tastes of an individual audience, however, in no way implies a lack of concern for the social purpose of art. Consuelo's identity as "child of the people" and the egalitarianism that seems to come so naturally to her enable her to conceptualize and to enact an aesthetic transcendence that is a kind of Kantian universal subjectivity that would be limited and deformed by concern for the responses of an individual audience. Her differences with her mentor Porpora, who cannot imagine opera or theater outside of the rivalries and corruptions necessitated by aristocratic patronage, lead her to elucidate a vision of art perfectly in accord with the social mission of Les Invisibles. For Porpora, aesthetic transcendence can only be imagined in metaphors of monarchical power: "God made you a queen," ("Dieu t'a faite reine") he exclaims to Consuelo, "he has placed upon your brow a diadem of beauty, intelligence, and power! Carry you into the midst of a free, intelligent, and sensible people (supposing that such exist) and you would be at once a queen, because you have only to show yourself and sing, in order to prove that you are queen by divine right" ("il t'a mis au front un diadème de beauté, d'intelligence et de force. Que l'on te mène au milieu d'une nation libre, intelligente et sensible (je suppose qu'il en existe de telles!), et te voilà reine, parce que tu n'as qu'à te montrer et à chanter pour prouver que tu es reine de droit divin"; *Romance*, p. 613; *Consuelo* vol. II, p. 329). Such a conception of the aristocracy of genius leads only to bitterness and disillusionment, to farcical performances before the idiotic nobility and the vulgar rich, as Porpora himself admits, given the ignorance and egotism of most patrons of the arts. Like one of E.T.A. Hoffmann's bourgeois musicians who rule only in their own kingdom of dreams,[20] object of their author's fondest satire, Porpora's conception of aesthetic transcendence is predicated upon both self-irony and contempt for his audience: "Oh! it is only when I am at the theater that I see clearly our true relations to society. The spirit of music unseals my eyes, and I see behind the footlights a true court, real heroes, lofty inspirations; while the miserable idiots who flaunt in the boxes upon velvet couches are the real actors" ("Oh! Quand je suis au théâtre je vois clair, moi! L'esprit de la musique me dessille les yeux, et je vois derrière la rampe de véritables héros, des inspirations de bon aloi; tandis que ce sont de véritables histrions et de misérables cabotins qui se pavanent dans les loges sur des fauteuils de velours"; *Romance*, p. 614; *Consuelo* vol. II, p. 329). Consuelo, on the other hand, firmly rejects such a notion of the misunderstood, alienated Romantic genius: I am still an artist and shall always be an artist. But I conceive a different aim, I shadow out a different destiny for art, than the rivalries of pride, and the vengeance of humiliation. I have another spring of action and it will sustain me ... I would make art loved and understood, without making the artist himself either feared or hated (Je suis encore artiste et je le serai toujours. Je conçois un autre but, une autre destinée à l'art que la rivalité de l'orgueil et la vengeance de l'abaissement. J'ai un autre mobile, et il me soutiendra ... J'ai pour mobile de faire comprendre l'art et de le faire aimer sans faire craindre et haïr la personne de l'artiste; *Romance*, p. 616; *Consuelo* vol. II, p. 332).

Consuelo's challenge to the Byronic Albert to abandon his reflective powers entirely and to descend into his heart provides the key to her conception of how to make art both loved and understood even as it remains impersonal and sublime. For Consuelo, descending into one's heart and there concentrating all of one's existence means practicing a life and an art of active compassion. This life is made possible for both Consuelo and Albert through initiation into the secret Illuminist society, Les Invisibles, who, by their collective efforts, rescue Albert when he is presumed dead and buried alive at the end of *Consuelo* and free Consuelo from her imprisonment in the dungeon at Spandau by Frederick the Great in the early chapters of *La Comtesse de Rudolstadt*. The Invisibles are a group of religious and political heretics – a term they employ with great respect – whose goal is nothing short of freeing the entire human race from all "intellectual and material tyranny" ("tyrannie intellectuelle et matérielle"; *Countess* vol. II, p. 118; *Comtesse*, p. 367).[21] Under the proleptic banner of "Liberty, Equality, and Fraternity," they seek to found a new egalitarian social order and a new and universal religion of humanity. Like her ideological opposite, the Jesuit Abbé Barruel whose *Histoire du Jacobinisme* (1797–8)[22] traces the origin of the French Revolution to Freemasonry and illuminism, Sand represents the Invisibles as one of innumerable secret societies termed by Consuelo's initiator as "subterranean laboratories in which is preparing a great revolution, the crater of which will be Germany or France" ("laboratoires souterrains où se prépare une grande révolution, dont le cratère sera l'Allemagne ou la France"; *Countess* vol. II, p. 124; *Comtesse*, p. 372). (Comparisons with Shelley's *Frankenstein* whose monster was created in Weishaupt's Ingolstadt are inevitable here.) Sand's narrator, in fact, credits

Adam Weishaupt and the historical Bavarian Illuminati, descendants of her fictional Invisibles, with shaking "for an instant all dynasties upon their thrones, ... and bequeathing to the French Revolution something like an electric current of sublime enthusiasm, ardent faith and terrible fanaticism" ("Il ébranla un instant toutes les dynasties sur leurs trônes, et succomba à son tour, en léguant à la Révolution française comme un courant électrique d'enthousiasme sublime, de foi ardente et de fanatisme terrible"; *Countess* vol. II, p. 277; *Comtesse*, p. 480).

As Consuelo's initiator into this mysterious web of conspirators proclaims, however, the Invisibles have moved beyond bloody revolt as they have renounced the violence and overt political warfare practiced by their ancestors: "We still expose ourselves to proscription and poverty, to captivity and death, for the methods of tyranny are still the same. But our methods are no longer an appeal to a material revolt and the bloody preaching of the cross and sword" ("nous nous exposons encore à la proscription, à la misère, à la captivité, à la mort; car les moyens de la tyrannie sont toujours les mêmes: mais nos moyens, à nous, ne sont plus l'appel à la révolte matérielle, et la prédication sanglante de la croix et du glaive"; *Countess* vol. II, p. 114; *Comtesse*, pp. 364–5). Hence the pivotal role played by artists and intellectuals in their movement:

> Our war is wholly intellectual, like our mission. We appeal to the mind. We act by the mind. It is not with the strong hand that we can overthrow governments now organized and based upon all the resources of brute force. We wage against them a slower, more secret and deeper war, – we attack them at the heart ... we destroy every prejudice, we hurl from our fortress against altars and thrones the fiery missiles of ardent truth and implacable reason.
>
> (*Countess* vol. II, pp. 114–15)

> Notre guerre est tout intellectuelle comme notre mission. Nous nous adressons à l'esprit. Nous agissons par l'esprit. Ce n'est pas à main armée que nous pouvons renverser des gouvernements, aujourd'hui organisés et appuyés sur tous les moyens de la force brutale. Nous leur faisons une guerre plus lente ...; nous détruisons tous les prestiges; nous lançons du haut de notre forteresse tous les boulets rouges de l'ardente vérité et de l'implacable raison sur les autels et sur les trônes.
>
> (*Comtesse*, p. 365)

Like Staël, Shelley, and Arnim, Sand's idealist vision emphasizes the power of thought as action at the same time that *Consuelo* moves beyond their novelistic meditations to suggest organized, political means for transforming the world through thought.

In *La Comtesse de Rudolstadt* we, as readers, witness Consuelo's initiation into Les Invisibles. Indeed, the sequel to *Consuelo* reads from beginning to end as a series of initiatory trials that Consuelo must endure and survive if she is to solve the mystery of her relation to Albert and fulfill her role as revolutionary artist: the test of loyalty to the Princess Amelia, Frederick the Great's sister, Cagliostro's ritual summoning of the dead Albert, imprisonment in Spandau, and finally of course the illuminist ritual in the dungeons of the Château du Graal. No other aspect of *Consuelo/La Comtesse de Rudolstadt* has received more critical attention or been the object of such subtle, suggestive and sophisticated analyses. For the most part these analyses are mythic, structural, and/or psychoanalytic, bringing together, into discussions of the "myth of the feminine," Consuelo's Orphic descent in *Consuelo* with her later trials as Psyche in relation to the masked or hidden Liverani/Albert and her final quest in the Château du Graal of Les Invisibles.[23]

Utopian future and the female *Bildungsroman*

As my aim in this chapter is to illuminate Sand's critique of the legacy bequeathed to her by earlier writers of Romanticism like Staël, Schiller, Goethe, and Byron, my focus here will be on the trials of initiation in *La Comtesse de Rudolstadt* as elements of a *Bildungsroman* that rewrites its model *Wilhelm Meisters Wanderjahre*. If *Die Günderode* challenges the complacency and conservatism of the *Lehrjahre*, *La Comtesse de Rudolstadt* stands in a similar relation to the *Wanderjahre* (1829) which was translated into French by the Baronness of Carlowitz and (most likely) immediately read by Sand as she was composing *La Comtesse* in 1843. As Cellier and Guichard have indicated, Sand owned a copy of this translation of the Goethe novel published by La Charpentier which was also the object of a *compte rendu* in the October 25, 1843 volume of the *Revue Indépendante*.[24]

Given Sand's earlier responses to Goethe's *Faust*, it is perhaps surprising that *Consuelo/La Comtesse de Rudolstadt* should bear such clear marks of his influence. Indeed, as Naomi Schor has argued, Sand's 1839 *Essay on Fantastic Drama*, a comparison of Goethe's *Faust*, Byron's *Manfred*, and Mickiewicz's *Konrad*, proclaims Goethe to be "the anti-Sand."[25] Sand in this essay writes of the materialist Goethe, that "Goethe does not seem to me to be the ideal of a poet, because he is a poet without an ideal." He is, furthermore, no philosopher, Schor notes, quoting Sand, "because for Sand philosophy is 'a philosophy of the future' and 'chained to the present, he [Goethe] painted things as they are and not as they should be'" (p. 13). Six years later, however, in 1845, Sand wrote a letter to Bettine von Arnim, thanking her for sending her a copy of the French translation of *Goethe's Correspondence with a Child*, a remarkable letter that evinces a radically different assessment of Goethe's cultural significance. Here, Sand transforms the Goethe of the *Wanderjahre* into a visionary communist. She suggests that if the Goethe of *Wilhelm Meister* lived currently in France, "he would be, in the matter of socialist ideas, our master, as he already is and will always be in matters of art."[26]

In fact, the passage to which Sand refers in Goethe's text is an unabashed apology for the privileges of the landed gentry, a self-satisfied bureaucratic version of what we now call "trickle down economics" that clearly justifies Sand's earlier judgment of Goethe as apologist for the status quo:

[A] man should cherish every sort of possession, should make himself the center from which all common property can issue forth; he must be an egoist, lest he become an egotist, must conserve, that he may contribute. What good is it to give goods and possessions to the poor? It is more laudable to act as an administrator for them. That is the meaning of the maxim "Possessions and Common Property": the capital should not be touched, for in the course of events the interest will in any case belong to everyone.[27]

Of particular significance for my argument is that Sand speaks in her letter with utter confidence that Arnim will welcome her utopian socialist reading – her perhaps willful misreading – of Goethe's *Wanderjahre*. Sand asserts unequivocally her confidence that her political aspirations to transform the future are one with those of her German counterpart. This was the one and only letter that passed between Sand and Arnim. After this letter was opened by German censors and its contents found their way into the press, Arnim chose to respond by a French translator rather than put anything to Sand down on paper. The Prussian authorities seem to have sensed the political power of these two courageous writers that was to be so clearly demonstrated in the important roles that both Arnim and Sand played in the impending 1848 revolutions in their respective countries.

Placing Sand's model of *Bildung* as it is developed in *La Comtesse de Rudolstadt* alongside that of Goethe in the *Wanderjahre* and of Arnim in *Die Günderode* will render evident the affinities that link the two women writers in their impatience with social and economic injustice and separate them from Goethe's resolute refusal of social critique.[28] The parallels between the *Wanderjahre* and *La Comtesse* – the quasi-masonic nature of the secret societies, the enforced separation from the betrothed, the mirroring of the gypsy-like familial wandering at the opening of the *Wanderjahre* in the epilogue of *La Comtesse* – are striking. Yet even if Sand read Goethe's novel only later, the comparison remains instructive as an exploration of two radically different novelistic visions of the structure of individual and social development as that structure takes form in and is guided by Sand's Invisibles and Goethe's *Turmgesellschaft*.

Clearly the political aims of the Society of the Tower and the Invisibles occupy opposite ends of the ideological spectrum. If the Invisibles dedicate their lives to the overthrow of existing governments and religious institutions, the members of the Society of the Tower, as their spokesman Lenardo asserts, have taken upon themselves two duties: "to honor every form of worship, since they are all more or less expressed in the Creed" and "to accept the validity of all forms of government, and, since all of them require and promote useful activity, to work within each according to its will" (p. 369). The new world undertaking upon which the members of this world confederation are about to embark is implausibly conceived as insulated from any need for governmental reform or transformation, even as it is clearly pictured by Odoardo as a colonialist project of domination.

The significant undertaking in which I have invited this throng of stalwart men to participate is not altogether unknown to you, for I have already discussed it with you in general terms. . . . Over there Nature has spread vast, wide spaces that lie untouched and wild, so that one hardly dares venture into them and engage them in battle. And yet it is easy for resolute men gradually to conquer this wilderness and assure themselves of partial possession. . . . Nature can be subdued through industry; men must be subdued through force or persuasion.

(p. 381)

It is precisely the horrific consequences of this subjection by force that Consuelo witnesses in the dungeons of the Château du Graal during her initiation into the Invisibles. Jarno/Montan makes clear his belief in the necessity of mental coercion of the lower orders as well to the elitist Society in his explanation of why Church and State may deem themselves infallible, even as the pursuit of scientific truth is conducted in total freedom by the privileged few who work for the benefit of distant ages: "Church and state may possibly find cause for declaring themselves unassailable, for they have to deal with the recalcitrant masses, and so long as order is maintained, the means do not matter" (pp. 405–6). Though one cannot, of course, equate Goethe's views with those of his characters, the absence of any perspectives that would counter the reactionary and authoritarian ones expressed in the novel speaks volumes.

My point here in comparing the radical egalitarianism of *La Comtesse de Rudolstadt* with Goethe's defense of the political and religious status quo is not to suggest that Sand conceived her own *Bildungsroman* as a systematic critique of Goethe's prototype. Her letter to Bettine von Arnim suggests only the most superficial knowledge of Goethe's novel, a limitation she attributes in that letter to her lack of knowledge of German and her unwillingness to draw conclusions about the novel based upon a translation. To imply that Sand's great novel was written primarily as a reaction to any other previous work of fiction would be to do it a great disservice and to fail to recognize its wild freedom. Rather I am suggesting here, as I have throughout this study, that Sand, like Staël, Shelley, and Arnim, shared intellectual and philosophical concerns with her male predecessors and contemporaries and that she shaped her responses to those concerns in a manner that reflected her gendered perspective and her republican and proto-socialist politics.

Franco Moretti, in his analysis of *Wilhelm Meisters Lehrjahre*, correctly emphasizes that Wilhelm's initiation into the Society of the Tower oddly involves no overt initiatory trial, no willingness to accept that time stop and one's own identity vanish, that one die to be reborn (p. 44). At the end of that novel, Wilhelm becomes a member of the Society almost without knowing how or why. Such cannot be said for the *Wanderjahre* which Moretti does not discuss in his analysis of the earlier novel as a classical *Bildungsroman*. This later novel, subtitled "Die Entsagenden" or "The Renunciants," describes the process by which individual identity is in a sense renounced or sacrificed to the group through the "curious obligations" (p. 119) that are imposed upon the renunciants during their trial period: they must take on new names, never stay more than three days in one location, and "if they encounter one another they should speak neither of the past nor the future, but only of the present" (p. 119). All of these requirements gently dissolve the sense of individual identity and prepare the renunciants for their dedication to the communal commitments delineated at the conclusion of the novel.

Consuelo's initiation is, on the other hand, harrowing and symbolically life threatening, in order, as the members of the supreme council inform her, to prepare her for the treacherous political battles that lie ahead of her. Though offered Liverani as a guide, Consuelo chooses to brave her journey through "the catacombs of feudality, of military or religious despotism" ("les catacombes de la féodalité, du despotisme militaire ou religieux") on her own (*Countess* vol. II, p. 251; *Comtesse*, p. 462). The one command to which she must adhere is that she never look back, obedience to this Orphic injunction, as I read it, signifying her willingness to abandon completely her past self and life. The Invisibles' reading of the significance of these dungeons is inscribed directly into the stone, in uninterrupted circular lines, as if to embody the power of liberatory language both to record and to transform the previously inescapable oppressive patterns of the past:

Here have perished, suffered, wept, cursed and blasphemed twenty generations of men, for the most part innocent and some of them heroic, all victims or martyrs, prisoners of war, serfs in revolt or too utterly crushed by taxes to pay new ones, religious reformers, sublime heretics, the unfortunate, the vanquished, fanatics, saints, villains, too. ... These are the abodes which powerful men built for men in slavery, to stifle the cries and conceal the corpses of their brothers conquered and in chains.

(*Countess* vol. II, p. 251)

Ici ont péri, ici ont souffert, ici ont pleuré, rugi et blasphémé vingt générations d'hommes, innocents pour la plupart, quelques-uns héroïques; tous victimes ou martyrs; des prisonniers de guerre, des serfs révoltés ou trop écrasés de taxes pour en payer de nouvelles, des novateurs religieux, des hérétiques sublimes, des infortunés, des vaincus, des fanatiques, des saints, des scélérats aussi. ... Voilà les demeures que les hommes puissants ont fait construire par des hommes asservis, pour étouffer les cris et cacher les cadavres de leurs frères vaincus et enchaînés.

(*Comtesse*, p. 462)

Sand makes clear that this brutal history of the abuse of human rights is the explicitly patriarchal history of class conflict:

Fleshless skulls, human bones, broken and dried, tears, blots of blood, – these are the meaning of your armorial emblems, if your fathers have bequeathed to you the dishonour of nobility; ... Yes, these are the foundations of the titles of nobility, the source of the hereditary glories and wealth of this world. ... This, this is what men have invented in order to hold themselves, from father to son, above other men!

(*Countess* vol. II, p. 252)

[D]es crânes décharnés, des os humains brisés et desséchés, des larmes, des taches de sang, voilà ce que signifient les emblèmes de tes armoiries, si tes pères t'ont légué la tache du patriciat; ... Oui, voilà le fondement des titres de noblesse, voilà la source des gloires et des richesses héréditaires de ce monde ... Voilà, voilà ce que les hommes ont inventé pour s'élever de père en fils au-dessus des autres hommes!

(*Comtesse*, pp. 462–3)

If her Orphic descent under the Schreckenstein in *Consuelo* reveals to her the voices of the past silenced by official history and brought to life by the folk melodies of Albert's violin, her initiation into the Invisibles brings her into direct contact with the physical remains of these oppressed and buried masses. And if Sand pays tribute explicitly in the Gothic romance of *Consuelo* to her model Ann Radcliffe, *La Comtesse de Rudolstadt* lays bare in the starkest and most graphic possible terms the historical and political underpinnings of that fictional mode as her heroine makes her way through the ossuary of the castle and the ashes of 20 generations of victims, coming face-to-face with hideous skeletal remains and instruments of torture. In this open collective grave into which Consuelo descends, Sand concretizes the history of class conflict, political repression, and persecution and makes it impossible for her reader to ignore or to rationalize. Overcome by this spectacle of violated and mutilated humanity, Consuelo faints and is proclaimed victorious in her ordeals by the Invisibles precisely for *not* reaching the end of her pathway and for instead having allowed her heart to be broken "by indignation and pity in presence of the palpable evidences of the crimes and misfortunes of humanity" ("d'indignation et de pitié devant les témoignages palpables des crimes et des maux de l'humanité"; *Countess* vol. II, p. 263; *Comtesse*, p. 470).

"The divine equality of man and woman"

The differences between the sexual politics of Sand's and Goethe's *Bildungsromane* are, if possible, even more radical than their understandings of class relations.[29] As Cellier and Guichard emphatically note, it appears that Sand set herself the ambitious task of offering France the equivalent of Goethe's prototypical novel, with the all important difference of the protagonist's gender.[30] As critics have frequently observed, Goethe's *Lehrjahre* records a process of development that is reserved for men and off-limits to women, with the women either sacrificed along the way as victims of the intensity of their unrequited and unlawful loves (Marianne, Mignon, and Aurelie) or totally dedicated to the care and nurture of men (Therese and Natalie).[31] For Goethe, "the gradual organic unfolding of inner capacities, culminating in active social involvement and civic responsibility" is, as Marianne Hirsch has shown, the prerogative of men; female *Bildung*, on the other hand, tends to the self-absorption and withdrawal from society typified by the example of the totally spiritualized Beautiful Soul. "Pushed into absolute subjectivity, the exceptional woman is cut off from social intercourse; pushed into the role of posthumous confessor, her narrative remains virtually separate from the rest of the plot" (p. 32). Similarly in the *Wanderjahre*, Makarie, who supposedly functions as the spiritual heart of this visionary company, is again, like the Beautiful Soul, totally disembodied and ethereal, described as "an angel of God upon the earth," with her words, like those of her counterpart in the earlier novel, appended awkwardly to the text in a final archive of sententious maxims and meditations. Furthermore, all those who debate, define, and promulgate the utopian ideals of the community to be founded in the new world by the Society of the Tower are men – Friedrich, Montan, Odoardo, Lenardo – while the women are left to imagine their tasks as purveyors of clothing or as educators of "a whole race of housewives guided and inspired to precision and neatness!" (p. 405).

Consuelo's initiators in *La Comtesse de Rudolstadt*, in contrast, leave no doubt whatsoever that the Invisibles have sworn their dedication to the destruction of power imbalances between men and women and to the full intellectual and political participation of women in their struggle. As the initiator who instructs Consuelo in their doctrines asserts, "[l]ike Albert, we profess the divine precept of equality between man and woman" ("Comme Albert, nous professons le précepte de l'égalité divine de l'homme et de la femme"; *Countess* vol. II, p. 125; *Comtesse*, p. 374). This initiator also makes it clear that Consuelo will know the secrets of the related fraternity, the Freemasons, though women are only permitted to join them "by adoption." (Among her sources on Freemasonry, Sand had been reading a newly published history by F.M. Clavel that praised these secret societies for opening their doors to women in nineteenth-century France.)[32] "We will treat you as a man" ("Nous te traiterons comme un homme"), the initiator proclaims, in an implicit challenge to the Freemasonic distinction of its women as adopted "sisters" to its full-fledged male members (*Countess* vol. II, p. 125; *Comtesse*, p. 373).[33] It is, he furthermore suggests, the faulty education and vulnerable social position of women that has rendered them less fit than men for the dangerous political mission of the Invisibles rather than any innate or essential difference between the sexes. Sand offers here one explanation for the jarring contrast between her theory and practice, between her feminist, egalitarian ideals and her often expressed sense of superiority to other women: "[c]ompelled to recognize in the unfortunate results of the education of your sex, of your social situation and habits, a dangerous levity and capricious instincts, we cannot practise this precept to its full extent. We can trust only a small number of women, and there are some secrets which we will intrust to you alone" ("... forcés de reconnaître dans les fâcheux résultats de l'éducation de ton sexe, de sa situation sociale et de ses habitudes, une légèreté dangereuse et de capricieux instincts, nous ne pouvons pratiquer ce précepte dans toute son étendue; nous ne pouvons nous fier qu'à un petit nombre de femmes, et il est des secrets que nous ne confierons qu'à toi seule"; *Countess* vol. II, p. 125; *Comtesse*, p. 374). Consuelo's specific task for the Invisibles will have the explicitly feminist aim, still utopian today, of the formation of an internationalist network of women, a network that will unite women of all social classes and walks of life in their struggle for freedom:

> You will institute among women new secret societies founded by us upon the principle of our own, but appropriate in their form and composition to the customs and manners of different countries and classes. You will bring about, so far as possible, the cordial and sincere association of the great lady and the bourgeoise, the rich woman and the humble worker, the virtuous matron and the adventurous artist.
>
> (*Countess* vol. II, pp. 126–7)

> Tu institueras parmi les femmes des sociétés secrètes nouvelles, fondées par nous sur le principe de la nôtre, mais appropriées, dans leurs formes et dans leur composition, aux usages et aux mœurs des divers pays et des diverses classes. Tu y opéreras, autant que possible, le rapprochement cordial et sincère de la grande dame et de la bourgeoise, de la femme riche et de l'humble ouvrière, de la vertueuse matrone et de l'artiste aventureuse.
>
> (*Comtesse*, p. 375)

From her indoctrination by this initiator, Consuelo moves to a private conference with a confessor to whom she divulges her doubts and fears about her passion for the mysterious Liverani. If the focus of the initiator is uniting women across nations and classes in a battle against material inequality, the confessor's aims are more socio-cultural – the liberation of women from the restrictions of domesticity and the transformation of the institution of marriage. Given the care with which Sand has created an entirely masculine realm in her world of Invisibles and their Château du Graal, a realm into which Consuelo is admitted as pioneering and exceptional woman, the moment when this hooded confessor discloses her identity as Albert's mother is shocking and arresting. Not only does Wanda von Prachlitz reveal that she has been a member of the supreme council for decades, she also emphasizes that she has presided over their conferences when necessary and participated fully in their intellectual and philosophical deliberations. Furthermore, she renders evident Sand's prefiguration of identity politics, her conception of the gendered nature of women's political and cultural perspectives, such that her own personal experiences enable her to understand Consuelo's dilemmas in a way impossible for her male counterparts:

> A man would not have been able to tell you what are woman's sacred rights and true duties in love. They have made their laws and formed their ideas

without consulting us, yet I have often enlightened the consciences of my associates in this respect, and they have had the courage and honesty to listen to me.

(*Countess* vol. II, p. 141)

Un homme n'eût pu vous dire quels sont dans l'amour les droits sacrés et les véritables devoirs de la femme. Ils ont fait leurs lois et leurs idées sans nous consulter; j'ai pourtant éclairé souvent à cet égard la conscience de mes associés, et ils ont eu le courage et la loyauté de m'écouter.

(*Comtesse*, p. 385)

She makes clear that it is her duty to save Consuelo from the "complete degradation" ("complet abaissement") and "eternal torture" (p. 141) ("éternelle souffrance"; p. 385) of a loveless marriage such as she herself endured with Albert's kind but archly conservative Catholic father.

Revealing to Consuelo the mystery of Albert's resurrection without letting her know that Albert and Liverani are one person, his mother is radically unequivocal in her response to the conflict in Consuelo between duty and passion, devotion to her husband Albert, and desire for Liverani. Far from advising that "such instincts [should] be stifled by our will" as Consuelo suggests, her confessor calls marriage without love "plighted prostitution," slavery, and servitude and asserts that God rejects such a sacrifice of female sexuality. Only those marriages based in reciprocity, affinity, and equality are hallowed by God. "When this reciprocity does not exist there is no equality, and where equality is broken there is no real union" ("Là où cette réciprocité n'existe pas, il n'y a pas d'égalité; et là où l'égalité est brisée, il n'y a pas d'union réelle"; *Countess* vol. II, p. 138; *Comtesse*, p. 383). Thus this sibylline figure proclaims with absolute certainty that it is her duty and her right to pronounce Consuelo's divorce from Albert so that she can unite herself with Liverani.

For much as Consuelo has respected and revered Albert, she never desired him and agreed to marry him only out of compassion on his deathbed. Thus Sand's deflationary critique of the Byronic and the melancholic hero extends to her depiction of these types as utterly unerotic, indeed repugnant to women – possessing none of the sexual magnetism of the seductive heroes of Staël's *Corinne* and Shelley's *Valperga* or of the infamously attractive Byron himself. Sand is furthermore quite explicit in her assertion that the revivified Albert is a new person, and that his transformation is the result of his freedom from Satanic will and concomitant melancholy.

As if to emphasize the gap between the monumental difficulty and importance of this tension between duty and desire, spirit and body in Consuelo, as they are traditionally conceived, and the reality of their consonance and harmony, Sand extends this conflict in her heroine throughout most of *La Comtesse* even though the reader strongly suspects, indeed assumes, that Liverani is Albert from his very first appearance. Even after the authority of her confessor's experienced and compassionate voice frees her to choose Liverani without guilt and her eavesdropping on Albert's conversation with Trenck reveals that he can release her without pain, Consuelo still refuses to abandon Albert, believing that her own sense of personal integrity demands loyalty to her marriage oath. Once again, the Sibyl must emphatically remind her that the Invisibles: "[w]ish to sanctify love, lost and profaned in this world, the free choice of the heart, the sacred and voluntary union of two beings equally in love. ... You have not the right to dispose of your being for sacrifice, you cannot stifle the love in your breast and deny the truth of your confession, unless we so authorize you" ("[veulent] ... sanctifier l'amour, perdu et profané dans le monde, le libre choix du cœur, l'union sainte et volontaire de deux êtres également épris. ... Tu n'as donc pas [le droit] de disposer de ton être pour le sacrifice, tu ne peux pas étouffer l'amour dans ton sein et renier la vérité de ta confession, sans que nous t'y ayons autorisée"; *Countess* vol. II, p. 271, trans. modified; *Comtesse*, p. 476). When this sibylline confessor finally hurls Consuelo into the arms of Liverani who is revealed to be none other than Albert, the effect is profoundly anti-climactic. Whether this effect is intended or not, Sand's plot strongly reinforces the reader's sense of the meaninglessness and artificiality of the desire/duty, body/spirit conflict. It furthermore suggests that a destiny beyond individual choice will ultimately dissolve this opposition in the truly spiritual being. Thus the plot of *Consuelo* moves from her immature passion for Anzoleto, to her asexual reverence and compassion for the forbidding and sickly Albert until that bond is finally transformed into a genuine union of healthy bodies and souls. One could hardly be farther from the sexual politics of Goethe's *Wanderjahre* that maintains till the very end, after disposing of the inconveniently and demandingly sexual Marianne, Mignon, and Aurelie, the opposition between the carefree and promiscuous Philine and the spiritual and disembodied Makarie.[34]

Sand's monumental novel, in contrast, concludes with the annulment of Consuelo's legal marriage to Albert and the celebration of her mystical union with Liverani, a kind of apotheosis of sensuous and spiritual pleasure. Though this union is consecrated by the Invisibles, who constitute "a chain of brotherly love and religious association" ("une chaîne d'amour fraternelle et association religieuse"; *Countess* vol. II, p. 286; *Comtesse*, p. 487), it is left to Wanda, Albert's spectral mother, transformed by enthusiasm into a sibylline prophetess, to pronounce the significance of this union to her male comrades. We witness here Sand's indebtedness to and sympathy with the social and political goals of the Saint-Simonian feminists of her day, in particular the call for sexual liberation and reform of marriage and for female leadership often cast in the role of symbolic "Mother." As with the Saint-Simoniennes, many of whom were lower middle-class or working-class, the feminist agenda of the Invisibles is explicitly socialist and egalitarian in its choice of Consuelo as its agent.[35] Whereas these men wish to seal this ceremony with an oath on their swords, Wanda utterly rejects the violence and masculinist history implicit in this gesture. Her transport becomes a vehicle for Sand's inimitable expression – both lengthy and emphatic – of her own rejection of bourgeois and patriarchal marriage as "the tomb of love, happiness and virtue" ("le tombeau de l'amour, du bonheur et de la vertu"), "sworn prostitution" ("prostitution jurée"; *Countess* vol. II, p. 293; *Comtesse*, p. 492), enforced by "law, with threats and punishments, an imposed slavery, with scandal, prisons and chains in case of infraction" ("une loi avec des menaces et des châtiments, un esclavage imposé, avec du scandale, des prisons, et des chaînes en cas d'infraction"; *Countess* vol. II, p. 292; *Comtesse*, p. 491). Through the vehicle of Wanda, Sand asserts most unequivocally the need for a profound revolution in the relations of the sexes as the bedrock upon which any positive transformation of society is to be founded. The protests against the institution of marriage that are implicit in the fates of the heroines of *Corinne*, *Valperga*, and *Die Günderode* are rewritten here into an explicit program of political and social change.

For Sand's prophetess, love is an ideal rooted in two people's free transfer to each other of their inalienable liberty. Accordingly, Consuelo's "wedding night" becomes a Midsummer Night's Dream of the ultimate harmony of body and mind, passion, and spirit:

> It seemed as though life in all its power, happiness in all its intensity, had taken possession of her in all her fibres, and that she was breathing them out through every pore. She did not count the hours – she would have wished this enchanted night never to end. Why can one not stop the sun beneath the horizon in certain night-watches when one feels [oneself] in all the plenitude of [one's] being, and when all the dreams of enthusiasm seem realized or realizable?
>
> (*Countess* vol. II, pp. 308–9)

> Il semblait que la vie dans toute sa puissance, le bonheur dans toute son intensité, se fussent emparés d'elle par toutes ses fibres, et qu'elle les aspirât par tous ses pores. Elle ne comptait pas les heures: elle eût voulu que cette nuit enchantée ne finît jamais. Pourquoi ne peut-on arrêter le soleil sous l'horizon, dans de certaines veillées où l'on se sent dans toute la plénitude de l'être, et où tous les rêves de l'enthousiasme semblent réalisés ou réalisables!
>
> (*Comtesse*, p. 503)

In its inseparability from the ideology of Les Invisibles and their celebration of the (female) body, the politicized and feminized nature of Sand's aesthetic of enthusiasm could not be any clearer. The novel proper ends with this ecstatic moment of erotic self-abandonment, as Consuelo leans "her burning brow" on Liverani's shoulder, pronounces his name and, in this instant, realizes her own dream of enthusiasm in a harmonic union of male and female that had eluded Sand's predecessors Staël, Shelley, and Arnim.

New horizons: from Zingarella to Zingara

Yet Sand refuses to conclude her narrative with this utopian moment, and, in her uniquely fluent fashion, continues her story in a 100-page Epilogue that attempts to trace the subsequent fates of Consuelo and Albert as they pursue their ardent and indefatigable pilgrimage across Europe in the name of liberty, equality, and fraternity. An obtrusive first-person narrator enters the text here, lamenting the obscurity and scarcity of reliable sources of information about the future destinies of the novel's protagonists and shifting the mode of the novel one last time from the Gothic to a complex medley of picaresque, realist, and meta-fictional modes. This dialogic conclusion facilitates both a clear (re)statement of the philosophical and ideological aims of the novel and an ironic challenging of these ideals. Up until this point in the novel, class conflict had had a powerful but abstract presence in the novel as the ideological framework around which the Invisibles had built their secret society, while Consuelo had been protected from need by aristocratic patronage and Albert by his vast inherited wealth. In the Epilogue, however, harsh economic realities dominate the lives of Consuelo and Albert as Sand makes clear that their mutual "dream of enthusiasm" cannot last in the world of bourgeois capital. Despite her artistic success, Consuelo is penniless, Sand is quick to point out, because of her refusal of the capitalist ethos of economic speculation:

> After ten years of work and journeys she was no richer than when she had set out, because she had not known how to speculate, and moreover had not been willing to do so – two conditions under which wealth does not come to seek, in spite of them, workers of any class. Besides, she had not laid up the often hard-won fruit of her labours: she had spent it in good works, and in a life secretly devoted to active propaganda. Even her own resources had not been sufficient: the central government of the Invisibles had sometimes contributed to it.
>
> (*Countess* vol. II, pp. 324–5)

> Après dix ans de travail et de courses, elle n'était pas plus riche qu'à son point de départ, elle ne l'avait pas su spéculer, et, de plus, elle n'avait pas voulu: deux conditions moyennant lesquelles la richesse ne vient chercher malgré eux les travailleurs d'aucune classe. En outre, elle n'avait point mis en réserve le fruit souvent contesté de ses peines; elle l'avait constamment employé en bonne oeuvres, et dans une vie consacrée secrètement à une active propagande, ses ressources mêmes n'avaient pas toujours suffi; le gouvernement central des Invisibles y avait quelquefois pourvu.
>
> (*Comtesse*, p. 516)

Through the agency of lawyers – scourge of the realist novel from Charlotte Smith's late eighteenth-century *The Old Manor House* (1793) to Dickens's *Bleak House* (1853) and beyond – who seek to take hold of the Rudolstadt estate and attempt to prove Albert an impostor when he returns to bid his aunt farewell in her dying days, Albert is imprisoned. Most tragically, imprisonment and persecution lead to the return of Albert's madness and Consuelo loses her incomparable voice in response to his suffering.

Thus, like Corinne and, to a certain extent, Euthanasia, Beatrice, and Karoline, Sand's prototypical female artist is silenced at the end of the novel after a career illuminated by moments of transcendent accomplishment. Feminist critics, myself included, have found it hard not to see in this silencing of Consuelo a reduction of this gloriously independent and strong heroine to domesticity and marriage.[36] Yet, in the end, though bound through love and devotion to her husband and children, Consuelo is never confined to home or hearth. Instead, she returns to the radical movement and freedom that she has always associated with her mother and her art. Sand, in fact, makes it clear throughout *Consuelo* that her heroine's true nature is that of the Zingarella and that a life of freedom is essential to the true artist, for her mother had always warned her that comfort and repose mean death to the soul of an artist. Just as the Epilogue emphasizes that Consuelo's entire career in the corrupt world of institutionalized theater has constituted "a long martyrdom" ("un long martyre"; *Countess* vol. II, p. 322; *Comtesse*, p. 515), so some of the novel's most lyrical passages celebrate this contrasting maternal legacy of liberty, the artist's wandering life, as the younger Consuelo calls out to the memory of her mother when she longs to leave the oppressive Rudolstadt castle for the open road that

[i]s the path for all humankind. ... It belongs to no master, to close and open it at pleasure. It is not only the powerful and rich that are entitled to tread its flowery margins and to breathe its rich perfume ... the highway is a land of liberty. ... O, my mother! ... Why canst thou not carry me on thy strong shoulders, and bear me far, far away, where the swallow skims onward to the blue and distant hills, and where the memory of the past and the longing after vanished happiness cannot follow the light-footed artist, who travels still faster than they do, and each day places a new horizon, a second world, between her and the enemies of liberty?

(*Romance*, pp. 341–2)

Et puis ce chemin, c'est le passage de l'humanité. ... Il n'appartient pas à un maître qui puisse le fermer ou l'ouvrir à son gré. Ce n'est pas seulement le puissant et le riche qui ont le droit de fouler ses marges fleuries et de respirer ses sauvages parfums. ... [L]e chemin est une terre de liberté. ... O ma mère! Ma mère! ... Que ne peux-tu me reprendre sur tes fortes épaules et me porter là-bas, là-bas où vole l'hirondelle vers les collines bleues, où le souvenir du passé et le regret du bonheur perdu ne peuvent suivre l'artiste aux pieds légers qui voyage plus vite qu'eux, et met chaque jour un nouvel horizon, un nouveau monde entre lui et les ennemis de sa liberté!

(*Consuelo* vol. I, pp. 390–1)

Sand provides in the conclusion of *La Comtesse de Rudolstadt* a vision of the anonymous gypsy artist that confirms this earlier celebration of artistic freedom and radically challenges the previous models of the Romantic artist based in pain, nostalgia, and unfulfilled longing that have been the objects of her critique throughout the novel as a whole.

The artist's wandering existence, as depicted and idealized by Sand, is, of course, also clearly a protest against private property and possessive individualism. Furthermore, and perhaps most importantly, Consuelo continues to compose music and to teach it, as well as her radical political philosophy, to the peasants and laborers encountered in her peregrinations. As Consuelo herself explains it, she and her husband "enter into the ideal" by bringing "art and enthusiasm to souls capable of feeling the one and breathing in the other. ... Every day we make new disciples of art" ("entrer ... dans l'idéal," "l'art et l'enthousiasme aux âmes susceptibles de sentir l'un et d'aspirer à l'autre. ... Chaque jour nous faisons de nouveaux disciples de l'art"; *Countess* vol. II, p. 366; *Comtesse*, pp. 547–8). Might not Sand then also be transforming the celebrated prima donna into an anonymous street musician who writes for and teaches to the lowest ranks of society what she can no longer sing, in order to honor, as Sand writes earlier, with reference to Les Invisibles, the "[m]any energetic labourers [who] have remained obscure, carrying into the tomb the secret of their missions" ("Beaucoup de travailleurs énergiques [qui] sont restés obscurs, emportant dans la tombe le secret de leur mission"; *Countess* vol. II, p. 278; *Comtesse*, p. 481)? George Eliot's *Armgart* (1871) certainly suggests that she read Sand's novel in that light. Eliot's Armgart, clearly an avatar of both Corinne and Consuelo, defines fame as "the benignant strength of the One, transformed/To joy of Many" (p. 195) and sees herself not as a prima donna but as "a happy spiritual star," an agent of "glory wide-diffused," of collective good.[37] Even after she tragically loses her voice at the end of the drama, she refuses to marry the Count who has pursued her throughout her career, choosing instead the life of an obscure teacher of music.[38]

La Comtesse de Rudolstadt, then, concludes under the sign of the Mother, with the sibylline prophecies of Albert's mother and the artistic path cut out by Consuelo's own gypsy mother guiding her future endeavors, both political and cultural. *Bildung*, in this maternal framework, aims for an egalitarian diffusion of knowledge and culture rather than the submission to hierarchy depicted in Goethe's secret society. Indeed, the parting image of this monumental novel replicates her earlier, idealized memory of her own mother quoted above in this parting vision of the heroine and her family in which Consuelo has matured from Zingarella to Zingara: "At last they vanished behind the pines, and, as the Zingara was about to disappear the last of all, we saw her raise her little Wenceslawa and place her upon her strong shoulder" ("Enfin, ils se perdirent derrière les sapins; et au moment où elle allait disparaître la dernière, nous vîmes la Zingara enlever sa petite Wenceslawa et la placer sur son épaule robuste"; *Countess* vol. II, p. 409; *Comtesse*, p. 579). This image of the maternal strength of the female artist bearing a female child into the future concludes Sand's masterpiece.[39] As David Powell observes, Sand here rejects the suicidal impulses that so often haunt the female *Bildungsroman* with the life-affirming triumph of her heroine: the conclusion of *Consuelo* offers "an illuminating example of Sand's feminism, of her desire to put a woman to an aesthetic and spiritual trial where she comes out victorious, strong, unadulterated, and successful on all counts."[40] It answers Corinne's replication of herself in the mini-improvisatrice Juliette with the suggestion that the predecessor's role is to support rather than to determine the form of future generations of artists. It also contrasts radically with the concluding scene of Goethe's *Wanderjahre* in which Wilhelm, now a surgeon and a father, bends over the virtually lifeless, naked body of his son Felix, who has nearly died in a drowning accident, a "lovely flower wilted in [the] arms" of his rescuers (p. 417). Wilhelm lances his arm from which "a rich stream of blood [springs] forth" (p. 417), father and son stand "in tight embrace" likened to the brothers Castor and Pollux, and Wilhelm exclaims, "You are always brought forth anew, ... and are always injured again straight away, wounded from within or without!" (p. 417). Here the symbolism of wounding and ejaculation suggests a relation of father and son, past and future, that is incestuous, pedophilic, necrophiliac, and narcissistic.[41] Consuelo, on the other hand, like Arnim's Bettine who disperses roses to future generations of students, gives life unconditionally to the future.

The Illuminati: organizers of destruction

Sand herself is clearly committed, like the Invisibles she depicts, to a class war that is fought by "wholly intellectual" means; in her companion piece to *Consuelo*, *Jean Ziska*, for example, she writes, that past spilling of blood has been replaced by the spilling of ink (p. 5). Here Sand makes a place beyond violence for herself as historical novelist and for her women readers by implication in this struggle. Given the mechanized brutality of the modern state, the weapons of the poor, the female, the exploited, must be mental, spiritual, and aesthetic rather than military, her Invisibles assert. Yet just as Sand cannot leave her reader with an image of ecstatic erotic union in the marriage ceremony of Albert/Liverani and Consuelo, so she also suggests in her Epilogue that the time has not yet come when Europe can radically transform itself without violence and chaos. And in *Jean Ziska*, powerfully contravening the gendered association of men with an ethic of justice and women with an ethic of care developed by Carol Gilligan, Sand makes clear that she understands even Ziska's most bloodthirsty and brutal acts as historical necessity, as instantiations of a historically determined idea of justice. "Justice is represented blindfolded. Ziska, this agent of God's justice, according to the Taborites, and of the human justice of his century in reality, like ancient Nemesis, had to be blind and insensitive to spectacles of horror and scenes of despair. He was a kind of abstract being whose hand did not soil itself in the blood of its victims, but whose name governed all and was the inspiration for all action" (p. 145).

Indeed, Albert's fate at the novel's conclusion suggests Sand's acknowledgment that Europe at the conclusion of the eighteenth century is after all not quite done with melancholy geniuses or the titanic violence and conflict that their guilt seeks to expiate. In the end, Albert's melancholy has returned, accompanied by the horrific visions that precipitate it. The concluding portrait of Albert, like that of Consuelo, tells the tale of his encounter with Adam Weishaupt (nicknamed Spartacus!), leader of the Bavarian Illuminati, from the point of view of Weishaupt's follower, the naïve enthusiast, dubbed Philo in secret society vernacular. When Weishaupt and his acolyte seek out Albert for his prophetic wisdom, we see him once again in the role of Ariadne, this time not as abandoned lover but as guide to the future, as "magus of our religion, this philosopher, both metaphysician and organizer, who was to provide us with Ariadne's thread, and enable us to find our way out of the labyrinth of past ideas and things" ("mage de notre religion, ce philosophe à la fois métaphysicien et organisateur, qui devait nous confier le fil d'Ariane et nous faire retrouver l'issue du labyrinthe des idées et des choses passées"; *Countess* vol. II, p. 355; *Comtesse*, p. 539). Albert makes explicit the wisdom of the philosophical heroines of Shelley and Arnim, that true politics springs from self-knowledge. Albert indeed sees Weishaupt as inheritor of the worldly political battles against social and religious despotism, of the efforts to persuade the learned, the patrician, and the rich that he himself had abandoned out of disillusionment and despair in favor of acting directly upon the people. "Heaven has made you an organizer of destruction; destroy and dissolve, that is your work" ("Le ciel t'a fait organisateur de destruction; détruis et dissous, voilà ton oeuvre"; *Countess* vol. II, p. 382; *Comtesse*, p. 558), he proclaims to Weishaupt, exhorting him to hasten to France, where he will play a predestined role analogous to Ziska with the Taborites. Finally, Albert's Leibnizian message asserts unequivocally the effectiveness of the Illuminist efforts: "Though the name and form of your work disappear, though you labour without a name, like me, your work will not be lost. ... [In] the crucible of the divine chemist every atom is counted at its exact value" ("Ton nom et la forme de tes oeuvres disparaîtraient, tu travaillerais *sans nom* comme moi, que ton oeuvre ne serait pas perdue. ... [D]ans le creuset du divin chimiste, tous les atomes sont comptés à leur exacte valeur"; *Countess* vol II, p. 385; *Comtesse*, p. 560).

Albert thus now sees that the apocalyptic predictions of the Invisibles will be confirmed, even as this confirmation in a sense challenges the relentless optimism of their teleology. With this emphasis upon the tension between ordered, divinely ordained progress and chaos and destruction, the reader is brought back to a recognition of the *conscious, purposeful naïveté* with which Sand imbues her portrait of the Invisibles, retrospectively considered against the bloodshed and slaughter of the French Revolution and the Napoleonic wars. This tension is nowhere better expressed than in the remarkable authorial interjection of a portrait of the eighteenth century that introduces the reader to the "historical" significance of the Invisibles. I quote only a fragment:

> But by degrees light will come out of chaos, and if our century ever comes to sum itself up, it will also sum up the life of its father, the eighteenth century, that immense logogriph, that brilliant nebula, in which so much cowardice is

opposed to so much greatness, so much knowledge to so much ignorance, barbarity to civilization, light to error, ... incredulity to faith, ... so much superstition to so much haughty reason ... that frightful laboratory in which so many heterogeneous forms have been thrown into the crucible that they have vomited forth in their monstrous ebullition a torrent of smoke in which we are still walking, enveloped in shadows and confused images.

(Countess vol. II, pp. 278–9)

Mais peu à peu la lumière sortira de ce chaos; et si notre siècle arrive à se résumer lui-même, il résumera aussi la vie de son père le dix-huitième siècle, ce logogriphe immense, cette brillante nébuleuse, où tant de lâcheté s'oppose à tant de grandeur, tant de savoir à tant d'ignorance, tant de barbarie à tant de civilization, tant de lumière à tant d'erreur, ... tant d'incrédulité à tant de foi, ... tant de superstition à tant de raison orgueilleuse ... laboratoire effrayant, où tant de formes hétérogènes ont été jetées dans le creuset, qu'elles ont vomi, dans leur monstrueuse ébullition, un torrent de fumée où nous marchons encore enveloppés de ténèbres et d'images confuses.

(Comtesse, p. 481)

As *La Comtesse de Rudolstadt* concludes, the reader knows that the Illuminist recipient of Philo's narrative, Martinowicz, will soon be violently sacrificed in this crucible of history. Yet the strongest impression that remains is the portrait of the loving, transformative bond between Albert, Consuelo, their children, and the future to come, a legacy celebrated in Philo's concluding credo that "Life is a journey which has life for its goal, and not death ..." ("la vie est un voyage qui a la vie pour but, et non la mort"; *Countess* vol. II, p. 410; *Comtesse*, p. 579) and his appeal to the readers of his letter to join this journey.

Sand's obscure Invisibles and their descendants the Illuminati do indeed continue their journey and live on in the future fictions of her fellow nineteenth-century writers. Their literary fate is nowhere more clearly recorded than in George Eliot's humanist prayer, "O May I Join the Choir Invisible."[42] Though the other, English George strips Sand's Invisibles of their overt socialism and their radical occultism, she nevertheless joins her predecessors Staël, Shelley, Arnim, and Sand in challenging despair, rejecting self-interest, and figuring a historical (female) sublime. Furthermore, she celebrates collective, progressive historical effort as more powerful than the work of the lone, isolated individual genius:

O May I join the choir invisible
Of those immortal dead who live again
In minds made better by their presence: live
In pulses stirred to generosity,
And deeds of daring rectitude, in scorn
For miserable aims that end with self,
In thoughts sublime that pierce the night like stars,
And with their mild persistence urge man's search

To vaster issues. So to live is heaven:
To make undying music in the world,
Breathing as beauteous order that controls
With growing sway the growing life of man.
So we inherit that sweet purity
For which we struggled, failed, and agonized
With widening retrospect that bred despair.

      *   *   *

This is life to come,
Which martyred men have made more glorious
For us to strive to follow. May I reach
That purest heaven, be to other souls
The cup of strength in some great agony,
Enkindle generous ardor, feed pure love,
Beget the smiles that have no cruelty –
Be the sweet presence of a good diffused,
And in diffusion ever more intense.
So shall I join the choir invisible
Whose music is the gladness of the world.

                                (pp. 286–7)

Eliot's humanist prayer, with the following epigraph from Cicero, could indeed stand at the head of each of the novels featured in the previous pages, as an echo of Staël's contemplation of the "vast tableau of destinies," Shelley's tracing of the "footsteps of the children of liberty," and Arnim's concourse with historical shades: "Longum illud tempus, quum non ero, magis me movet, quam hoc exiguum. – That long time, when I shall not be, moves me more than this brief life" (Cicero, Letter to Atticus, xii. 18).[43]

Epilogue

Comic flight and the winds of fate: Isak Dinesen's *The Dreamers*

The personal is the destroyer of the spiritual; and to the former everything is now referred.

Letitia Landon

In the twentieth century, the Danish modernist Isak Dinesen (née Karen Dinesen) pays ironic tribute to the legacy of Corinne and Consuelo in her artistic manifesto *The Dreamers* from *Seven Gothic Tales* (1934). Like the nineteenth-century novels included in this study, this novella records a vision of selfhood and creativity that aims at impersonality, detached spirituality, and collective transcendence even as it is rooted in Dinesen's experiences as a highly individualistic modern European woman. *The Dreamers*, the first tale written after the great tragedy of her life, the loss of her beloved African farm and the freedom and fullness of existence it had meant to her, was remembered decades later by Dinesen as "a scream, a lion's roar."[1] Yet this tale is above all else a masterpiece of comic detachment, a testimony to the hypnotic power of Dinesen's almost otherworldly perspective on life. It constitutes a courageous, if only partially successful, attempt to lift into comic flight the tragic fate of the female artist bequeathed to her by her Romantic predecessors.

I begin with a brief synopsis of this intricate frame tale. The heroine of *The Dreamers*, Pellegrina Leoni, is a Venetian opera singer of transcendent talent and accomplishment who loses her incomparable voice in a fire that ravages her opera house during a performance in Mozart's *Don Giovanni*. From this moment on, the heroine abandons her identity as Pellegrina and adopts a series of flagrantly stereotypic identities as prostitute, revolutionary conspirator, and saint-like widow that allow her near complete freedom and detachment from the interests and concerns of her previous identity as prima donna. Supported by her one friend and confidant, the Dutch Jew Marcus Cocoza, Pellegrina maintains her mobile existence until she is finally hunted down in an Alpine blizzard by three obsessed lovers, each of whom has known her in one of her respective incarnations as Olalla, Madame Lola, or Rosalba. Seeking to escape her former lovers' relentless demands to know who she "really" is, Pellegrina jumps to her death, in an effort at failed flight, into an Alpine ravine. After her death, Marcus

Cocoza recounts her story to her three despondent and frustrated suitors. One of them, the English Lincoln Forsner, includes it as the heart of the tale of his own life which he relates, in the frame tale that encompasses Pellegrina's tragedy, to the archetypal storyteller, Mira Jama, whose own life history and aesthetic practice, in turn, frame Lincoln's narrative and open and close this remarkable tale.

At the same time that *The Dreamers* bears unmistakable similarities to the previously discussed novels of Staël, Shelley, Arnim, and Sand, it also challenges the teleology of that tradition, as I have traced it, in provocative, daring, and disturbing ways that suggest its post-Nietzschean genesis.[2] Dinesen's work is in a sense emblematic of the modernist and even postmodernist fate of the nineteenth-century female *Künstlerroman* as I have traced it in this study. It begins where the novels of her predecessors leave off, with the silencing and metaphoric death of its artist-heroine. Above all else, *The Dreamers* explodes, in explicit and spectacular fashion, all received notions of a coherent, individual self in favor of an imaginatively constructed collective selfhood that comes into being through performance. As Dinesen weaves the tale of her mysterious, iconoclastic, and compelling artist, she takes up one by one the tropes that were the object of emulation, scrutiny, and critique for the nineteenth-century women novelists who preceded her and pushes those tropes to their tragi-comic limits and beyond into a realm of mystical epiphany and detachment. The figures of Staël's abandoned woman, the Byronic hero, Sand's artist of the people, as well as conceptions of Romantic melancholy or spleen, passionate, Romantic love, and the paradigmatic North/South, sublime/beautiful dichotomies familiar from Staël, Schiller, and Schlegel, are all celebrated in playful parody that exposes their blatant artifice. Most significantly, the Enlightenment doctrine of perfectibility and evolution, so dear to Staël and Sand, is replaced in Dinesen by a conception of historical process not unlike that of Nietzsche according to Foucault; rather than "gradually progress[ing] from combat to combat until it arrives at universal reciprocity, where the rule of law finally replaces warfare; humanity installs each of its violences in a system of rules and thus proceeds from domination to domination."[3] The ideal of collective historical and political progress so vital to the novelistic projects of Staël, Shelley, Arnim, and Sand dissolves into a myth of eternal return directed by a wry, mischievous, unpredictable, and ultimately inscrutable Fate.

If one begins with the figure of the abandoned woman – which is where all female *Künstlerromane* following *Corinne* must begin – we find in Pellegrina Leoni both an acknowledgment of its cultural currency and an absolute refusal to play this role as it has been cast previously. Indeed *The Dreamers* radically extends the critique, common to her nineteenth-century predecessors, of Romantic love and bourgeois marriage as it takes shape in a patriarchal society by suggesting, beyond the inevitable disillusionment with Romantic passion, the impossibility of egalitarian, companionate heterosexual love as well. Thus it is fitting that her only confidant and the one person who stands by her throughout her life, the Jew Marcus Cocoza, is a friend but never a lover. The relationship between Marcus and Pellegrina thus bears clear affinities to the friendship between Ephraim and

Bettine that concludes *Die Günderode*. With her focus on social construction and artifice, Dinesen, however, unlike Arnim, manipulates the most common and destructive anti-semitic stereotype of the "filthy rich" Jew in her repeated references to Marcus as a "fabulously rich Jew" (p. 287), such that for a good portion of the narrative, the reader is taken in by the narrator Lincoln Forsner's assumption of Marcus's uncanny and demonic power over his beautiful friend as "an evil spirit in her life" (p. 287).[4] The reversal of this assumption near the conclusion of the tale, then, with the revelation of Marcus as an embodiment of wisdom, selflessness, and devotion, works powerfully indeed to highlight the blind egotism and self-absorption of Pellegrina's three lovers. This movement from demonization to idealization replicates, in some sense, the tensions present in Arnim's representation of Jews and, as with Arnim, asks the reader to evaluate the relationship between stereotype and ideal.

Marcus's character is, however, then given a remarkable singularity in his sensitive and compelling narrative of Pellegrina's life as the most celebrated and gifted opera singer, the greatest soprano in all of Europe. Before the tragic loss of her voice, her position exactly parallels that of Corinne at the beginning of Staël's novel; she is an internationally renowned artist and salonnière who has led a public life of cultural and sexual freedoms. Yet whereas Corinne is held up to restrictive patriarchal norms of feminine behavior and found wanting by Oswald, Marcus leaves no doubt that Pellegrina embodies and longs for ideals that contemporary social realities cannot even begin to approach. As a young woman, she is filled with inordinate idealism and is thus perpetually disappointed in her love affairs, a feeling, Marcus sympathetically imagines, "that many women, in their love affairs, must feel" (p. 337). Pellegrina, then, is not only the archetypal artist, but the archetypal woman as well. Marcus remembers teasingly calling her "Donna Quixotta de la Mancha":

> The phenomena of life were not great enough for her; they were not in proportion with her own heart. ... When she was hurt in her love affairs, it was not her vanity which was wounded. ... But she was badly hurt and disappointed because the world was not a much greater place than it is, and because nothing more colossal, more like the dramas of the stage, took place in it, not even when she herself went into the show with all her might.
>
> (p. 336)

Like Sand's Consuelo, her youthful operatic debut takes place in Venice and her artistic talents come to fruition after her experience of disillusionment with passionate love. Once Pellegrina abandons hope for happiness in romantic love, she achieves "a lightness in such things which was not hers by birth" and her art reaches new heights of "perfection, on the stage, in the part of the young innocent girl in love" (pp. 337–8). Impersonality, detachment, and humor then triumph over melancholy to the benefit of art.

Telling her of his doctrine of love as an "aspect of toxicology," Marcus in fact asserts an understanding of sexual passion as battle, as a struggle for domination that owes much to Schopenhauer, Nietzsche, and Freud. Eros is here inseparable from Thanatos:

> [Your lovers] are like little vipers or scorpions, proud of their bite, and proof against poison proportionate to their own virulence. To most of them love is a mutual distribution of poisons and counterpoisons. . . . But you, Pellegrina, are no venomous snake, but a python . . . you have no poison whatever in you, and if you kill it is by the force of your embrace. This quality upsets your lovers, who are familiar with little vipers, and who have neither the strength to resist you, nor the wisdom to value the sort of death which they might obtain with you.
>
> (p. 337)

In the voice of this wise, worldly, and appealing outsider, Dinesen is attacking one stereotype of "femininity" after the next: that women are weak, that they are petty, that they are fearful, that they are vain. She is also perhaps suggesting, in her use of essentializing animal metaphors, that sexual passion, perhaps everywhere and for all time, is inseparable from power struggles that render harmonious, egalitarian relationship impossible. Her position here, then, is much closer to Shelley's in parts of *Valperga* than to the utopianism of Arnim and Sand, for whom belief in the power of collective Eros is fundamental to their humanitarianism. Dinesen's position also undercuts faith in political action, feminist or otherwise, by rendering problematic any notion of human agency and progress, be it individual or collective. Thus, in the development of her artist heroine, Dinesen traces the trajectory of the female *Künstlerroman* from its nineteenth-century idealism into twentieth-century nihilism. As a student of Nietzsche herself, she anticipates Foucault's reading of Nietzsche's genealogy of human social interaction as constituted by one "single drama, . . . the endlessly repeated play of dominations."[5]

Disappointed in personal love, the prima donna Pellegrina is, however, fully satisfied in her passion for her audience, as she subjects herself to its power. Rather than nursing her wounds or glorifying her suffering as does the archetypal abandoned woman, she relinquishes any hope of happiness in a love affair and devotes herself entirely to her audience. It was not, Marcus recounts, the famous or the wealthy and the powerful she loved to entertain, but the galleries. "Those poor people of the back streets and market places, . . . she loved them beyond everything in the world" (pp. 333–4). In "her passion for those lowest in the world," she is "like [a] holy flame," clearly a Christ figure who perversely and paradoxically asserts the originary, egalitarian spirit of Christianity (p. 334). "She would have died for them," he asserts. "'Oh, must we all be cut to the same pattern' she asked me . . . 'and be sinners worshiping the divinities? Come, let me be what I am, Marcus, and choose to be. Let me be a divinity worshiping the sinners'" (pp. 336–7). Thus the ideal artist created by Dinesen, so often accused of elitism, is an artist of the people, a servant of the masses.

Pellegrina's story, then, mirrors that of Consuelo who brings her experience of aesthetic perfection and transcendence to the peasants and the proletariat. And, like Consuelo, her mother stems from lowly Spanish stock. Yet when Pellegrina loses her voice, as did Consuelo, her life takes a radically different turn from that of the underground political activist and teacher. And her love affair with her audience cannot really be termed an activist effort to transform oppressive social realities, for Dinesen evinces little faith in the artist's *direct* ameliorative social function. Furthermore, after her tragedy, she comes to believe that she has been selfish in her glorification of the prima donna Pellegrina and deluded in her sense of self-importance. Dinesen, in fact, as I have previously suggested, dares to begin her tale where Staël, Shelley, and Sand conclude theirs – after the silencing of the public voices or the deaths of their respective heroines. Thus the narratives at the core of *The Dreamers*, the tales of Pellegrina's love affairs as prostitute with Lincoln Forsner, female revolutionary with Friederich Hohenemser, and saintly widow with the Swedish Baron Guildenstern, take place after the spectacular identity of the prima donna Pellegrina Leoni has dissolved into anonymity, collectivity and perpetual performance. Indeed, Dinesen's heroine declares her former self officially dead and has a marble plate erected in her honor inscribed with the simple words, "By the grace of God" (p. 344). From this moment on, her public mourns her loss and she takes flight into an infinite series of masquerades, vowing to free herself from enslavement to one inevitably stereotypic female identity. From this moment on, as well, we recognize Dinesen's creation of a new character who embodies what Foucault, following Baudelaire, sees as distinguishing marks of modernity as legacy of the Enlightenment: the will to invent and produce the self as well as the ironic heroization of the present that captures *within* the fleeting moment traces of death and eternity.[6]

Pellegrina herself has now been given the chance for rebirth into a new life and a new and even higher art form. Asking Marcus to help her declare the death of Pellegrina Leoni, she explains her new philosophy of life, that she will never again be attached to one self, to one ego, that she will be many selves, many people:

> And if ... I come to think very much of what happens to ... one woman, why I shall go away, at once, and be someone else. ... There are many that I can be. If they are happy or unhappy, or if they are fools or wise people, those women, I shall not think a great deal about that. ... Never again will I have my heart and my whole life bound up with one woman, to suffer so much.
>
> (p. 345)

Crucially, Pellegrina presents her choice of future paths as an intellectual decision, the choice of a *philosophy* of life that she believes is generalizable to all humankind. And, as female philosopher, she advises Marcus to follow her example:

I should like you to be easy, your little heart to be light again. You must, from now, be more than one, many people, as many as you can think of. I feel, Marcus – I am sure – that all people in the world ought to be, each of them, more than one, and they would all, yes, all of them, be more easy at heart. They would have a little fun. Is it not strange that no philosopher has thought of this, and that I should hit upon it?

(pp. 345–6)

Dinesen seems to be suggesting that no philosopher has hit upon this because, up until the twentieth century, philosophers were by definition male. Furthermore, Dinesen makes it clear that the capacity for multiplicity and a concomitant disinterest comes much more easily to her heroine than to her male characters, for the three men who fall in love with Pellegrina in her various incarnations become obsessed with possessing her freedom, trapped as they are in their own limited identities ruled by desire for power and control (Lincoln Forsner), competitive urges (Baron Guildenstern), and fears of nothingness (Friederich Hohenemser). These masculine identities come across as flat and ludicrous variations on the Byronic and melancholy heroes I have traced throughout this study.

As Susan Hardy Aiken has so convincingly shown, Dinesen clearly prefigures contemporary French feminist understandings of female subjectivity articulated by Kristeva, Kofman, Cixous, and Irigaray, as fluid and multiple in ways quite foreign to masculine selfhood.[7] In my opinion, Dinesen's conception of woman's multiplicity and fluidity *also* incorporates a strong emphasis upon performance and social-construction that is lacking in these psychoanalytically based theorists. What is striking and distinctive in Dinesen is her playful and highly self-conscious assertion, nearly half a century before the second wave of feminism brought forth these feminist theorists, of an explicit artistic credo based upon performing the multiplicity of female selfhood. It is the central narrator of *The Dreamers*, Lincoln Forsner, who, in describing Pellegrina's effect upon him to the storyteller Mira Jama, links her presence to aesthetic experience:

To this woman I owe it that I have ever understood, and still remember, the meaning of such words as tears, heart, longing, stars, which you poets make use of. Yes, as to stars in particular, Mira, there was much about her that reminded one of a star. ... Perhaps you too have met in the course of your life women of that sort, who are self-luminous and shine in the dark, who are phosphorescent, like touchwood.

(pp. 282–3)

Pellegrina's life has become a work of art, her presence embodying that unimpeded, incandescent freedom from self and ego that characterizes the mind of the great artist as Virginia Woolf describes it in *A Room of One's Own*.[8] The quality, then, that renders Dinesen's heroine self-luminescent is not stereotypic female beauty, but strength, a strength that arises from abandonment of personal self to the collective forces of nature and fate, a woman's version of Nietzsche's *amor fati*. Lincoln explains,

> If all your life you had been tacking up against the winds and the currents, and suddenly, for once, you were taken on board a ship which went, as we do tonight, with a strong tide and before a following wind, you would undoubtedly be much impressed with the power of that ship. You would be wrong; and yet in a way you would also be right, for the power of the waters and the winds might be said rightly to belong to the ship, since she had managed, alone amongst all vessels, to ally herself with them. . . . In the arms of this woman I felt myself in accord with them all, lifted and borne on by life itself. This, to my mind then, was due to her great strength. And still, at that time I did not know at all to what extent she had allied herself with all the currents and winds of life.
>
> (pp. 283–4)

Clearly Lincoln distinguishes Pellegrina's female philosophy of life, her art of living, from the patriarchal, utilitarian, and instrumental dictates of his father who thought it was "his duty ... to turn the chaotic world into a universe of order, and to see that all things were made useful – which, to him, meant making them useful to him himself" (p. 281). As Lincoln explains, his father had taught him to battle and resist nature instead of welcoming it: "Thus had I, all my life, under my father's ægis, been taught to tack up against all the winds and currents of life" (p. 283). In choosing the prostitute Olalla/prima donna Pellegrina as his lover and accepting her philosophy of life, then, Lincoln becomes the antithesis of Corinne's Oswald as he courts and accepts the utter rejection contained in his father's final letter to him almost gladly. Lincoln's father responds:

> You have refused to make, by your example, virtue attractive and the reward of good conduct obvious. [You have] my blessing in the completion of a career which may make filial disobedience, weakness, and vice a usefully repugnant and deterring example to your generation of our family.
>
> (p. 291)

Dinesen could not make any clearer her desire to thumb her nose at the patriarchal moral authority Corinne and her author ultimately found so hard to resist.

Lincoln's efforts to find and possess Olalla, in the hopes of claiming her philosophy of life for himself, lead him as well as her two other former lovers to the encounter in the Alpine Hotel Andermatt that has such fatal consequences for their object of prey. Their collective obsession with possessing her suggests an ironic reversal of Freud's infamous penis envy, in which Dinesen's male characters all seek to appropriate for themselves female fluidity, freedom from fixed identity, and liberation from personal ego or what Woolf terms "the straight dark bar shaped like the letter 'I'" (p. 103). Their tales of Madame Lola, the revolutionary, and Rosalba, the saint-like widow of the monarchist general, both marked by a snake-like scar from ear to collarbone, "the brand of the witch" (p. 312), alert Lincoln to the fact that all three men are, in fact, seeking the same mysterious woman, a sibylline figure who carries on the tradition, so troubling to male consciousness, of Staël's Circean Corinne, Shelley's prophetess Beatrice and her witch Mandragola. That the opera house fire that silenced Pellegrina's voice and branded her as a witch is, as Sara Stambaugh argues, a sign of

> male revenge against an autonomous woman who is sexually free is implicit in the imagery of rape that Marcus Cocoza uses to describe it. Searching for an image adequate to express her experience, Marcus thinks of a royal bride traveling to meet her bridegroom but raped on the way. The image of rape continues as Cocoza refers to Pellegrina as "the ravished royal virgin."[9]

Pellegrina's virginity is clearly sacerdotal and symbolic rather than literal. Compounding this emphasis upon Pellegrina's victimization by male fear and jealousy is Marcus's suggestion that he write a ballet about her fate entitled *Philomela*, after the mythical princess whose tongue is cut out by her rapist in order to prevent her telling of her tale.

In the end, then, the fate of Dinesen's Pellegrina suggests that the masculinist strictures that had destroyed her predecessor Corinne still haunt the twentieth-century woman writer, though her manner of depicting and challenging them has moved from melodrama and tragedy to irony and comedy. It is thus particularly fitting that Pellegrina is hunted to her death in the Alps, quintessential locus of Romantic sublimity and juncture between north and south, Romantic and Classic, spirit and senses, ideal and real, oppositions that Staël herself had formulated as the key tensions in European literature, binaries that were temporarily transcended in Corinne's art and person, but that have ever since worked so fiercely against the interests of women's creativity and dignity. Dinesen's aesthetic treatise both exploits to the fullest and mocks this utterly outworn schema of the division between, as she puts it, "the North, where things were cold and dead," and "the blue and voluptuous South" (p. 280), the worlds of the British Lincoln Forsner and the Italian Pellegrina.

And, finally, Dinesen's Pellegrina, despite the narrator's repeated references to her as a bird – nightingale, crane, owl, albatross, black martin, and swan – is unable to sustain her sublime flights of imagination, her challenge to cultural assumptions of woman's earthbound nature, and is brought back to earth by Lincoln's demand to know who she is. She ends her life in a movement, both sublime and grotesque, of failed flight:

> But the next moment she did what I had always feared that she might do: she spread out her wings and flew away. Below the round white moon she made one great movement, throwing herself away from us all, and the wind caught her and spread out her clothes. . . . For one second she seemed to lift

herself up with the wind, then, running straight across the road, with all her might she threw herself from the earth clear into the abyss, and disappeared from our sight.

(p. 327)

In the demise of Pellegrina Leoni, then, Dinesen seems to move backwards from the quiet, obscure but powerful triumph of Sand's Consuelo at the conclusion of her story toward the tragic victimization of the early nineteenth-century artist heroines, Corinne, Beatrice, Euthanasia, and Karoline. Yet *The Dreamers* does not conclude on this dark note. Rather, in the novella's frame-tale, both Lincoln and the archetypal storyteller Mira Jama archly assert that Pellegrina is not dead after all, but has instead decided to inhabit the African landscape as a "pretty little jackal." As Lincoln confesses:

I have imagined that so vividly that on a moonlight night I have believed that I heard her voice amongst the hills. And I have seen her, then, running about, playing with her own small graceful shadow, having a little ease of heart, a little fun.

"Ah, la, la," said Mira, ... "I have heard that little jackal too. ... She barks: 'I am not one little jackal, not one; I am many little jackals.'"

(pp. 353–4)

The female artist lives on beyond the death of her individual being, in Dinesen's modernist tale, then, as her nineteenth-century predecessors do, though that life is sustained by *natural* rather than *historical* process. The progressive historical telos of Staël, Shelley, Arnim, and Sand is displaced by images of eternal return akin to those evoked in the voices of the animal companions of Nietzsche's Convalescent in *Thus Spoke Zarathustra*.[10] Yet if Nietzsche's animals proclaim the eternal return of the exact, selfsame life of the overman or superman who begins again his proclamations, Dinesen's jackal celebrates the return of playful multiplicity and change. Dinesen, who as a young woman posed as Byron and who honored him as the central character in one of her most moving last tales, "Second Meeting," ultimately challenged and parodied Byron's legacy and that of his descendant Nietzsche, in making it her own. Furthermore, her story-teller Mira Jama embraces a trickster god known for humor rather than Nietzschean cruelty and infliction of suffering: "I have been trying for a long time to understand God. Now I have made friends with him. To love him truly you must love change, and you must love a joke, these being the true inclinations of his own heart" (p. 355). Fittingly, Mira Jama's anti-humanism is a sly reversal of Christ's parable of turning water into wine: "[W]hat is man, when you come to think upon him, but a minutely set, ingenious machine for turning, with infinite artfulness, the red wine of Shiraz into urine?" (p. 275).

And, in the end, the boundaries between Mira, Lincoln, and Pellegrina herself seem to vanish as Mira claims her tale as his own, when he says to Lincoln: "I know all your tale. ... I believe that I made it myself" (p. 354). And if Pellegrina fails to sustain her transcendent artistry, Mira (her mirror image) in fact succeeds. Having been, as a youth, symbolically castrated when his ears and nose were cut off, Mira now stands as a grotesque emblem of impersonal humanity beyond sex and gender, personal ambition, and desire. "I have become too familiar with life; it can no longer delude me into believing that one thing is much worse than the other. The day and the dark, an enemy and a friend – I know them to be about the same" (p. 274). This transcendence of desire allows him the perspective on himself necessary to the creation of great, comic art, or what Dinesen, through her alter ego Mira, terms the art of dreaming: "The air in my dreams ... is always very high, and I generally see myself as a very small figure in a great landscape" (pp. 276–7). Mira's philosophy of dreaming becomes a kind of grotesque, modernist rendering of Staël's previously discussed conception of meditative self-possession, the acceptance of fate instead of railing against it and allowing oneself, as she puts it, "to drift at the will of the wind." Mira's perspective indeed allows him to give himself up to "the winds of fate," and to dream, as "the world creates itself around [him] without any effort on [his] part" (p. 276). As he perversely mouths the Christian piety that "all things work together for good to them that love God" (p. 355), he also acknowledges his acceptance of the will of a trickster God who, above all else, loves a joke.

Thus the teleology of divine providence and resultant human progress that underlies the idealism of the nineteenth-century novels previously examined in this study is replaced in Dinesen's *The Dreamers* by the celebration of natural, material realities and the mischievous comic fate that rules them. Although this relinquishing of enlightenment ideology does perhaps necessitate the abandonment of any faith in the efficacy of direct political statement or activism on the part of the artist, Dinesen's tales do, nevertheless, as should by now be obvious, contain powerful elements of social criticism. They are anything but reassuring representations of the status quo. Indeed Dinesen's work might well be termed oppositional, as the term is so brilliantly defined in Ross Chambers's *The Writing of Melancholy: Modes of Opposition in Early French Modernism*. Like the texts that are the focus of Chambers's study, Dinesen's work is characterized by duplicity in the sense that it, like its heroine, cannot be pinned down; its subversiveness results from "a certain way of confusing the categories so as to be classifiable as both 'for' and 'against,' and hence neither 'for' nor 'against.'"[11] For Chambers, oppositional modernism comes into being in France through the disillusionment with the possibilities of collective political action experienced in the wake of the failures of the revolutions of 1830 and 1848 by writers such as Nerval, Baudelaire, and Flaubert and the repressed, inner-directed anger that was the result. According to Chambers, "this anger could be expressed only in a sublimated (and hence repressed) form by becoming a writing of melancholy. For melancholia is anger vaporized. ... [And] melancholic writing is not necessarily writing that thematizes sadness; rather it espouses the decentering and vaporization of being that are the principal features of melancholia" (p. 33). This fragmented, unstable self is, for Chambers, the key to oppositional textuality: "Between these extremes of resistance and retreat, the decentered self of the melancholic subject – that vaporized, faltering, lacking subject of a new textuality – occupies a precarious middle ground of semi-resistance and semi-retreat, a ground neither of resistance nor of retreat, which is that of the oppositional or the 'depolitified'" (p. 59). Chambers might well be describing here the subject of Dinesen's seemingly apolitical textuality – Pellegrina's mobile, plural, fluid self – as figured in *The Dreamers*, such that after all we seem to have moved through the nineteenth century only to return once more to our beginnings in Romantic melancholy.

Yet if *The Dreamers* is grounded in anger – the anger of both the author and her heroine at the harshness of fate and the stupidity of men – that anger becomes laughter, not melancholia or the bitterness of Baudelaire, the cynicism of Flaubert, in Dinesen's world, when it is sublimated or vaporized. As Karen Blixen is true to her chosen pen name "Isak," meaning "the one who laughs," we once again witness the woman writer's resistance to the inertia and passivity of Romantic melancholy and disenchantment. The "scream, the lion's roar" that Dinesen herself heard in *The Dreamers*, when she spoke of it many years later, and that is echoed in the heroine's death rattle, that "strange sound, like the distant roar of a great animal" (p. 352), that is recorded by Lincoln Forsner, suggests the intensity of that anger. One can only imagine Karen Blixen's fury at her husband for his utter ineptitude as a coffee farmer that ruined her financially and for having infected her with syphilis in the first year of their marriage, a disease that would render her unable to bear children and cripple her in later life. But just as Blixen/Dinesen archly claimed that she had made a pact with the Devil and accepted syphilis gladly with the understanding that the rest of her life would be transformed into art, so her heroine's loss of voice compels her to an even greater performance than the operatic stage afforded. This comic performance, this art of dreaming, or, as Mira Jama terms it, "the well-mannered people's way of committing suicide" (p. 277), vaporizes or disperses the individual ego into a shifting plurality of selves such that the concept of self-interest loses all meaning. Thus, Lincoln admits, his tale will indeed "prove useful" (p. 279) after all; it will demonstrate to the young Said, travelling with and listening to "the dreamers" and bent upon the destruction of his enemies, the futility of vengeance. As Mira notes, [Said] says, "I shall show no mercy, and I ask for none. But that is where Said is mistaken. He will be showing mercy before he has done with all of us" (pp. 278–9).

The Dreamers concludes with the blending of identities of Pellegrina Leoni, Lincoln Forsner, Mira Jama, and the pretty little philosophical jackals who assert Dinesen's oppositional message of female freedom. At the end of *The Dreamers*, Lincoln imagines that if Pellegrina had lived and traveled to Africa, she would have been honored by the Kenyan tribes as "a great witch" (p. 353). This figure of the witch, both anarchic and pantheist, mythic and profoundly social, perhaps best encompasses the contradictions of Dinesen's feminism and her belief in the power of oppositional spirituality. In her later *Daguerreotypes* (1951), Dinesen explains her ironic understanding of the social and sexual significance of the witch with reference to the contemporary women's movement:

But there was a woman who, long before the words "emancipation of women" came into use, existed independently of a man and had her own center of gravity. She was the witch. . . . One may suppose that for most men the explanation is, that a woman who can exist without a man certainly also can exist without God, or that a woman who does not want to be possessed by a man necessarily must be possessed by the devil.[12]

(p. 36)

It is precisely in the witch's connection to a uniquely female tradition of spirituality that Dinesen sees her power to effect social change. And when she quotes a worldly-wise friend, whom she terms "my old friend and teacher in the art of witchcraft," Dinesen, who can never resist a sly joke, is also deeply serious:

Women's organizations could achieve far more, indeed would make shortcuts directly to their goals if, instead of forming committees, making speeches, and writing articles – all tame and simple imitations of men – they would let it be known the country over that they would meet on the heath and on the commons under a waning moon.

(p. 36)

We return here, then, to the witch as a figure for women's desire for power that Mary Shelley saw so clearly embodied in her bitterly mythic and self-destructive Mandragola. With Dinesen and her characters, this bitter self-destructiveness becomes a sly oppositionality rooted in a conviction of the "difference" – social, biological, and historical – of women's experience.

In conclusion, then, *The Dreamers* renders ridiculous the self-important posturing and melancholy brooding of the stereotypical Romantic artist seen from the perspective of a clear-sighted feminist irreverence. Similarly, Dinesen's *The Poet* with its many references, both explicit and implicit, to Goethe, can be read as a devastating satire of his self-importance and arrogance and, as Hannah Arendt suggests, as "a story about the vices of *Bildung*."[13] One registers in the work of Dinesen, then, once again, the remarkable coherence of the constellation of Romantic themes, topoi, and aesthetic, moral, and philosophical preoccupations traced in this study from Staël even into the twentieth century. To recognize the power of the tradition of female *Bildungsromane* identified here well beyond what we now term the Romantic period, one need only think of the artist heroine in Lou-Andreas Salomé's *Eine Ausschweifung* (1898) who rejects Romantic love and marriage in favor of life as an artist because of the historical and collective legacy of female masochism that she sees as essential to heterosexual love. Moving outside of Europe, Thea Kronborg, the operatic heroine of Willa Cather's magnificently flawed masterpiece, *The Song of the Lark* (1915), could never, I think, have been conceived without *Corinne* and *Consuelo*. We see, once again, in Cather's novel, the sad incapacity of the institution of marriage to nurture or suit her artist's talents and dreams. And the depiction of Thea's affinities for the music of the restless Spanish Johnny and the Mexican Americans of her community owes

much to Sand's portrait of Consuelo's Spanish "gypsy" roots. Similarly, Thea's
relations to her music teachers, the troubled, romantic Professor Wunsch and the
exacting Hungarian Harsani, are undoubtedly indebted to Sand's vivid portrait
of Niccola Porpora. We also recognize the emphasis upon the collective past,
both historical and mythic, so prominent in the tradition I have been tracing, as
the source of the art of Cather's heroine. I conclude with Thea's meditation in
response to the transcendent beauty and mystery of the ancient Native American
art that she discovers in the caves of the cliff-dwellers in the American southwest,
scenery reminiscent of the sibylline caves of the Preface to *The Last Man* and that
Ellen Moers has termed "the most thoroughly elaborated female landscape in
literature" (p. 252). Thus Thea's words also connect her with the artists featured
in this study as her more immediate ancestors:

> A dream had been dreamed there long ago, in the night of ages, and the
> wind had whispered some promise to the sadness of the savage. In their own
> way, those people had felt the beginnings of what was to come. These
> potsherds were like fetters that bound one to a long chain of human
> endeavor.[14]

For Cather, women's art becomes an ideal union of transcendent, collective life,
and the individual female body:

> The stream and the broken pottery: what was any art but an effort to make a
> sheath, a mould in which to imprison for a moment the shining, elusive
> element which is life itself, – life hurrying past us and running away, too
> strong to stop, too sweet to lose? The Indian women had held it in their jars.
> ... In singing, one made a vessel of one's throat and nostrils and held it on
> one's breath, caught the stream in a scale of natural intervals.

> (pp. 254–5)

Notes

Introduction

1 Margaret Fuller, *Woman in the Nineteenth Century*, intro. Bernard Rosenthal (New York: Norton, 1971), p. 119. Fuller compares Sand with Staël and with Arnim only to find all lacking in "self-rule" and strength of heart. See Bell Gale Chevigny, *The Woman and the Myth: Margaret Fuller's Life and Writings* (New York: The Feminist Press, 1976), pp. 57–8.

2 Naomi Schor, *George Sand and Idealism* (New York: Columbia University Press, 1993), p. 54.

3 For gender complementary models of Romanticism, see Margaret Homans, *Women Writers and Poetic Identity: Dorothy Wordsworth, Emily Brontë, and Emily Dickinson* (Princeton: Princeton University Press, 1980); Stuart Curran, "The I Altered," *Romanticism and Feminism*, ed. Anne K. Mellor (Bloomington: Indiana University Press, 1988), pp. 185–207; Marlon Ross, *The Contours of Masculine Desire: Romanticism and the Rise of Women's Poetry* (Oxford: Oxford University Press, 1989); Meena Alexander, *Women in Romanticism* (London: Macmillan, 1989); and Anne Mellor, *Romanticism and Gender* (New York: Routledge, 1993). My position is closer to that of Julie Ellison who in *Delicate Subjects: Romanticism, Gender and the Ethics of Understanding* (Ithaca: Cornell University Press, 1990) writes: "But what is the place of romanticism in a theory of gender? Feminist theory has exhibited sustained dislike for the romantic. Nonetheless, feminism and romanticism share an anxiety about aggression and violence; a critique of authority; a commitment to the cognitive validity of feeling and atmosphere; an identification with the victim; an intrigue with the construction and deconstruction of subjectivity. Both psychoanalysis and Marxism, the most prestigious influences within feminist theory, have a romantic prehistory that is powerfully revised but not negated by feminist thinkers. Given this large and endlessly disputable common ground, can one say that feminism is not romantic? Or that a feminist ethics is not descended from the gendered figurations of romantic criticism?" (pp. 10–11).

4 Anne K. Mellor, *Mothers of the Nation: Women's Political Writing in England, 1780–1830* (Bloomington: Indiana University Press, 2000), pp. 85–102.

5 Doris Kadish's *Politicizing Gender: Narrative Strategies in the Aftermath of the French Revolution* (New Brunswick: Rutgers University Press, 1991) does bring together, in exemplary fashion, the novels of Staël, Shelley, and Charlotte Brontë. Another more recent exception is Denise Dupont's "Masculinity, Femininity, Solidarity: Emilia Pardo Bazán's Construction of Madame de Staël and George Sand," *Comparative Literature Studies*, XL (2003), pp. 372–94.

6 Ellen Moers's belittling of *Corinne* in *Literary Women: The Great Writers* (New York: Doubleday, 1976), pp. 263–319, exemplifies the limitations of contemporary critical reaction to Staël's novels. For a wonderful response to Moers, written on the occasion of *Signs'* 20 years' commemoration of *Literary Women*, see Madelyn Gutwirth, "Taking

Corinne Seriously: A Comment on Ellen Moers's *Literary Women*," *Signs: Journal of Women in Culture and Society*, XXV (2000), pp. 895–9.

7   Franco Moretti, *The Way of the World: The Bildungsroman in European Culture* (London: Verso, 1987), p. 9.

8   Germaine de Staël, *Corinne, or Italy*, trans. and ed. Avriel Goldberger (New Brunswick: Rutgers University Press, 1987), p. 29. All subsequent page references to *Corinne* in English are to this edition and will appear in the text.

9   Elizabeth Abel, Marianne Hirsch, and Elizabeth Langland, eds. *The Voyage In: Fictions of Female Development* (Hanover: University Press of New England, 1983) (hereafter Abel, Hirsch, and Langland); Susan Fraiman, *Unbecoming Women: British Women Writers and the Novel of Development* (New York: Columbia University Press, 1993), and Lorna Ellis, *Appearing to Diminish: Female Development and the British Bildungsroman: 1750–1850* (Lewisburg: Bucknell University Press, 1999). For work on the female *Bildungsroman*, see Laura Sue Fuderer, *The Female Bildungsroman in English: An Annotated Bibliography of Criticism* (New York: MLA, 1990).

10 See Sharon Spencer, "'Femininity' and the Woman Writer: Doris Lessing's *The Golden Notebook* and the *Diary of Anaïs Nin*," *Women's Studies*, Vol. 1, No. 3 (1973), p. 247 and Patricia Meyer Spacks, *The Female Imagination* (New York: Knopf, 1975), pp. 199–200. These statements are puzzling, in any case, given such superb, well-known English and American novels as Virginia Woolf's *To the Lighthouse* and *Orlando* and Willa Cather's *The Song of the Lark*. For a comparatist study of the *Künstlerroman* and *Künstlernovelle* that includes German and American writers and is written from a psychoanalytic perspective, see Ursula R. Mahlendorf, *The Wellsprings of Literary Creation: An Analysis of Male and Female "Artist Stories" from the German Romantics to American Writers of the Present* (Columbia: Camden House, 1985).

11 Moers's *Literary Women* does, of course, provide a generously comparatist approach to women's writing. I am indebted to her chapter "Performing Heroinism: The Myth of Corinne," pp. 263–319, for an early outline of the tradition I am studying here.

12 Evy Varsamopoulou, *The Poetics of the Künstlerinroman and the Aesthetics of the Sublime* (Aldershot: Ashgate, 2002), pp. 248–9.

13 Abel, Hirsch, and Langland 1983, p. 7. Among these earlier studies are Susanne Howe's *Wilhelm Meister and His English Kinsmen: Apprentices to Life* (New York: Columbia University Press, 1930) and Jerome Hamilton Buckley, *Season of Youth: The Bildungsroman from Dickens to Golding* (Cambridge: Harvard University Press, 1974). For an excellent history of the genre, see Fraiman 1993, pp. 3–13.

14 See Linda Huf, *The Portrait of the Artist as a Young Woman: The Writer as Heroine in American Literature* (New York: Frederick Ungar, 1983), pp. 10–11.

15 For a rich and suggestive treatment of the German tradition of the *Künstlerroman*, see Ernst Bloch, "A Philosophical View of the Novel of the Artist," *The Utopian Function of Art and Literature*, trans. Jack Zipes and Frank Mecklenburg (Cambridge: MIT Press, 1988), pp. 265–77. Bloch asserts that the focus on artistic process, creation, and the not yet realized in the artist novel gives it an anticipatory, utopian function. This applies to the novels I am discussing even more than to the novels and novellas of Hoffmann and Mann, with their valorization, albeit ironic, of sickness and melancholy.

16 Rita Felski, *Beyond Feminist Aesthetics: Feminist Literature and Social Change* (Cambridge: Harvard University Press, 1989), p. 122.

17 For discussion of the influence of *Corinne* on nineteenth-century women poets in particular, see Moers's *Literary Women*, as well as Angela Leighton, *Victorian Women Poets: Writing Against the Heart* (Hemel Hempstead: Harvester/Wheatsheaf, 1992), Margaret Linley, "Sappho's Conversions in Felicia Hemans, Letitia Landon, and Christina Rossetti," *Prism(s)*, IV (1996), pp. 15–42, and Margaret Reynolds, "'I lived for art, I lived for love': The Woman Poet Sings Sappho's Last Song," *Victorian Women Poets: A Critical Reader*, ed. Angela Leighton (Oxford: Blackwell, 1996), pp. 277–306.

18 See Patrick Henri Vincent, *Elegiac Muses: Corinne and the Engendering of the Romantic Poetess, 1820–1840* (Hanover: University Press of New England, 2004) for an illuminating treatment of this international response to *Corinne*. For Staël and nineteenth-century German women novelists, see Judith Martin, "Between Exaltation and Melancholy: Madame de Staël's *Corinne* and the Female Artist Novel in Early Nineteenth-Century Germany," *JAISA*, II (2000), pp. 29–50 and "Nineteenth-Century German Women's Reception of Madame de Staël," *Women in German Yearbook*, XVIII (2002), pp. 133–57.

19 For an excellent discussion of British women's historiography in the late eighteenth-century, see Devoney Looser, *British Women Writers and the Writing of History, 1670–1820* (Baltimore: Johns Hopkins, 2000), pp. 1–27. Looser writes, "As historiography gained scientific credentials and as fiction gained readers and respect, gendered associations adhered to each genre in a more subtle way. History was never completely 'male' in its production and content, just as novels were not wholly 'female,' but the effect of nineteenth-century historical scientificity – though it did not literally force women out of historiography – appears to have limited how far audiences were prepared to see women's historical writings as authoritative or successful. The conditions for women's historiography that came before that moment remain unclear and largely unexplored" (p. 9).

20 Michel de Certeau, *The Writing of History*, trans. Tom Conley (New York: Columbia University Press, 1988), p. 35. De Certeau, in a sense, traces his own lineage to such contemporaries of Sand and Arnim as Michelet and is thus a particularly appropriate voice for theorizing these nineteenth-century European perspectives.

21 William Godwin, "On History and Romance," *Things as They are, or The Adventures of Caleb Williams*, ed. Maurice Hindle (London: Penguin, 1987), p. 367.

22 British examples include Charlotte Smith's *Desmond* (1792), Mary Robinson's *The Natural Daughter* (1799), and Helen Craik's *Adelaide de Narbonne, with Memoirs of Charlotte de Cordet* [sic] (1800). In Germany, see Therese Huber's *Die Familie Seldorf: Eine Erzählung der französischen Revolution* (1796) and Caroline de Fouqué's later *Magie der Natur: Eine Revolutions-Geschichte* (1812).

23 For a fuller treatment of this question of historiography, see my "Children of Liberty: Idealist Historiography in Staël, Shelley and Sand," *PMLA*, CXVIII (May 2003), pp. 502–20. Paragraphs of this essay are reprinted by permission of the copyright owner, The Modern Language Association of America.

24 Jon Mee, *Romanticism, Enthusiasm, and Regulation* (Oxford: Oxford University Press, 2003), pp. 1–19.

25 See *Foreign Quarterly Review*, XXVII, 1841, pp. 205–6 and XXIX, 1845, pp. 304–6.

26 We witness here the influence of Shaftesbury via Diderot and Rousseau. For Shaftesbury's writings on enthusiasm, see Mee, pp. 37–49.

27 All subsequent references to Staël's non-fiction works will appear in the text by page number and, with the exception of quotes from *Reflections on Suicide*, are from *An Extraordinary Woman: Selected Writings of Germaine de Staël*, trans., intro., and ed. Vivian Folkenflik (New York: Columbia University Press, 1987).

28 Greg Kucich, "Mary Shelley's *Lives* and the Reengendering of History," *Mary Shelley in her Times*, eds Betty T. Bennett and Stuart Curran (Baltimore: Johns Hopkins University Press, 2000), pp. 209–10.

29 George Sand, *Jean Ziska*, *Oeuvres complètes*, XIX (Genève: Slatkine, 1980), p. 15. All subsequent references are my translations of this edition and will appear in the text.

30 In his Introduction to Staël's *De la littérature considérée dans ses rapports avec les institutions sociales* (Geneva: Librairie Droz, 1959), p. lxi, Paul Van Tieghem quotes Sainte-Beuve's description of *De la littérature* as "le prospectus d'un romantisme futur."

31 Hans Robert Jauß, *Literaturgeschichte als Provokation* (Frankfurt: Suhrkamp, 1970), pp. 67–106.

32 The question of influence and priority here is a tricky one because Staël could not yet read German when she wrote *On Literature*. As John Isbell suggests in *The Birth of*

European Romanticism (Cambridge: Cambridge University Press, 1994), it is likely that Staël's friend Wilhelm von Humboldt introduced her to ideas from *Naïve and Sentimental Poetry* during conversations between September 1798 and the publication of *On Literature* in 1800. Isbell nevertheless ultimately concludes that "[i]t seems certain that the broad framework of Staël's dialectic was in place before any encounter with the Germans" (p. 154) and that "Staël spontaneously coined her own Romantic system in *De la littérature*" (p. 156).

33 Coleridge nevertheless paraphrases Schiller and Staël quite closely in his delineation of the opposition ancient Greek/modern: "The Greeks idolized the finite, and therefore were the masters of all grace, elegance, proportion, fancy, dignity, majesty – of whatever, in short, is capable of being definitely conceived by defined forms or thoughts. The moderns revere the infinite, and affect the indefinite as a vehicle of the infinite; hence their passions, their obscure hopes and fears, their wanderings through the unknown, their grander moral feelings, their more august conception of man as man, their future rather than their past – in a word, their sublimity." Samuel Taylor Coleridge, *Literary Remains*, Vol. II, ed. Henry Nelson Coleridge (London: W. Pickering, 1836–9; rpt. New York: AMS, 1967), p. 23.

34 David Simpson, *Romanticism, Nationalism, and the Revolt Against Theory* (Chicago: University of Chicago Press, 1993). My effort to define Romanticism as an international movement whose *own* members saw in it a certain coherence also flies in the face of current trends in scholarship on British Romanticism to see only Romanticism(s), as any monolithic picture of the era's poetic production is brought into question by particularity of focus on women writers, radical and working-class authors, or writers of satire and the Gothic, for example. This contradiction fades, however, if one remembers that I am speaking of an emerging *canonical* Romanticism that the novelists I study here positioned themselves both *in* and *against*. The definition I am tracing bears resemblance to that of M.H. Abrams in *Natural Supernaturalism*, with this important difference: he accepted this definition as valid today, whereas my attribution of it to the Romantics themselves is more historically specific and open to current critical questioning.

35 Friedrich Schiller, *Naïve and Sentimental Poetry and On the Sublime*, trans. and intro. Julias Elias (New York: Ungar, 1966), p. 13, p. 150. All subsequent references will be to this edition and will appear in the text.

36 Charles Baudelaire, *L'art romantique*, ed. Lloyd James Austin (Paris: Garnier-Flammarion, 1968), p. 21. The title of this posthumously published collection of Baudelaire's criticism was chosen by his friends Théodore de Banville and Charles Asselineau.

37 See Claire Gaspard, "Madame de Staël et les Historiens de la Révolution," *Cahiers Staëliens*, LI (2000), pp. 7–19. Gaspard asserts that nineteenth-century French historians were not prepared to take a woman seriously as a political/historical writer. She also emphasizes that these historians of the Revolution – Thiers, Quinet, Michelet, Louis Blanc – had working-class, egalitarian leanings that conflicted with Staël's assumption of elite privilege and her economic liberalism. She concludes that Staël's current increased visibility reflects the fact that historians are only now really able to comprehend her thought (p. 18). For another recent work that highlights Staël's gifts as a historian, see Laure Lévêque, *Corinne, ou l'Italie de Madame de Staël: Poétique et Politique* (Paris: Editions du Temps, 1999).

38 Jean-François Lyotard, "The Sign of History," *The Differend: Phrases in Dispute* (Minneapolis: University of Minnesota Press, 1988), pp. 151–81.

39 Mary Shelley, *The Last Man*, ed. Anne McWhir (Peterborough: Broadview, 1996), p. 90.

1 "The vast tableau of destinies"

1 Margaret Fuller, *Memoirs*, I, in *The Woman and the Myth: Margaret Fuller's Life and Writings*, ed. Bell Gale Chevigny (Old Westbury: The Feminist Press, 1976), p. 58. Fuller is actually speaking of George Sand here and comparing her with Corinne.

2 Margaret Fuller, *Woman in the Nineteenth Century*, intro. Bernard Rosenthal (New York: W.W. Norton, 1971), p. 94.

3 Mary Shelley, *Germaine de Staël, 1766–1817*, in *Lives of the Most Eminent Literary and Scientific Men of France*, II, *Cabinet Cyclopedia*, ed. Rev. Dionysius Lardner (London: Longman, 1839), p. 331.

4 For a summary of the crudely biographical approach that has dominated criticism of Staël's work until recently see Noreen J. Swallow, "The Weapon of Personality: A Review of Sexist Criticism of Mme de Staël, 1785–1975," *Atlantis*, VIII (Fall 1982), pp. 78–82.

5 Madelyn Gutwirth, *Germaine de Staël, Novelist: The Emergence of the Artist as Woman* (Urbana: University of Illinois Press, 1978), p. 295.

6 See, for example, English Showalter's "Corinne as an Autonomous Heroine," *Germaine de Staël: Crossing the Borders*, ed. Madelyn Gutwirth, Avriel Goldberger, and Karyna Szmurlo (New Brunswick: Rutgers University Press, 1991), p. 188, hereafter Gutwirth, Goldberger, and Szmurlo.

7 Nancy K. Miller, "Performances of the Gaze: Staël's *Corinne, or Italy*," *Subject to Change: Reading Feminist Writing* (New York: Columbia University Press, 1988), p. 182, hereafter Miller.

8 All subsequent references to Staël's non-fiction works will appear in the text by page number and, with the exception of quotes from *Reflections on Suicide*, are from *An Extraordinary Woman: Selected Writings of Germaine de Staël*, trans., intro., and ed. Vivian Folkenflik (New York: Columbia University Press, 1987).

9 For enthusiasm and 1790s radicalism, see Mee, pp. 82–128. See p. 32 for British attempts to define the term in opposition to fanaticism.

10 Simone Balayé notes the importance of unresolved pairs of opposing or complementary concepts such as decadence and perfectibility, regret and hope, melancholy and audacity in Staël's work. See "À Propos du 'Préromantisme': Continuité ou rupture chez Mme de Staël," *Le Préromantisme: hypothèque ou hypothèse?*, ed. Paul Viallaneix (Paris: Klincksieck, 1975), p. 164. Subsequent references to this essay appear in the text.

11 Bonnie G. Smith is correct in asserting that Staël was "a genius at doing history," and that, in *Corinne*, she depicted "a historical sensibility constructed around a woman's genius" and, in so doing, raises the question of female historical agency. Bonnie G. Smith, "History and Genius: The Narcotic, Erotic, and Baroque Life of Germaine de Staël," *French Historical Studies*, XIX (Autumn 1996), pp. 1059–60.

12 Shelley writes in *Germaine de Staël*, "her *Germany*, perhaps, deserves the highest rank, from its research, and the great beauty of its concluding chapters" (p. 343).

13 See Balayé, p. 167.

14 For an excellent discussion of Staël's thought as embodying the continuity between Enlightenment and Romantic world views see Roland Mortier's "Madame de Staël et l'héritage des 'Lumières'," *Madame de Staël et l'Europe* (Paris: Klincksieck, 1970), pp. 129–44.

15 Madame de Staël, *Reflections on Suicide*, trans. from the French (London: Longman, Hurst, Orme, and Brown, 1813), pp. 32–3. All subsequent page references to *Reflections on Suicide* are to this edition and will appear in the text by page number.

16 For insightful analyses of the role of the narrator in *Corinne*, see Miller, pp. 196–7 and Carla Peterson, *The Determined Reader: Gender and Culture in the Novel from Napoleon to Victoria* (New Brunswick: Rutgers University Press, 1986), pp. 60–1.

17 Virginia Woolf notes the deep fear of publicity that haunts nineteenth-century women writers. "Currer Bell, George Eliot, George Sand, all the victims of inner strife as their writings prove, sought ineffectively to veil themselves by using the name of a man." *A Room of One's Own* (London: Harcourt, Brace, Jovanovich, 1929), p. 52.

18 Elaine Showalter, *The New Feminist Criticism: Essays on Women, Literature, and Theory* (New York: Pantheon, 1985), pp. 243–70.

19 Teresa de Lauretis, *Technologies of Gender: Essays on Theory, Film, and Fiction* (Bloomington: Indiana University Press, 1987), p. 25.
20 Jean Starobinski, "Suicide et mélancolie chez Madame de Staël" in *Madame de Staël et l'Europe*, p. 251; my translation.
21 Margaret R. Higonnet, "Suicide as Self-Construction," Gutwirth, Goldberger, and Szmurlo, p. 73.
22 Lawrence Lipking, *Abandoned Women and Poetic Tradition* (Chicago: University of Chicago Press, 1988), pp. 209–44.
23 Deborah Heller, "Tragedy, Sisterhood, and Revenge in *Corinne*," *PLL*, XXVI (Spring 1990), p. 213.
24 Germaine de Staël, *Corinne, or Italy*, trans. and ed. Avriel Goldberger (New Brunswick: Rutgers University Press, 1987), p. 125. All subsequent page references to *Corinne* in English are to this edition and will appear in the text. All subsequent page references to *Corinne* in the original French are to *Corinne, ou L'Italie* (New York: Leavitt & Allen, 1864), and will appear in the text. See p. 129. This chapter was completed before the publication of what will undoubtedly be the standard and authoritative edition: *Corinne, ou L'Italie*, ed. and intro. Simone Balayé (Paris: Champion, 2000).
25 See Frank Paul Bowman, "*Corinne* et la religion," *L'Éclat et le silence*, ed. Simone Balayé (Paris: Honoré Champion, 1999), pp. 156–60.
26 Marie-Claire Vallois, "Old Idols, New Subject: Germaine de Staël and Romanticism," Gutwirth, Goldberger, and Szmurlo, p. 92.
27 Juliana Schiesari, *The Gendering of Melancholia: Feminism, Psychoanalysis, and the Symbolics of Loss in Renaissance Literature* (Ithaca: Cornell University Press, 1992). Further references by page number to this study will appear in the text.
28 Sigmund Freud, "Mourning and Melancholia," *Collected Papers*, Vol. 4, trans. Joan Riviere (New York: Basic Books, 1959), p. 157. All subsequent references to Freud are from this edition and will appear in the text.
29 See Margaret Waller's discussion of *Corinne* in *The Male Malady: Fictions of Impotence in the French Romantic Novel* (New Brunswick: Rutgers University Press, 1993), pp. 57–92.
30 Moers writes in *Literary Women* (New York: Doubleday, 1976) that "the politicizing of genius, that is, the demonstration of genius by means of public acclamation, by an actual crowning, was Mme de Staël's principal intention, before self-aggrandizement, before feminism, when she wrote Book 2 of *Corinne*" (p. 277).
31 Georges Poulet, "The Role of Improvisation in *Corinne*," *ELH*, XLI (Winter 1974), p. 608.
32 Corinne cannot even speak to her friend Prince Castel-Forte coherently. See p. 374.
33 See *Corinne*, p. 378.
34 See Freud's description of the sado-masochism of melancholia, p. 162. "The self-torments of melancholiacs, which are without doubt pleasurable, signify, just like the corresponding phenomenon in the obsessional neurosis, a gratification of sadistic tendencies and of hate, both of which relate to an object and in this way have both been turned round upon the self. ... It is this sadism, and only this, that solves the riddle of the tendency to suicide which makes melancholia so interesting – and so dangerous."
35 Dorish Kadish, *Politicizing Gender: Narrative Strategies in the Aftermath of the French Revolution* (New Brunswick: Rutgers University Press, 1991), pp. 15–36. Kadish's emphasis is on Corinne's attempt, in replacing father and king, "to propose meaningful alternatives to traditional patriarchal and aristocratic figures of power" (p. 24). In contrast, my reading suggests that, once Corinne has accepted the role of substitute father, she is complicit with and imbricated in patriarchal structures of domination, both psychic and political.
36 See Waller, pp. 75–7
37 John Claiborne Isbell, *The Birth of European Romanticism* (Cambridge: Cambridge University Press, 1994), p. 105, p. 107.

38 Moers, of course, in *Literary Women* initiates the study of the history of *Corinne*'s influence on subsequent generations of women writers. Moers writes that *"Corinne* stands alone in Mme de Staël's *oeuvre*, in its silliness as in its enormous influence upon literary women" (p. 264). Joan DeJean, in "Staël's *Corinne*: The Novel's Other Dilemma," *Stanford French Review*, XI (Spring 1987), pp. 77–88, also reads the conclusion of the novel as a "revenge fantasy," in which the name "Juliette" calls forth Rousseau's heroine, as well as Wolmar's child-marionette daughter Henriette, from *La nouvelle Héloise*. DeJean thus sees Staël as predicting the "silencing of [woman's] conversational voice, a lesson borne out by the future of women's writing in nineteenth-century France" (p. 87).

2 "The sweet reward of all our toil"

1 Shelley is actually quoting a French critic to whom she refers as M. Année in the concluding pages of her biography of Staël.
2 In her biography of Staël, "Madame de Staël, 1766–1817," from *The Cabinet Cyclopedia: Eminent Literary and Scientific Men of France*, ed. Dionysius Lardner, II (London: Longman, *et. al.*, 1839), Shelley writes that Staël's novels "do not teach the most needful lesson – moral courage" (p. 343).
3 For a more thorough comparison, see my "Sibylline Leaves: Mary Shelley's *Valperga* and the Legacy of *Corinne*," *Cultural Interactions in the Romantic Age*, ed. Gregory Maertz (Albany: State University of New York Press, 1998), pp. 157–76.
4 Mary Shelley, *Valperga; or, The Life and Adventures of Castruccio, Prince of Lucca*, ed. by Tilottama Rajan (Peterborough: Broadview, 1998), p. 397, p. 440. All subsequent references to *Valperga* will be to this edition and will appear in the text.
5 For an instructive analysis of the significance of the ways in which Machiavelli and Mary Shelley "alter and manipulate the facts" surrounding Castruccio's life, see Betty Bennett, "Machiavelli's and Mary Shelley's Castruccio: Biography as Metaphor," *Romanticism: The Journal of Romantic Culture and Criticism*, III (1997), pp. 139–51.
6 J.G.A. Pocock, *The Machiavellian Moment: Florentine Political Thought and the Atlantic Republican Tradition* (Princeton: Princeton University Press, 1975).
7 See Betty T. Bennett, "The Political Philosophy of Mary Shelley's Historical Novels: *Valperga* and *Perkin Warbeck*," *The Evidence of the Imagination: Studies of Interactions between Life and Art in English Romantic Literature*, eds Donald H. Reiman, Michael C. Jaye, and Betty T. Bennett (New York: New York University Press, 1978), pp. 354–71 and Tilottama Rajan, "Mary Shelley's *Mathilda*: Melancholy and the Political Economy of Romanticism," *Studies in the Novel*, XXVI (1994), pp. 43–68.
8 In "Melancholy and the Political Economy of Romanticism," Rajan (1994) asserts that Beatrice, like the eponymous heroine of *Mathilda*, embodies a critique of Percy's idealism: "As a version of Mathilda, Mary's figure for her withdrawal from Percy's idealism, Beatrice also refers to his literary failure to deal through gender with the material realities of history" (p. 63).
9 For a moving account of Mary Shelley's personal feelings toward Byron, see Ernest J. Lovell, Jr., "Byron and Mary Shelley," *Keats–Shelley Journal*, I (1952), pp. 35–49.
10 For a related reading of this passage, see Joseph W. Lew, "History and Ideology in *Valperga*," in *The Other Mary Shelley: Beyond Frankenstein*, eds Audrey A. Fisch, Anne K. Mellor, and Esther Schor (Oxford: Oxford University Press, 1993), p. 165. Lew terms this exclamation a "Manfred-like statement" and writes: "This passage provides an unexpectedly dark portrait of Imagination, that human quality so admired by the male Romantics, providing the novel's first clear indication of the links between male Romantic ideology and the growth of empire" (p. 165).
11 George Gordon, Lord Byron, *Byron's Poetry*, ed. Frank D. McConnell (New York: W.W. Norton, 1978), p. 59.
12 Pamela Clemit, *The Godwinian Novel: The Rational Fictions of Godwin, Brockden Brown, Mary Shelley* (Oxford: Clarendon Press, 1993), p. 177.

13 Shelley's portrait of Guinigi is particularly significant in that it completely rewrites the figure of Guinigi, depicted in her historical source, Machiavelli's *Life of Castruccio*, as an emblem of armed conflict. See the excerpt in Rajan's edition of *Valperga*, pp. 475–8. See also Bennett (1997), "Biography as Metaphor," p. 140.

14 Ronald Paulson, *Representations of Revolution, 1789–1820* (New Haven: Yale University Press, 1983), pp. 215–47.

15 For a discussion of the clear lineage and power of influence that connects Byron and Nietzsche, see the final chapter of Peter Thorslev's *The Byronic Hero* (Minneapolis: University of Minnesota Press, 1962) and, more recently, James Soderholm, "Byron, Nietzsche, and the Mystery of Forgetting," *CLIO*, XXIII (Autumn 1993), pp. 51–63.

16 James Rieger, *The Mutiny Within: The Heresies of Percy Bysshe Shelley* (New York: George Braziller, 1967), pp. 121–8.

17 See Emily Sunstein, *Mary Shelley: Romance and Reality* (Boston: Little, Brown & Co., 1989), p. 53, p. 164.

18 Jane Blumberg, *Mary Shelley's Early Novels* (Iowa City: University of Iowa Press, 1993), p. 100. Barbara O'Sullivan, in "Beatrice in *Valperga*: A New Cassandra," *The Other Mary Shelley*, pp. 140–58, writes that "in her development of the Cassandra figure she made a ground-breaking attempt to express the creative potential of women" (p. 155).

19 In *Mary Shelley's Early Novels*, p. 105, Blumberg suggests that Mary Shelley was likely to have known of Sade's *Justine* from Byron and Matthew Lewis.

20 James Miller, *The Passion of Michel Foucault* (New York: Simon & Schuster, 1993), pp. 259–73.

21 Daniel Schierenbeck, "'Lofty enthusiasm' and 'vulgar superstitions': Shelley, Hume, and Religion's Role in History," 24 August 2002. NASSR Conference, University of Western Ontario.

22 Germaine de Staël, *De l'Allemagne*, II (Paris: Garnier Flammarion, 1968), p. 316.

23 Similarly, Staël, in *Corinne*, writes, "You cannot take one step in Rome without bringing together present and past, without juxtaposing different pasts. But seeing the eternal mobility of man's history, you learn to take the events of your own day calmly; in the presence of so many centuries which have all undone the work of their predecessors, you feel somewhat ashamed of your own agitation" (p. 72).

24 See Lew, p. 177.

25 Lew writes that "[d]espite her hardwon appreciation of history, Euthanasia decontextualizes literature with the ruthless rigor of a New Critic" (p. 177).

26 Bennett (1978), "The Political Philosophy of Mary Shelley's Historical Novels," p. 356.

27 For a Freudian analysis of Euthanasia's cave, see William D. Brewer, "Mary Shelley's *Valperga*: The Triumph of Euthanasia's Mind," *European Romantic Review*, V (1995), pp. 141–2.

28 Michael Schiefelbein, "'The Lessons of True Religion': Mary Shelley's Tribute to Catholicism in *Valperga*," *Religion and Literature*, XXX (1998), pp. 59–79. Schiefelbein further argues that Euthanasia is "morally victorious" at the conclusion of *Valperga* and that she "expresses Shelley's own idealism" (pp. 73–4).

29 See Rajan's (2000) notes to *Valperga*, p. 446. Indeed Schiefelbein argues that, like her heroine Euthanasia, Shelley "found spiritual nourishment in both study and contemplation. As much as she prized the 'intellectual liberty' that Protestantism represented for her, in her philosophical sensibilities she resembled Medieval mystics or theologians more than the radical Protestants of her own day" (p. 70).

30 See Pocock, pp. 49–79.

31 Elizabeth Grosz summarizes this recognition well: "The alternatives faced by feminist theorists are all in some sense 'impure' and 'implicated' in patriarchy. There can be no feminist position that is not in some way or other involved in patriarchal power relations; it is hard to see how this is either possible or desirable, for a purity from patriarchal 'contamination' entails feminism's incommensurability with patriarchy and thus the inability to criticize it." "Sexual Difference and the Problem of

Essentialism," *The Essential Difference*, ed. Naomi Schor and Elizabeth Weed (Bloomington: Indiana University Press, 1994), pp. 94–5.

32 Biddy Martin, "Feminism, Criticism and Foucault," *Feminism and Foucault: Reflections on Resistance*, ed. Irene Diamond and Lee Quinby (Boston: Northeastern University Press, 1988), p. 10.

33 Mary Shelley, *Mary Shelley's Journal*, ed. Frederick Jones (Norman: University of Oklahoma Press, 1947), pp. 169–70.

34 See also Michael Rossington, "Future Uncertain: The Republican Tradition and its Destiny in *Valperga*," in *Mary Shelley in her Times*, ed. Betty T. Bennett and Stuart Curran (Baltimore: Johns Hopkins University Press, 2000), pp. 103–18. He writes that Euthanasia represents an ideal that survives "beyond an actuality that seems to have defeated it" and that this is "presumably what P.B. Shelley meant in describing *Valperga* as expressing 'the ... romantic truth of history'" (p. 118).

35 Mary Shelley, *The Last Man*, ed. Anne McWhir (Peterborough: Broadview, 1996), p. 1.

36 See Sandra Gilbert and Susan Gubar, *The Madwoman in the Attic: The Woman Writer and the Nineteenth-Century Literary Imagination* (New Haven: Yale University Press, 1979), p. 98.

37 Rajan (1994), for example, writes in "Mary Shelley's *Mathilda*" that "[a]s a figure for a feminist history, Euthanasia is, of course, ineffectual" (p. 65). Mellor asserts that *Valperga* "emphasizes the inability of women, whether as adoring worshippers (like Beatrice) or active leaders (like Euthanasia), to influence political events or to translate an ethic of care – whether embodied in the domestic affections or in a political program of universal justice and peace – into historical reality" (p. 210). Daniel E. White, in "Mary Shelley's *Valperga*: Italy, and the Revision of Romantic Aesthetics," *Mary Shelley's Fictions: From Frankenstein to Falkner*, ed. Michael Eberle-Sinatra (New York: St. Martin's, 2000), describes *Valperga* as one of the most relentlessly pessimistic texts of the Romantic period, and reads its focus on a will to power as a critique of "the idealism we associate with *Prometheus Unbound*" (p. 91). Whereas I emphasize the historical potentiality embodied in Euthanasia's philosophy and her relationship with Beatrice, for White, the feminine enclave of Beatrice and Euthanasia "provides only a temporary and profoundly inconsequential respite before the inevitable emptiness of the conclusion" (p. 84). Much more troubling and in my opinion completely false to the tone of the novel are Blumberg's judgmental assertions that Euthanasia's self-reliance is a "damning characteristic" that "she denies her need for domestic love" and "betrays herself and her lover through an egocentric devotion to her own ideal" (p. 92). Of Beatrice and Euthanasia, Blumberg concludes: "Both women, childless, die excluded from salvation; even their final spiritual states are left blank. They are completely annihilated, the failure of their lives extending into eternity" (p. 112).

38 See Gary Kelly, "Last Men: Hemans and Mary Shelley in the 1820s," *Romanticism: the Journal of Romantic Culture and Criticism*, III (1997), pp. 198–208, for an excellent discussion of Hemans's and Shelley's critiques of masculine historiography. See Bennett (1997) in "Biography as Metaphor" on Castruccio's end as portrayed by Shelley: "Castruccio's funeral in *Valperga* emulates Beatrice's in pomp. Its particular hypocrisy is exposed in the words on Castruccio's actual memorial in the Church of San Francesco, ... which, in its irony, recalls Shelley's 'Ozymandias.' This inscription first celebrates the glory of his soldiery and family, confesses he has sinned and suffered, but then asks that 'Men of good will, help a devout soul in need'" (p. 145). See also p. 144 for illuminating parallels between Mary's descriptions of the deaths of Euthanasia and Percy.

39 Tilottama Rajan (2000), "Between Romance and History: Possibility and Contingency in Godwin, Leibniz, and Mary Shelley's *Valperga*," in Bennett and Curran, p. 101.

40 Bennett (1978), "The Political Philosophy of Mary Shelley's Historical Novels," p. 363.

3 Beyond impossibility

1 See Nancy A. Kaiser, "A Dual Voice: Mary Shelley and Bettina von Arnim," in *Identity and Ethos: A Festschrift for Sol Liptzin on the Occasion of His 85th Birthday*, ed. Mark H. Gelber (New York: Peter Lang, 1986), pp. 211–33, for an illuminating comparison of the conflicted authorial identities of both Shelley and Arnim.

2 Marjanne Goozé, "Desire and Presence: Bettine von Arnim's Erotic Fantasy Letter to Goethe," *Michigan Germanic Studies*, XIII, 1 (1987), p. 52.

3 See Patricia Anne Simpson, "Letters in Sufferance and Deliverance: The Correspondence of Bettina Brentano-von Arnim and Karoline von Günderrode," in *Bettina Brentano-von Arnim: Gender and Politics*, ed. Elke P. Frederiksen and Katherine R. Goodman (Detroit: Wayne State University Press, 1995), pp. 247–77. Hereafter Frederiksen and Goodman. Simpson's sensitive discussion focuses upon Arnim's metaphor of the kiss of nature as the power of figurative language that, in *Die Günderode*, gives "voice to the dead" in "an uncanny kind of mouth-to-mouth resuscitation" (p. 249).

4 Konstanze Bäumer, in *Bettina von Arnim* (Stuttgart: J.B. Metzler, 1995), p. 32, emphasizes that one of Arnim's central aims in writing *Die Günderode* was to call attention to her friend's writings. According to Bäumer, Günderode's work was all but forgotten when Arnim's tribute was published in 1840. Friedrich Goetz was the editor of the 1857 volume of her collected works.

5 For Arnim's heartwrenching account of the suicide and her own response to it, see *Goethe's Correspondence with a Child* (Boston: Ticknor & Fields, 1859), pp. 50–67. Subsequent references will appear in the text.

6 Here I distinguish between the historical personages and authors, Bettine von Arnim and Karoline von Günderode, and the auto/biographical fictions created by Arnim for *Die Günderode* which I refer to as Bettine and Karoline. The names of both Arnim and Günderode vary in spelling: Bettine/Bettina and Günderode/Günderrode. For simplicity's sake, I have chosen the spellings used in the Deutscher Klassiker Verlag edition of the novel for the historical personages as well.

7 Bettine von Arnim, *Die Günderode, Werke und Briefe*, ed. Walter Schmitz and Sibylle von Steinsdorff (3 vols, Frankfurt: Deutscher Klassiker Verlag, 1986), I, p. 724. All further references to *Die Günderode* are to this edition and will appear in the text. All English translations are from the only extant translation begun by Margaret Fuller and completed by Minna Wesselhoeft, after Fuller's death: *Correspondence of Fraülein Günderode and Bettine von Arnim* (Boston: T.O.H.P. Burnham, 1861), p. 325. I have replaced archaic pronoun and verb forms (i.e. thee, thou, hast, dost) with modern forms and revised occasional errors or awkwardnesses. Otherwise, the text here conforms to this translation.

8 Bettine von Arnim had met Germaine de Staël in the spring of 1808 in Frankfurt. According to Ingeborg Drewitz, Staël's response to Bettine was also decidedly negative, causing Achim von Arnim to feel compelled to defend Bettine against the criticism by the "femme célèbre." See *Bettine von Arnim: Romantik, Revolution, Utopie* (Düsseldorf: Eugen Diederichs Verlag, 1969), p. 53, hereafter Drewitz. For Arnims's epistolary references to Staël, see Arthur Helps and Elizabeth Jane Howard, *Bettina: A Portrait* (London: Chatto & Windus, 1957), pp. 88–95. Arnim's full account of her meeting with Staël in Mainz is found in *Goethe's Correspondence with a Child*, pp. 40–1. Here Bettine claims that she treads a laurel leaf dropped by Staël underfoot and describes Staël's brain as "an ant-hill of thoughts" (p. 41).

9 In powerful and unequivocal fashion, Günderode had, in fact, proposed an act of Liebestod, a mutual suicide, to Friedrich Creuzer. See the letter of March 1805 in *Karoline von Günderrode: Der Schatten eines Traumes*, ed., intro. Christa Wolf (Darmstadt: Luchterhand, 1981), p. 221.

10 Ursula Liebertz-Grün, *Ordnung im Chaos: Studien zur Poetik der Bettine Brentano-von Arnim* (Heidelberg: Carl Winter Universitätsverlag, 1989), p. 38.

11 Arnim herself registered the depth of her psychic involvement in this project through comparison of the writing process with that of *Goethe's Correspondence with a Child*: "wie denn überhaupt mein Briefwechsel mit der Günderode mein ganzes Innere viel gründlicher betätigt, als der mit Goethe es vor den Augen der Welt tun kann," as quoted in Bäumer, p. 32.

12 Elke Frederiksen and Monika Shafi make a similar point in their groundbreaking article, "'Sich im Unbekannten suchen gehen': Bettina von Arnim's *Die Günderode* als weibliche Utopie," *Akten des VII. Internationalen Germanisten-Kongresses*, Göttingen, 1985, VI, *Frauensprache-Frauenliteratur?*, ed. Inge Stephan and Carl Pietzcker (Tübingen: Niemeyer, 1986), pp. 54–61, that highlights the utopian aspects of the novel as well as its suspension of the gulf between theory and practice.

13 Kant writes, "By the public use of one's reason I understand the use which a person makes of it as a scholar before the reading public. Private use I call that which one may make of it in a particular civil post or office which is entrusted to him" (p. 265). Such uses would by definition exclude early nineteenth-century women. In "What is Enlightenment?" Kant does seem to advocate eventual enlightenment for "the entire fair sex" by critiquing their willingness to be treated as "domestic cattle" (p. 263). Immanuel Kant, *Philosophical Writings*, ed. Ernst Behler (New York: Continuum, 1993), pp. 263–9.

14 See Patricia Anne Simpson's discussion of the publication history of Günderode's works and the question of the impossibility of distinguishing fact from fiction in these letters (pp. 249–55). In particular, Simpson quotes Waldemar Oehlke's early twentieth-century study of Arnim, *Bettina von Arnims Briefromane* (Berlin: Mayer & Mueller, 1905) in which Oehlke, after attempting to determine which letters are historical and which fictional, concludes: "For, the attempt to classify the material, compiled from letters, as an epistolary publication on the grounds that it fulfills the conditions of the genre, leads to the opposite result. We have before us an individually crafted work of art, which, on the one hand exhibits historical accuracy, but on the other, a completely disorderly use of the limited authentic material; not letters, not even parts of letters: epistolary thoughts are the components of this book" (p. 255). As Katherine Goodman asserts in *Dis/Closures: Women's Autobiography in Germany Between 1790 and 1914* (New York: Peter Lang, 1986), "Generally speaking, Arnim dismantled actual letters and dispersed their parts throughout a given correspondence" (p. 91).

15 For a fine discussion of the theoretical implications of Arnim's fictionalization of auto/ biographical experience, see Lisabeth M. Hock's *Replicas of a Female Prometheus: The Textual Personae of Bettina von Arnim* (New York: Peter Lang, 2001). Hock identifies two prominent tendencies in the attempts of literary critics to deal with Arnim's blurring of the boundaries between art and life. The referential or biographical makes little or no attempt to distinguish between Arnim and her literary Bettine and "has been employed to foreground Arnim's interest in and activity on behalf of oppressed groups such as minorities and women" (p. 7). The textual approach encourages "multiple and conflicting readings of the author and her figures" at the same time that it seeks to identify in her works "a portrait of … Arnim's inner or ideal self" (p. 8). In my admiration for Arnim as a remarkably courageous historical personage *and* my own strong agreement with her belief in the political and ethical value of idealization, my analysis hovers self-consciously between these two poles. It is my hope that this movement brings to bear on my discussion the tensions between societal discourse and individual agency that Hock, following Teresa de Lauretis, sees as formative of individual historical subjectivity.

16 See Roswitha Burwick's (1986) discussion of the dynamic relationship between Bettine and Karoline as partners in a dialogue that stimulates the reader to a highly active, sophisticated, and ironic reading of the text in "Bettina von Arnims *Die Günderode*. Zum Selbstverständnis der Frau in der Romantik," *Kontroversen, alte und neue. Akten des VII.*

Internationalen Germanisten-Kongresses, Göttingen, pp. 62–7. Indeed Burwick sees the text as a paradigmatic realization of romantic aesthetics: "Das Buch wird geradezu zum Paradebeispiel von romantischer Ironie" (p. 65). See also Lisa C. Roetzel's "Acting Out: Bettine as Performer of Feminine Genius," *Women in German Yearbook*, eds. Sara Friedrichsmeyer and Patricia Herminghouse, XIV (1998), pp. 109–25, that emphasizes the emancipatory, feminist, and activist implications of Arnim's construction of a concept of genius that "redefines feminine genius as the courage to act" (p. 122).

17 For a discussion of the significance of Arnim's representation of her relationship to her brother Clemens as exemplifying the radicality of her sexual politics in contrast to his conservative standards for female behavior, see Katherine R. Goodman, "Through a Different Lens: Bettina Brentano-von Arnim's views on Gender," in Frederiksen and Goodman, pp. 118–27. See also Liebertz-Grün, pp. 94–134, for a fine treatment of the elements in *Frühlingskranz* that parody early nineteenth-century and Romantic ideals of the feminine. For *Die Günderode* as a challenge to the distinction between the genres of biography and autobiography, see Anna K. Kuhn, "The 'Failure' of Biography, the Triumph of Women's Writing: Bettina von Arnim's *Die Günderode* and Christa Wolf's *The Quest for Christa T.*," in *Revealing Lives: Autobiography, Biography, and Gender*, ed. Susan Groag Bell and Marilyn Yalom (Albany: State University of New York Press, 1990), pp. 13–28.

18 Edith Waldstein's *Bettine von Arnim and the Politics of Romantic Conversation* (Columbia: Camden House, 1988) compares *Die Günderode* with Arnim's fictional correspondences with men and finds the latter wanting; "None of her fictional correspondences with men completely reaches the goal of total communication. The epistolary partners are never equal" (p. 58). For the influence of "Romantische Geselligkeit" in Arnim's life and work, see also Gisela Dischner, *Bettina von Arnim: Eine weibliche Sozialbiographie aus dem neunzehnten Jahrhundert* (Berlin: Wagenbach, 1977), pp. 19–34.

19 Fuller, Preface, p. x.

20 For Bettine von Arnim's relation to the politics of German Romanticism, see Dischner, pp. 19–33 and pp. 149–52 and Christa Wolf (1995), "Your Next Life Begins Today: A Letter About Bettine," in Frederiksen and Goodman, where she describes Arnim as "the one, in the circle of the Romantics, who resurfaced in the 1830s with her Romantic principles intact, and who ... earned the title of herald of the revolution for later generations" (p. 38).

21 Christina Crosby, *The Ends of History: Victorians and the "Woman Question"* (New York: Routledge, 1991), p. 148.

22 Ann Rigney, *Imperfect Histories* (Ithaca: Cornell University Press, 2001), pp. 1–2.

23 See Crosby, p. 1.

24 For discussion of Arnim's political activism, see Drewitz, pp. 150–289, Dischner, pp. 149–80, and Waldstein, pp. 59–93. See also Ulrike Landfester, "'Die echte Politik muss Erfinderin sein': Uberlegungen zum Umgang mit Bettine von Arnims politischem Werk," in *Beiträge eines Wiepersdorfer Kolloquiums zu Bettina von Arnim*, ed. Hartwig Schultz (Berlin: Saint Albin, 1999), pp. 1–37, and Heinz Härtl, "Bettinas Salon der 'edlen' Weltverbesserer," *Internationales Jahrbuch der Bettina-von-Arnim-Gesellschaft*, ed. Uwe Lemm and Walter Schmitz, VIII/IX (1996–7) (Berlin: Saint Albin), pp. 163–76 and Landfester, "Das Schweigen der Sibylle: Bettine von Arnims Briefe über die Revolution von 1848," *Internationales Jahrbuch der Bettina-von-Arnim-Gesellschaft*, ed. Wolfgang Bunzel, Uwe Lemm, and Walter Schmitz, XI/XII (1999–2000), pp. 121–43.

25 Rigney defines the historical sublime in Carlyle as the outcome of his struggle "to deal with the complexity of the past" (p. 10). In Arnim and her Karoline, the historical sublime results from a related effort, both painful and inspiring, to make emotional and intellectual contact with the dead, to understand them.

26 Christa Wolf, in Frederiksen and Goodman, p. 52.

27 Drewitz asserts that "[d]ie Papiere aus Arnims Nachlaß zeigen seine langsame Abkehr von Meinungen und Vorurteilen in der 'christlich-deutschen Tischgesellschaft.' Bettines Einfluß ist spürbar" (p. 286).

28 For a history of the myth of the Wandering Jew, Ahasverus, see Paul Lawrence Rose, *Revolutionary Antisemitism in Germany from Kant to Wagner* (Princeton: Princeton University Press, 1990), pp. 23–43.

29 Baldwin provides a useful historical sketch of the status of Jews in nineteenth-century Prussia as well as an incisive discussion of Arnim's last published novel as "a sustained argument" for the legal emancipation of Jews in "Questioning the 'Jewish Question': Poetic Philosophy and Politics in *Conversations with Demons*," in Frederiksen and Goodman, pp. 213–24. For less convincing essays that question the sincerity of Arnim's commitment to the cause of Jewish rights and freedoms, see Helmut Hirsch, "Jüdische Aspekte im Leben und Werk Bettine von Arnims," *Internationales Jahrbuch der Bettina-von-Arnim-Gesellschaft*, I (1987), pp. 61–76 and "Zur Dichotomie von Theorie und Praxis in Bettines Äußerungen über Judentum und Juden," *Internationales Jahrbuch*, III (1989), pp. 153–72. The question of Arnim's attitudes toward and textual representations of Jews is a complex and understandably controversial one. For two recent discussions, see Lisabeth M. Hock, "'Sonderbare', 'heißhungrige', und 'edle' Gestalten: Konstrukte von Juden und Judentum bei Bettina von Arnim," in *Salons der Romantik: Beiträge eines Wiepersdorfer Kolloquiums zu Theorie und Geschichte des Salons*, ed. Hartwig Schultz (Berlin: Walter de Gruyter, 1997), pp. 317–41 and Peter-Anton von Arnim, "'Der eigentliche Held in dieser Zeit, die einzige wahrhaft freie und starke Stimme': Die jüdischen Aspekte in Leben und Werk Bettina von Arnims als Herausforderung," in *Beiträge eines Wiepersdorfer Kolloquiums zu Bettina von Arnim*, pp. 163–216. Hock's article is valuable in its demonstration of the ways in which Arnim cannot transcend the anti-semitic prejudices of her day and in its tracing of the development of Arnim's social and political attitudes throughout her life toward greater activism in the cause of Jewish emancipation and increasingly positive literary portraits of Jews and Judaism. Hock equates Arnim's idealization of Jews like Ephraim with stereotyping. For Arnim, however, idealization serves a utopian function lacking in stereotypes. Furthermore, as Peter-Anton von Arnim points out, many of the portraits of Jews as depicted by Arnim hardly constitute stereotypes since she was one of the first to create them. Taking on previous critics one by one, he emphasizes, in contrast to Hock and Hirsch, the courage and consistency of Arnim's battles, textual and political, for Germany's Jews.

30 Here, in her 1840 letter offering *Die Günderode* to Levysohn, Arnim sets forth, in her inimitable fashion, a political program in brief: "Ich gebe Ihnen mein Buch aus drei Gründen, erstens, weil Sie Jüde sind, zweitens, weil Sie eine Säbelschmarre tragen, und drittens, weil Sie Ihre Frau aus Liebe geheiratet haben," as quoted in Hock (1997), p. 329. This good will did not prevent her from taking legal action against Levysohn in 1843 over financial dealings related to book sales.

31 See Rose, pp. 44–50 and pp. 165–70.

32 For interpretations of Mignon that focus on gender, see Sabine Groß's "Diskursregelung und Weiblichkeit: Mignon und ihre Schwestern," and Ulrike Rainer's "A Question of Silence: Goethe's Speechless Women," in *Goethes Mignon und ihre Schwestern: Interpretationen und Rezeption*, ed. Gerhard Hoffmeister (New York: Peter Lang, 1993), pp. 83–100 and pp. 101–12. For a study devoted to "Mignon's extra-textual afterlife" (p. 21), see Carolyn Steedman's *Strange Dislocations: Childhood and the Idea of Human Interiority, 1780–1930* (London: Virago, 1995). That Steedman does not even *mention* Bettine von Arnim renders evident the urgent need for more genuinely comparatist studies of such significant nineteenth-century European cultural phenomena.

33 For associations of the Harper and Jews, see Chapter 11 in which Wilhelm sends the Harper to seek for news of a mysterious lady until "the Harper was obliged to return, in order not to be taken for a Jewish spy because of his beard; but had no good news to

report to his master." Johann Wolfgang von Goethe, *Wilhelm Meister's Apprenticeship*, ed. and trans. Eric A. Blackall in cooperation with Victor Lange, *Goethe's Collected Works*, IX (New York: Suhrkamp, 1989), p. 142. For the Harper as a Wandering Jew figure, see pp. 122–3. The Protestant pastor who treats the Harper for madness suggests that it is indeed his difference from others, symbolized by his appearance, that threatens him with madness (p. 210).

34 As quoted in Drewitz, p. 166.

35 See Ruth-Ellen B. Joeres, "'We are adjacent to human society': German Women Writers, the Homosocial Experience, and a Challenge to the Public/Domestic Dichotomy," *Women in German Yearbook*, ed. Jeanette Clausen and Sara Friedrichsmeyer, X (1995), pp. 39–57.

36 Hegel writes, "God is understood as spirit only by being known as the Trinity. This new principle is the hub around which world history revolves. History is divided by going forward to this point, and starting from it." *The Philosophy of History* in *The Philosophy of Hegel*, ed. Carl J. Friedrich (New York: Random House, 1953), p. 86.

37 Goodman, *Dis/Closures*, p. 110.

38 For her contemporaries' responses to Bettine's "eccentricities," see Helps and Howard, pp. 36–7, pp. 96–7, and pp. 150–1 in particular. Her brother Franz wrote of her as a young woman, worried that she would never marry: "Bettine kann gut werden, wenn sie einfach und natürlich bleibt und nicht eigne Länder entdecken will, wo keine weibliche Glückseligkeit zu entdecken ist," as quoted in Drewitz, p. 26. Drewitz emphasizes that Bettine was clearly seen as the black sheep of her family (p. 27).

39 For a relatively recent and comprehensive discussion of the history of Bettina Brentano-von Arnim criticism, see Marjanne Goozé, "The Reception of Bettina Brentano-von Arnim as Author and Historical Figure," in Frederiksen and Goodman, pp. 349–420. Hildegard Platzer Collins and Philip Allison Shelley demonstrate the predominance of the Goethe book in the critical picture of Arnim outside of Germany in "The Reception in England and America of Bettina von Arnim's *Goethe's Correspondence with a Child*," in *Anglo-German and American-German Crosscurrents*, ed. Philip Allison Shelley with Arthur O. Lewis, Jr., Vol. II (Chapel Hill: University of North Carolina, 1962), pp. 97–174.

40 As quoted in Waldstein, p. 40.

41 Heinrich Heine, *Die Romantische Schule* (München: Wilhelm Goldmann Verlag, 1964), p. 41.

42 An anonymous English reviewer (identified to me by Fred Burwick as one Lady Eastlake) in the *Foreign Quarterly Review* also reads an implicit critique of Goethe's formality into the text: "Bettina Brentano is an honest girl – and this is the real charm of the book. Göthe, with all his dignity, and propriety, and courtier-like composure, and what the Germans call Vornehmtheit [sic], cuts a poor figure before the visionary girl, whose letters are instinct with a Promethean fire of poetry, with the want of which his own productions have been often, and not altogether unjustly, reproached." As quoted in Collins and Shelley, p. 106. See also Drewitz, p. 164.

43 Friedrich Schiller, *On the Aesthetic Education of Man*, trans. and intro. Reginald Snell (London: Routledge & Kegan Paul, 1954; repr. New York: Ungar, 1977), pp. 120–1.

44 Michel Foucault, "Nietzsche, Genealogy, History," in *The Foucault Reader*, ed. Paul Rabinow (New York: Pantheon, 1984), p. 95.

45 See David Simpson's *Romanticism, Nationalism, and the Revolt Against Theory*, pp. 104–25. Simpson's focus is Anglo-American culture, but his point holds true for Germany as well. For a brilliant discussion of the ideological significance, in relation to Arnim, of Friedrich Schlegel's definition of women as natural philosophers, see Friedrich Kittler's "Writing into the Wind, Bettina," trans. Marilyn Wyatt, *Glyph*, VII (1980), pp. 32–69.

46 In "Through a Different Lens," Goodman (1995) emphasizes "the radicality of Arnim's views on gender," (p. 115) and shows that her challenging of male–female polarities has profound political significance, culminating in her desire for an active

and "heroic" role in the public world and her rejection of woman's relegation to the domestic realm.

47 Elisabeth Moltmann-Wendel, "Bettina von Arnim und Schleiermacher," *Evangelische Theologie*, XXXI (1971), pp. 395–414.

48 See Moltmann-Wendel's discussion of the distinction between Opfer (victim) and Selbstaufgabe (self-sacrifice) in Schleiermacher's theology, his critique of bourgeois, individualistic subjectivity, and his conception of the sublation of the individual in the "Transcendenz der Liebe" (pp. 404–6).

49 See Moltmann-Wendel, p. 405.

50 See Moltmann-Wendel, pp. 397–9.

51 For a discussion of Arnim's representation of Hölderlin in *Die Günderode* and past critical reception of that representation, see Bäumer, *Bettina von Arnim*, pp. 34–44. See also Liebertz-Grün, pp. 60–75.

52 See Liebertz-Grün, p. 60.

53 Translation from *Bitter Healing: German Women Writers From 1700–1850*, ed. Jeannine Blackwell and Susanne Zantop (Lincoln: University of Nebraska Press, 1990), p. 1.

54 See Juliana Schiesari, "*Soverchia maninconia*: Tasso's Hydra," in *The Gendering of Melancholia* (Ithaca: Cornell University Press, 1992), pp. 191–232.

55 Anne Mellor, "English Women Writers and the French Revolution," in *Rebel Daughters: Women and the French Revolution*, ed. Sara E. Melzer and Leslie Rabine (New York: Oxford University Press, 1992), p. 265.

56 Roswitha Burwick, "Liebe und Tod in Leben und Werk der Günderode," *German Studies Review*, III (1980), p. 209. Burwick quotes the following from a letter to Gunda Brentano: "Warum ward ich kein Mann! ich habe keinen Sinn für weibliche Tugenden, für Weiberglückseligkeit. Nur das Wilde Große, Glänzende gefällt mir. Es ist ein unseliges aber unverbesserliches Misverhältniß in meiner Seele; und es wird und muß so bleiben, denn ich bin ein Weib, und habe Begierden wie ein Mann, ohne Männerkraft. Darum bin ich so wechselnd, und so uneins mit mir" (p. 208).

57 Two critics have made convincing cases for the influence of *Die Günderode* on Dickinson: Rebecca Patterson, "Emily Dickinson's Debt to *Günderode*," *The Midwest Quarterly VII* (1967), pp. 331–54 and Barton Levi St. Armand, "Veiled Ladies: Dickinson, Bettine, and Transcendental Mediumship," in *Studies in the American Renaissance* (Charlottesville: University Press of Virginia, 1987), pp. 1–51.

58 For a suggestive discussion of the labyrinth motif in *Die Günderode*, see Liebertz-Grün, pp. 72–5.

59 She writes that "it was the epoch in which I first became conscious of myself" in *Goethe's Correspondence with a Child*, p. 50.

60 For a discussion of Arnim's relation to the women's movement of her time, see Barbara Becker-Cantarino, "Zur politischen Romantik. Bettina von Arnim, die 'Frauenfage' und der 'Feminismus,'" in *Beiträge eines Wiepersdorfer Kolloquiums zu Bettina von Arnim*, pp. 217–48. Goodman points out, in "Through a Different Lens," that although Arnim was not directly involved with the "feminist activity undertaken by younger women like Louise Aston, Louise Otto-Peters, Fanny Lewald, Mathilde Anneke or others" (p. 116), her writings certainly expressed ideas that were consonant with their politics and their goals.

61 Lisabeth Hock (2001) speculates (pp. 71–2) that Arnim the author may have been influenced by Günderode's hesitancy to act in the cause of women, and her own belief, expressed in the novel, that the time for such outward action had not yet come.

62 See Ulrike Landfester, "Von Frau zu Frau? Einige Bemerkungen über historische und ahistorische Weiblichkeitsdiskurse in der Rezeption Bettine von Arnims," *Internationales Jahrbuch der Bettina-von-Arnim-Gesellschaft*, VIII/IX (1996–7), pp. 201–19. Landfester's excellent article is critical of the ahistorical bent she perceives in much work on Arnim. The hermeneutic developed in the dialogue "Die Manen" from *Die Günderode* and Arnim's own commitment to idealization complicate such a critique, in my opinion.

4 Rewriting Romanticism

1 Madelyn Gutwirth, "*Corinne* and *Consuelo* as Fantasies of Immanence," *George Sand Studies*, VIII (1986–7), p. 21. For other discussions of Sand's relation to Staël, see Nancy Rogers, "George Sand and Germaine de Staël: The Novel as Subversion," *West Virginia George Sand Conference Papers*, edited by Armand E. Singer, Mary W. Singer, Janice S. Spleth, and Dennis O'Brien (Morgantown: West Virginia University, 1981), pp. 61–73 and Eve Sourian, "L'Influence de Mme de Staël sur les premières oeuvres de George Sand," *George Sand Studies*, VII (1984–5), pp. 37–45. Sourian terms Staël "un modèle écrasant" (p. 44) for Sand.

2 George Sand, *Consuelo: A Romance of Venice*, no trans. (New York: Da Capo, 1979), pp. 62–3. All subsequent page references to *Consuelo* (in English) will be to this edition and will appear in the text as *Romance*.

3 George Sand, *Consuelo* [et] *La Comtesse de Rudolstadt*, 3 vols, ed. and introd. Léon Cellier and Léon Guichard (Paris: Garnier, 1959), Vol. I, p. 87. All subsequent page references to *Consuelo* and *La Comtesse de Rudolstadt* will be to this edition and will appear in the text.

4 Corilla is also named after the famous eighteenth-century Florentine improvisatrice, Corilla Olympia, who is described by such English travelers as Hester Piozzi and John Moore in their writings about Italy. I am indebted here to the work of Orianne Smith, in particular a paper delivered at the 2002 NASSR Conference, "Romantic Women Writers and the Figure of the Improvisatrice."

5 Sand's later novel *Lucrezia Floriana* (1846), the tale of a retired actress with four children from different fathers, none of whom she ever married, and who is destroyed by her love affair with a judgmental and melancholy aristocrat with a mother fixation, should be read in tandem with *Consuelo*, as a brave, bitter, and psychologically "realistic" re-writing of *Corinne*.

6 For an intriguing analysis of Albert as a new and utopian male hero, both maternal and egalitarian, see Pierrette Daly, "*Consuelo*: The Fiction of Feminism," *George Sand Studies*, XI (Spring 1992), pp. 43–8.

7 David A. Powell, *While the Music Lasts: The Representation of Music in the Works of George Sand* (Lewisburg: Bucknell University Press, 2001), p. 51.

8 George Sand, *Lettres d'un voyageur*, trans. Sacha Rabinovitch and Patricia Thomson (London: Penguin, 1987), p. 179. All subsequent references are to this edition and will appear in the text.

9 Isabelle Hoog Naginski, *George Sand: Writing for her Life* (New Brunswick: Rutgers University Press, 1991), p. 5.

10 "Sand's obscurity owes more to the valorization of the male *mal du siècle* in the French canon (and thus of the reassertion of male power in French culture) than to any weakness in her themes." Françoise Massardier-Kenney, *Gender in the Fiction of George Sand* (Amsterdam: Rodopi, 2000), p. 183.

11 Naginski writes that "the entire scene is a retelling of the Orpheus myth but with the genders reversed" (p. 205). Naginski also provides illuminating discussions of the Cupid/Psyche and the Demeter/Persephone myths in this same chapter, "*Consuelo* and *La Comtesse de Rudolstadt*: From Gothic Novel to Novel of Initiation." For a more traditional reading of Consuelo's mythic descent as an exchange of female virginity for male protection, see François Laforge, "Structure et fonction du mythe d'Orphée dans *Consuelo* de George Sand," *Revue d'Histoire littéraire de la France*, LXXXIV (1984), pp. 53–66.

12 See Naginski, for example, pp. 16–34.

13 See Jean-Pierre Lacassagne, "Albert et Pierre Leroux," *La Porporina: Entretiens sur Consuelo*, ed. Léon Cellier (Grenoble: Presses Universitaires de Grenoble, 1976), pp. 31–40. Lacassagne writes that "à cause de sa charge philosophique le personnage [Albert] prend une dimension hors de pair dans le project romanesque" (p. 31). For Leroux's philosophy and French Romanticism, see David Evans, *Le socialisme*

romantique: Pierre Leroux et ses contemporains (Paris: M. Rivière, 1948). For Leroux's influence on the novel, see also Léon Cellier, "L' Occultisme dans *Consuelo* and *La Comtesse de Rudolstadt*" in *Consuelo* and *La Comtesse de Rudolstadt*, ed. and intro. Léon Cellier and Léon Guichard (Paris: Garnier, 1959), pp. lxi–lxvi. For Sand's position on Leroux's doctrine of metempsychosis which was also shared by Enfantin, Fourier, Lamennais, and Reynaud, see pp. lxiv–lxvi.

14 George Sand, *Correspondance*, ed. Georges Lubin, VI (Paris: Garnier, 1969), p. 329.

15 Albert Sonnenfeld, "George Sand: Music and Sexualities," *Nineteenth-Century French Studies*, XVI (Spring–Summer 1988), p. 321.

16 For histories of French Freemasonry, see Alec Mellor, *La vie quotidienne de la franc-maçonnerie française du XVIIIe siècle à nos jours* (Paris: Hachette, 1973), Pierre Chevallier, *Histoire de la franc-maçonnerie française* (Paris: Fayard, 1974), and Michel Taillefer, *La franc-maçonnerie toulousaine: 1741–1799* (Paris: E.N.S.B.-C.T.H.S., 1984). For women and Freemasonry, see Janet M. Burke, "Freemasonry, Friendship and Noblewomen: The Role of the Secret Society in Bringing Enlightenment Thought to Pre-Revolutionary Women Elites," *History of European Ideas*, X (1989), pp. 283–93 and Margaret C. Jacob, "Freemasonry, Women, and the Paradox of the Enlightenment," *Living the Enlightenment: Freemasonry and Politics in Eighteenth-Century Europe* (New York: Oxford University Press, 1991), pp. 120–42. For European and British Freemasonry, see also Margaret C. Jacob, *The Radical Enlightenment: Pantheists, Freemasons, and Republicans* (London: Allen & Unwin, 1981).

17 George Sand, *Jean Ziska*. I have not translated these reader addresses in order to preserve the feminine French nouns.

18 George Sand, *Correspondance*, VI (Paris: Garnier, 1969), p. 179.

19 Fredric Jameson, *The Political Unconscious: Narrative as a Socially Symbolic Act* (Ithaca: Cornell University Press, 1981), pp. 19–20.

20 E.T.A. Hoffmann was a powerful influence on Sand, particularly in his predilection for artist-musician protagonists. See Robert Godwin-Jones, "Consuelo's Travels: The German Connection," *The Traveler in the Life and Works of George Sand*, ed. Tamara Alvarez-Detrell and Michael G. Paulson (Troy: Whitston, 1994), pp. 107–14, Elaine Boney, "The Influence of E.T.A. Hoffmann on George Sand," *George Sand: Collected Essays*, ed. Janis Glasgow (Troy: Whitston, 1985), pp. 42–52. Indeed, in a footnote to the Epilogue of *La Comtesse de Rudolstadt*, Sand mentions the openendedness of *Kater Murr* as an example to be emulated. According to Cellier and Guichard, Sand purchased a translation of Hoffmann's works in 1834.

21 George Sand, *The Countess Rudolstadt*, 2 vols, trans. Frank H. Potter (New York: Dodd, 1891), Vol. II, p. 118. All subsequent English translations will be from this edition and will appear in the text.

22 Sand knew Barruel's work, as Cellier points out in "L'occultisme dans *Consuelo* et *La Comtesse de Rudolstadt*," p. lxxii. Cellier also provides a list of no less than nine late eighteenth-century and early nineteenth-century masonic or anti-masonic works from the library catalogue at Nohant, pp. lxxi–lxxii.

23 See, for example, in addition to Naginski and Laforge quoted above, Léon Cellier, "Le roman initiatique en France au temps du romantisme," *Parcours initiatiques*, intro. Ross Chambers (Neuchâtel: La Baconnière, 1977), pp. 118–37, Simone Vierne, "Le mythe de la femme dans *Consuelo*," in *La Porporina*, pp. 41–52 and Lucienne Frappier-Mazur, "Desire, Writing, and Identity in the Romantic Mystical Novel: Notes for a Definition of the Feminine," *Style*, XVIII (Summer 1984), pp. 328–54. For structural analyses, see Gérard Schaeffer, "*Consuelo*, le temps et l'espace, lieux symboliques et personnages," in *La Porporina*, pp. 53–67, and *Espace et Temps Chez George Sand* (Neuchâtel: Baconnière, 1981), pp. 51–73.

24 In their introduction, Cellier and Guichard emphasize the importance of the influence of *Wilhelm Meister* despite the lack of formal proof. Goethe's Freemasonic lodge, Amalia, for example, was connected to a lodge named Rudolstadt (pp. xvii–xx).

25 Naomi Schor, *George Sand and Idealism* (New York: Columbia University Press, 1993), p. 13.
26 George Sand, *Correspondance*, ed. Georges Lubin, VI (Paris: Garnier, 1969), p. 826.
27 Johann Wolfgang von Goethe, *Wilhelm Meister's Journeyman Years or The Renunciants*, trans. Krishna Winston, ed. Jane K. Brown, *Goethe's Collected Works*, Vol. 10 (New York: Suhrkamp, 1989), p. 141.
28 My feminist reading of the *Wanderjahre* clearly differs profoundly from Marc Redfield's position in *Phantom Formations: Aesthetic Ideology and the Bildungsroman* (Ithaca: Cornell University Press, 1996) that the novel "diagnoses the violence of the Aesthetic State as the effect of a technicity that proves all the more haunting when violence itself is aestheticized as pragmatism" (p. 124). My much more straightforward reading suggests that, rather than diagnosing the ills of bureaucratic or technical pragmatisms, the novel reflects them in a manner and tone that seem to preclude rather than invite cultural critique.
29 The question of Sand's feminism is enormously complex and vexed, not the least because of the disparity between her frankly and courageously feminist texts like the virtually unknown *Jean Ziska* and her infamous dismissal of her nomination by a group of feminists as a candidate to the National Assembly in 1848. I do not propose to resolve the larger question here, of the feminism of Sand's art and life. My focus is instead on *Consuelo* and *La Comtesse de Rudolstadt* as unequivocally feminist texts. For an excellent discussion of the feminist implications of Sand's early novels, see Françoise Massardier-Kenney, "Textual Feminism in the Early Fiction of George Sand," *George Sand Studies*, XIII (Spring 1994), pp. 11–17. Massardier-Kenney also provides a good bibliography of previous articles on Sand and feminism. Her later book, *Gender in the Fiction of George Sand*, offers a strong argument for Sand as a major feminist writer. For analysis of *Lucrezia Floriani*, Sand's treatment of the professional woman artist, see pp. 126–57. For Sand's (anti-)feminism, see also Donna Dickenson, *George Sand: A Brave Man, The Most Womanly Woman* (Oxford: Berg Publishers, 1988), pp. 45–76 and Schor, pp. 68–81. Maryline Lukacher in *Maternal Fictions: Stendhal, Sand, Rachilde and Bataille* (Durham: Duke University Press, 1994) suggests that Sand's ambivalence about women's political emancipation and her opposition to women's suffrage had their roots in "her low opinion of her mother" (p. 11).
30 See Sand pp. xix–xx.
31 Hirsch writes in "Spiritual Bildung," *The Voyage In*, that "[b]y killing the emotional Mignon and the spiritual Beautiful Soul, by elevating the Amazon mother, Nathalie, as an ideal of femininity, Goethe protects society from the subversive extremes into which women are channeled" (p. 32).
32 Egbuna Modum in "Une Initiation à caractère maçonnique: L'exemple de *Consuelo* et *La Comtesse de Rudolstadt* de George Sand," *Nineteenth-Century French Studies*, XI (1983), pp. 268–77. Modum discusses F.M. Clavel's 1843 history of secret societies that examines their evolution in matters of gender equality.
33 Margaret Jacob writes in *Living the Enlightenment* that "[t]he admission of women to eighteenth-century [Masonic] societies of 'equals' gives us one of the first moments in Western culture when liberal idealism about merit and equality had to face the reality of socially constructed gender differences" (p. 124).
34 Moretti writes pointedly that "the episode that decides [Mignon's] death – one of the most disagreeable in all world literature – embodies without half-tones the eighteenth-century repudiation of premature and passionate desire. ... [W]hen Goethe shows us his philistine side, he does absolutely nothing to appear affable" (p. 47).
35 See Claire Goldberg Moses, "'Difference' in Historical Perspective: Saint-Simonian Feminism," Claire Goldberg Moses and Leslie Wahl Rabine, *Feminism, Socialism, and French Romanticism* (Bloomington: Indiana University Press, 1993), pp. 17–84, for an excellent portrait of this feminist movement, its program, and economic and cultural contexts.

36 For a survey of the wide variety of plausible and conflicting interpretations of this conclusion, see Robert Godwin-Jones, p. 113.

37 George Eliot, *Armgart* in *Theophrastus Such, Jubal, and Other Poems* (Chicago: Belford, Clarke & Co., 1887; rpt. Chicago: Donahue & Henneberry, 1987), p. 195.

38 Thanks to Tricia Lootens for suggesting this parallel to me.

39 Thanks to Mariarosa Mettifogo for pointing out to me the crucial significance of this concluding maternal image.

40 Powell, p. 57.

41 Conclusions of the *Wanderjahre* vary with editions. I choose to accept Eric Blackall's judgment in *Goethe and the Novel* (Ithaca: Cornell University Press, 1976) that Wilhelm's resurrection of Felix constitutes the "real ending of the novel" (p. 259), since it concludes the "narrative" devoted to Wilhelm. See Redfield, pp. 100–2 and pp. 125–6, for an excellent discussion of the question of the novel's ending(s).

42 For Sand's crucial influence on George Eliot, see Patricia Thomson, *George Sand and the Victorians: Her Influence and Reputation in Nineteenth-Century England* (London: Macmillan, 1977), pp. 152–84. My thanks once again to Tricia Lootens for pointing out the connection between Sand's Invisibles and Eliot's "choir invisible."

43 My thanks to Seth Schein for his translation of this passage.

Epilogue

1 Her words to her protégé, Thorkild Bjornvig, quoted in Judith Thurman's *Isak Dinesen: The Life of a Storyteller* (New York: St. Martin's, 1982), p. 283.

2 Nietzsche, introduced to her by the works of the prominent Danish scholar Georg Brandes, was clearly *the* formative philosophical influence on Dinesen's intellectual development. See Thurman, pp. 52–4. Robert Langbaum in *The Gayety of Vision: A Study of Isak Dinesen's Art* (New York: Random House, 1964) asserts that "[in] endowing the artist with both priestly and Dionysian or demonic elements, Isak Dinesen is romantic. But she moves to a late phase of romanticism, the phase, say, of Flaubert or Nietzsche, when she denies the artist the benefit of remorse and of our pity – when she denies him a personality, preferring that the artist and his work be superhuman" (p. 29). Brandes would also have likely introduced Dinesen to Staël, having written on her in *Hovedstromninger i det 19de aarhundreded Literatur* (Copenhagen: F. Hegel, 1872). Dinesen also likely knew Arnim's work from Brandes's "Rahel, Bettina, Charlotte Stieglitz," in *Main Currents of Nineteenth Century Literature*, VI (New York: Macmillan, 1905), pp. 277–304.

3 "Nietzsche, Genealogy, History," *The Foucault Reader*, ed. Paul Rabinow (New York: Pantheon, 1984), p. 85, hereafter "Genealogy."

4 Isak Dinesen, *Seven Gothic Tales* (1934; reprinted New York: Vintage, 1991). All subsequent references to *The Dreamers* will be to this edition and will appear in the text.

5 "Genealogy," p. 85.

6 Foucault, "What is Enlightenment?," *The Foucault Reader*, pp. 39–42.

7 See Chapters 2 and 3 of Susan Hardy Aiken, *Isak Dinesen and the Engendering of Narrative* (Chicago: University of Chicago Press, 1990), pp. 26–64.

8 Woolf, pp. 58–9.

9 For the theme of the witch, so central to Dinesen's work, see Sara Stambaugh, *The Witch and the Goddess in the Stories of Isak Dinesen* (Ann Arbor: University of Michigan Research Press, 1988). For her discussion of *The Dreamers*, see pp. 100–7 and 109–12. Stambaugh provides an excellent account of the influence of E.T.A. Hoffmann on this tale and of the significance of Mozart's *Don Giovanni* as the opera in which Pellegrina is performing when she is struck down and loses her voice in the theater fire. According to Stambaugh, Dinesen rejects Kierkegaard's reading of Don Giovanni in *Either/Or* as an incarnation of erotic power in favor of Hoffmann's critique of him as potential rapist and woman hater.

10 Friedrich Nietzsche, *Thus Spoke Zarathustra: A Book for All and None*, trans. Walter Kaufmann (New York: Random House, 1954), pp. 215–21. That Dinesen knew *Thus Spoke Zarathustra* is indicated by her choice of an epigraph for *Out of Africa* from that text: "To ride, to shoot with a bow, to tell the truth." See Thurman, p. 53.
11 Ross Chambers, *The Writing of Melancholy: Modes of Opposition in Early French Modernism* (Chicago: University of Chicago Press, 1993), p. 33.
12 Isak Dinesen, *Daguerreotypes and Other Essays*, Fwd. Hannah Arendt (Chicago: University of Chicago Press, 1979), p. 33. In the same volume, see also "Oration at a Bonfire, Fourteen Years Late," for another essay expressing Dinesen's complex and conflicted relationship to contemporary feminism. For Dinesen's views on marriage, see *On Modern Marriage and Other Observations*, trans. Anne Born, intro. Else Cederborg, Aftw. Frank Egholm Andersen (New York: St. Martin's, 1986).
13 Arendt, Fwd., *Daguerreotyes and Other Essays*, p. xxiii.
14 Willa Cather, *The Song of the Lark* (London: Penguin, 1999), pp. 256–7.

References

Abel, Elizabeth, Marianne Hirsch, and Elizabeth Langland (eds). *The Voyage In: Fictions of Female Development*. Hanover: University Press of New England, 1983.

Aiken, Susan Hardy. *Isak Dinesen and the Engendering of Narrative*. Chicago: University of Chicago Press, 1990.

Alexander, Meena. *Women in Romanticism*. London: Macmillan, 1989.

Arnim, Bettina von. *Correspondence of Fraülein Günderode and Bettine von Arnim*. Margaret Fuller and Minna Wesselhoeft (trans.). Boston: T.O.H.P. Burnham, 1861.

—— *Goethe's Correspondence with a Child*. Boston: Ticknor & Fields, 1859.

—— *Die Günderode. Werke und Briefe*. Walter Schmitz and Sibylle von Steinsdorff (eds). Frankfurt: Deutscher Klassiker Verlag, 1986, 3 vols.

Arnim, Peter-Anton von. "'Der eigentliche Held in dieser Zeit, die einzige wahrhaft freie und starke Stimme': Die jüdischen Aspekte in Leben und Werk Bettina von Arnims als Herausforderung," in *Beiträge eines Wiepersdorfer Kolloquiums zu Bettina von Arnim*, Hartwig Schultz (ed.). Berlin: Saint Albin, 1999, pp. 163–216.

Balayé, Simone. "A Propos du 'Préromantisme': Continuité ou rupture chez Mme de Staël," in *Le Préromantisme: hypothèque ou hypothèse?*, Paul Viallaneix (ed.). Paris: Klincksieck, 1975, pp. 153–68.

Baldwin, Claire. "Questioning the 'Jewish Question': Poetic Philosophy and Politics in Conversations with Demons," in *Bettine Brentano-von Arnim: Gender and Politics*, Elke P. Frederikson and Katherine R. Goodman (eds). Detroit: Wayne State University Press, 1995, pp. 213–24.

Baudelaire, Charles. *L'art romantique*. Lloyd James Austin (ed.). Paris: Garnier-Flammarion, 1968.

Bäumer, Konstanze. *Bettina von Arnim*. Stuttgart: J.B. Metzler, 1995.

Becker-Cantarino, Barbara. "Zur politischen Romantik. Bettina von Arnim, die 'Frauenfage' und der 'Feminismus,'" in *Beiträge eines Wiepersdorfer Kolloquiums zu Bettina von Arnim*, Hartwig Schultz (ed.). Berlin: Saint Albin, 1999, pp. 217–48.

Bennett, Betty T. "Machiavelli's and Mary Shelley's Castruccio: Biography as Metaphor," *Romanticism: The Journal of Romantic Culture and Criticism* III (1997): 139–51.

—— "The Political Philosophy of Mary Shelley's Historical Novels: *Valperga* and *Perkin Warbeck*," in *The Evidence of the Imagination: Studies of Interactions between Life and Art in English Romantic Literature*, Donald H. Reiman, Michael C. Jaye, and Betty T. Bennett (eds). New York: New York University Press, 1978, pp. 354–71.

Blackall, Eric. *Goethe and the Novel*. Ithaca: Cornell University Press, 1976.

Blackwell, Jeannine and Susanne Zantop (eds). *Bitter Healing: German Women Writers From 1700–1850*. Lincoln: University of Nebraska Press, 1990.

Bloch, Ernst. *The Utopian Function of Art and Literature: Selected Essays*, Jack Zipes and Frank Mecklenburg (trans.). Cambridge: MIT Press, 1988, pp. 265–77.

Blumberg, Jane. *Mary Shelley's Early Novels*. Iowa City: University of Iowa Press, 1993.

Boney, Elaine. "The Influence of E.T.A. Hoffmann on George Sand," in *George Sand: Collected Essays*. Janis Glasgow (ed.). Troy: Whitston, 1985, pp. 42–52.

Bowman, Frank Paul. "*Corinne* et la religion," in *L'Éclat et le silence*, Simone Balayé (ed.). Paris: Honoré Champion, 1999, pp. 145–60.

Brandes, Georg. 'Rahel, Bettina, Charlotte Stieglitz.' *Main Currents of Nineteenth Century Literature VI*. New York: Macmillan, 1905, pp. 277–304.

—— *Hovedstromninger i det 19de aarhundreded Literatur*. Copenhagen: F. Hegel, 1872.

Brewer, William D. "Mary Shelley's *Valperga*: The Triumph of Euthanasia's Mind." *European Romantic Review*, II (Winter 1995): 133–48.

Buckley, Jerome Hamilton. *Season of Youth: The Bildungsroman from Dickens to Golding*. Cambridge: Harvard University Press, 1974.

Burke, Janet M. "Freemasonry, Friendship and Noblewomen: The Role of the Secret Society in Bringing Enlightenment Thought to Pre-Revolutionary Women Elites." *History of European Ideas* X (1989): 283–93.

Burwick, Roswitha. "Bettina von Arnims *Die Günderode*. Zum Selbstverständnis der Frau in der Romantik." *Kontroversen, alte und neue. Akten des VII. Internationalen Germanisten-Kongresses, Göttingen*. Tübingen: Niemeyer, 1986.

—— "Liebe und Tod in Leben und Werk der Günderode." *German Studies Review* III (1980): 207–23.

Byron, George Gordon, Lord. *Byron's Poetry*, Frank D. McConnell (ed.). New York: W.W. Norton, 1978, p. 59.

Cather, Willa. *The Song of the Lark*. London: Penguin, 1999.

Cellier, Léon. "L'Occultisme dans *Consuelo* and *La Comtesse de Rudolstadt*." *Consuelo* and *La Comtesse de Rudolstadt*. Léon Cellier and Léon Guichard (eds and intro.). Paris: Garnier, 1959, pp. xlvii–lxxvii.

—— "Le roman initiatique en France au temps du romantisme," in *Parcours initiatiques*, Ross Chambers (intro.). Neuchâtel: La Baconnière, 1977, pp. 118–37.

—— (ed.) *La Porporina: Entretiens sur Consuelo*. Grenoble: Presses Universitaires de Grenoble, 1976.

Chambers, Ross. *The Writing of Melancholy: Modes of Opposition in Early French Modernism*. Chicago: University of Chicago Press, 1993.

Chevallier, Pierre. *Histoire de la franc-maçonnerie française*. Paris: Fayard, 1974.

Chevigny, Bell Gale. *The Woman and the Myth: Margaret Fuller's Life and Writings*. New York: The Feminist Press, 1976.

Clemit, Pamela. *The Godwinian Novel: The Rational Fictions of Godwin, Brockden Brown, Mary Shelley*. Oxford: Clarendon, 1993.

Coleridge, Samuel Taylor. *Literary Remains*. Vol. II, Henry Nelson Coleridge (ed.). London: W. Pickering, 1836–9; reprinted New York: AMS, 1967, 4 vols.

Collins, Hildegard Platzer and Philip Allison Shelley. "The Reception in England and America of Bettina von Arnim's *Goethe's Correspondence with a Child*," in *Anglo-German and American-German Crosscurrents*, Philip Allison Shelley (ed.) with Arthur O. Lewis, Jr. Vol. II. Chapel Hill: University of North Carolina Press, 1962, pp. 97–174.

Crosby, Christina. *The Ends of History: Victorians and the "Woman Question."* New York: Routledge, 1991.

Curran, Stuart. "The I Altered," in *Romanticism and Feminism*, Anne K. Mellor (ed.). Bloomington: Indiana University Press, 1988, pp. 185–207.

Daly, Pierrette. "*Consuelo*: The Fiction of Feminism." *George Sand Studies* XI (Spring 1992): 43–8.

de Certeau, Michel. *The Writing of History*, Tom Conley (trans.). New York: Columbia University Press, 1988.

DeJean, Joan. "Staël's *Corinne*: The Novel's Other Dilemma." *Stanford French Review* XI (Spring 1987): 77–88.

Dickenson, Donna. *George Sand: A Brave Man, The Most Womanly Woman*. Oxford: Berg Publishers, 1988.

Dinesen, Isak. *Daguerreotypes and Other Essays*, Hannah Arendt (fwd.). Chicago: University of Chicago Press, 1979.

—— *The Dreamers. Seven Gothic Tales.* 1934; reprinted New York: Vintage, 1991.

—— *On Modern Marriage and Other Observations*, Anne Born (trans.), Else Cederborg (intro.), Frank Egholm Andersen (aftw.). New York: St. Martin's, 1986.

Dischner, Gisela. *Bettina von Arnim: Eine weibliche Sozialbiographie aus dem neunzehnten Jahrhundert.* Berlin: Wagenbach, 1977.

Drewitz, Ingeborg. *Bettine von Arnim: Romantik, Revolution, Utopie.* Düsseldorf: Eugen Diederichs Verlag, 1969.

Dupont, Denise. "Masculinity, Femininity, Solidarity: Emilia Pardo Bazán's Construction of Madame de Staël and George Sand." *Comparative Literature Studies* XL (2003): 372–94.

Eliot, George. *Theophrastus Such, Jubal, and Other Poems.* Chicago: Belford, Clarke & Co., 1887; reprinted Chicago: Donahue & Henneberry, 1987.

Ellis, Lorna. *Appearing to Diminish: Female Development and the British Bildungsroman: 1750–1850.* Lewisburg: Bucknell University Press, 1999.

Ellison, Julie. *Delicate Subjects: Romanticism, Gender and the Ethics of Understanding.* Ithaca: Cornell University Press, 1990.

Evans, David. *Le socialisme romantique: Pierre Leroux et ses contemporains.* Paris: M. Rivière, 1948.

Felski, Rita. *Beyond Feminist Aesthetics: Feminist Literature and Social Change.* Cambridge: Harvard University Press, 1989.

Foucault, Michel. "Nietzsche, Genealogy, History," in *The Foucault Reader*, Paul Rabinow (ed.). New York: Pantheon, 1984, pp. 76–100.

—— "What is Enlightenment?," in *The Foucault Reader*, Paul Rabinow (ed.). New York: Pantheon, 1984, pp. 32–50.

Fraiman, Susan. *Unbecoming Women: British Women Writers and the Novel of Development.* New York: Columbia University Press, 1993.

Frappier-Mazur, Lucienne. "Desire, Writing, and Identity in the Romantic Mystical Novel: Notes for a Definition of the Feminine." *Style* XVIII (Summer 1984): 328–54.

Frederiksen, Elke and Monika Shafi. "'Sich im Unbekannten suchen gehen': Bettina von Arnim's *Die Günderode* als weibliche Utopie," in *Akten des VII. Internationalen Germanisten-Kongresses*, Göttingen, 1985, VI, *Frauensprache-Frauenliteratur?* Inge Stephan and Carl Pietzcker (eds). Tübingen: Niemeyer, 1986, pp. 54–61.

Freud, Sigmund. "Mourning and Melancholia." *Collected Papers.* Vol. IV, Joan Riviere (trans.). New York: Basic Books, 1959, 5 vols.

Fuderer, Laura Sue. *The Female Bildungsroman in English: An Annotated Bibliography of Criticism.* New York: MLA, 1990.

Fuller, Margaret. *Memoirs.* Vol. I. *The Woman and the Myth: Margaret Fuller's Life and Writings.* Bell Gale Chevigny (ed.). Old Westbury: The Feminist Press, 1976.

—— *Woman in the Nineteenth Century*, Bernard Rosenthal (intro.). New York: Norton, 1971.

Gaspard, Claire. "Madame de Staël et les Historiens de la Révolution." *Cahiers Staëliens* LI (2000): 7–19.

Gilbert, Sandra and Susan Gubar. *The Madwoman in the Attic: The Woman Writer and the Nineteenth-Century Literary Imagination*. New Haven: Yale University Press, 1979.

Godwin, William. "On History and Romance." *Things as They are, or The Adventures of Caleb Williams*, Maurice Hindle (ed.). London: Penguin, 1987, pp. 359–73.

Godwin-Jones, Robert. "Consuelo's Travels: The German Connection," in *The Traveler in the Life and Works of George Sand*, Tamara Alvarez-Detrell and Michael G. Paulson (eds). Troy: Whitston, 1994, pp. 107–14.

Goethe, Johann Wolfgang von. *Wilhelm Meister's Journeyman Years or The Renunciants*, Vol. X, Krishna Winston (trans.), Jane K. Brown (ed.), *Goethe's Collected Works*. New York: Suhrkamp, 1989. 12 vols.

—— *Wilhelm Meister's Apprenticeship*, Vol. IX, Eric A. Black (ed. and trans.), *Goethe's Collected Works*, Victor Lange (ed.). New York: Suhrkamp, 1989. 12 vols.

Goodman, Katherine R. *Dis/Closures: Women's Autobiography in Germany Between 1790 and 1914*. New York: Peter Lang, 1986.

—— "Through a Different Lens: Bettina Brentano-von Arnim's views on Gender," in *Bettine Brentano-von Arnim: Gender and Politics*, Elke P. Frederiksen and Katherine R. Goodman (eds). Detroit: Wayne State University Press, 1995, pp. 118–27.

Goozé, Marjanne. "Desire and Presence: Bettine von Arnim's Erotic Fantasy Letter to Goethe." *Michigan Germanic Studies* XIII, 1 (1987): 41–57.

—— "The Reception of Bettina Brentano-von Arnim as Author and Historical Figure," in *Bettine Brentano-von Arnim: Gender and Politics*, Elke P. Frederiksen and Katherine R. Goodman (eds). Detroit: Wayne State University Press, 1995, pp. 349–420.

Groß, Sabine. "Diskursregelung und Weiblichkeit: Mignon und ihre Schwestern," in *Goethes Mignon und ihre Schwestern: Interpretationen und Rezeption*, Gerhard Hoffmeister (ed.). New York: Peter Lang, 1993, pp. 83–100.

Grosz, Elizabeth. "Sexual Difference and the Problem of Essentialism," in *The Essential Difference*, Naomi Schor and Elizabeth Weed (eds). Bloomington: Indiana University Press, 1994, pp. 82–97.

Günderode, Karoline von. *Der Schatten eines Traumes*. Christa Wolf (ed. and intro.). Darmstadt: Luchterhand, 1981.

Gutwirth, Madelyn. "*Corinne* and *Consuelo* as Fantasies of Immanence." *George Sand Studies* VIII (1986–7): 21–7.

—— *Germaine de Staël, Novelist: The Emergence of the Artist as Woman*. Urbana: University of Illinois Press, 1978.

—— "Taking *Corinne* Seriously: A Comment on Ellen Moers's *Literary Women*." *Signs: Journal of Women in Culture and Society* XXV, 3 (2000): 895–9.

Härtl, Heinz. "Bettinas Salon der 'edlen' Weltverbesserer," in *Internationales Jahrbuch der Bettina-von-Arnim-Gesellschaft*, Uwe Lemm and Walter Schmitz (eds). VIII/IX (1996–7). Berlin: Saint Albin, pp. 163–76.

Hegel, Georg Wilhelm Friedrich. *The Philosophy of History* in *The Philosophy of Hegel*, Carl J. Friedrich (ed.). New York: Random House, 1953.

Heine, Heinrich. *Die Romantische Schule*. München: Wilhelm Goldmann Verlag, 1964.

Heller, Deborah. "Tragedy, Sisterhood, and Revenge in *Corinne*." *PLL* XXVI (Spring 1990): 212–32.

Helps, Arthur and Elizabeth Jane Howard. *Bettina: A Portrait*. London: Chatto & Windus, 1957.

Higonnet, Margaret R. "Suicide as Self-Construction," in *Germaine de Staël: Crossing the Borders*, Madelyn Gutwirth, Avriel Goldberger, and Karyna Szmurlo (eds). New Brunswick: Rutgers University Press, 1991, pp. 69–81.

Hirsch, Helmut. "Jüdische Aspekte im Leben und Werk Bettine von Arnims." *Internationales Jahrbuch der Bettina-von-Arnim-Gesellschaft* I (1987): 61–75.

—— "Zur Dichotomie von Theorie und Praxis in Bettines Äußerungen über Judentum und Juden." *Internationales Jahrbuch* III (1989): 153–72.

Hirsch, Marianne. "Spiritual Bildung: The Beautiful Soul as Paradigm," in *The Voyage In: Fictions of Female Development*, Elizabeth Abel, Marianne Hirsch, and Elizabeth Langland (eds). Hanover: University Press of New England, 1983, pp. 23–48.

Hock, Lisabeth M. *Replicas of a Female Prometheus: The Textual Personae of Bettina von Arnim.* New York: Peter Lang, 2001.

—— "'Sonderbare', 'heißhungrige', und 'edle' Gestalten: Konstrukte von Juden und Judentum bei Bettina von Arnim," in *Salons der Romantik: Beiträge eines Wiepersdorfer Kolloquiums zu Theorie und Geschichte des Salons*, Hartwig Schultz (ed.). Berlin: Walter de Gruyter, 1997, pp. 317–41.

Homans, Margaret. *Women Writers and Poetic Identity: Dorothy Wordsworth, Emily Brontë, and Emily Dickinson.* Princeton: Princeton University Press, 1980.

Howe, Susanne. *Wilhelm Meister and His English Kinsmen: Apprentices to Life.* New York: Columbia University Press, 1930.

Huf, Linda. *The Portrait of the Artist as a Young Woman: The Writer as Heroine in American Literature.* New York: Frederick Ungar, 1983.

Isbell, John. *The Birth of European Romanticism.* Cambridge: Cambridge University Press, 1994.

Jacob, Margaret C. *Living the Enlightenment: Freemasonry and Politics in Eighteenth-Century Europe.* New York: Oxford University Press, 1991.

—— *The Radical Enlightenment: Pantheists, Freemasons, and Republicans.* London: Allen & Unwin, 1981.

Jameson, Fredric. *The Political Unconscious: Narrative as a Socially Symbolic Act.* Ithaca: Cornell University Press, 1981.

Jauß, Hans Robert. *Literaturgeschichte als Provokation.* Frankfurt: Suhrkamp, 1970.

Joeres, Ruth-Ellen B. "'We are adjacent to human society': German Women Writers, the Homosocial Experience, and a Challenge to the Public/Domestic Dichotomy." *Women in German Yearbook*, Jeanette Clausen and Sara Friedrichsmeyer (eds), X (1995): 39–57.

Kadish, Doris. *Politicizing Gender: Narrative Strategies in the Aftermath of the French Revolution.* New Brunswick: Rutgers University Press, 1991.

Kaiser, Nancy A. "A Dual Voice: Mary Shelley and Bettina von Arnim," in *Identity and Ethos: A Festschrift for Sol Liptzin on the Occasion of His 85th Birthday*, Mark H. Gelber (ed.). New York: Peter Lang, 1986, pp. 211–33.

Kant, Immanuel. *The Conflict of the Faculties/Der Streit der Fakultäten.* Mary J. Gregor (trans. and intro.). Lincoln: University of Nebraska Press, 1979.

—— *Philosophical Writings*, Ernst Behler (ed.). New York: Continuum, 1986; reprinted 1993.

Kelly, Gary. "Last Men: Hemans and Mary Shelley in the 1820s." *Romanticism: The Journal of Romantic Culture and Criticism* III, 2 (1997): 198–208.

Kittler, Friedrich. "Writing into the Wind, Bettina," Marilyn Wyatt (trans.). *Glyph* VII (1980): 32–69.

Kucich, Greg. "Mary Shelley's *Lives* and the Reengendering of History," in *Mary Shelley in her Times*, Betty T. Bennett and Stuart Curran (eds). Baltimore: Johns Hopkins University Press, 2000, pp. 198–213.

Kuhn, Anna K. "The 'Failure' of Biography, the Triumph of Women's Writing: Bettina von Arnim's *Die Günderode* and Christa Wolf's *The Quest for Christa T.*," in *Revealing Lives: Autobiography, Biography, and Gender*, Susan Groag Bell and Marilyn Yalom (eds). Albany: State University of New York Press, 1990, pp. 13–28.

Lacassagne, Jean-Pierre. "Albert et Pierre Leroux," in *La Porporina: Entretiens sur Consuelo*, Léon Cellier (ed.). Grenoble: Presses Universitaires de Grenoble, 1976, pp. 31–40.

Laforge, François. "Structure et fonction du mythe d'Orphée dans *Consuelo* de George Sand." *Revue d'Histoire littéraire de la France* LXXXIV (1984): 53–66.

Landfester, Ulrike. "'Die echte Politik muss Erfinderin sein': Uberlegungen zum Umgang mit Bettine von Arnims politischem Werk," in *Beiträge eines Wiepersdorfer Kolloquiums zu Bettina von Arnim*, Hartwig Schultz (ed.). Berlin: Saint Albin, 1999, pp. 1–37.

—— "Das Schweigen der Sibylle: Bettine von Arnims Briefe über die Revolution von 1848." *Internationales Jahrbuch der Bettina-von-Arnim-Gesellschaft*, Wolfgang Bunzel, Uwe Lemm, and Walter Schmitz (eds), XI/XII (1999–2000): 121–43.

—— "Von Frau zu Frau? Einige Bemerkungen über historische und ahistorische Weiblichkeitsdiskurse in der Rezeption Bettine von Arnims." *Internationales Jahrbuch der Bettina-von-Arnim-Gesellschaft*. Uwe Lemm, and Walter Schmitz (eds), VIII/IX (1996–7): 201–19.

Langbaum, Robert. *The Gayety of Vision: A Study of Isak Dinesen's Art.* New York: Random House, 1964.

Lauretis, Teresa de. *Technologies of Gender: Essays on Theory, Film, and Fiction.* Bloomington: Indiana University Press, 1987.

Leighton, Angela. *Victorian Women Poets: Writing Against the Heart.* Hemel Hempstead: Harvester/Wheatsheaf, 1992.

Lévêque, Laure. *Corinne, ou l'Italie de Madame de Staël: Poétique et Politique.* Paris: Editions du Temps, 1999.

Lew, Joseph W. "History and Ideology in *Valperga*," in *The Other Mary Shelley: Beyond Frankenstein*, Audrey A. Fisch, Anne K. Mellor, and Esther Schor (eds). Oxford: Oxford University Press, 1993, pp. 159–84.

Liebertz-Grün, Ursula. *Ordnung im Chaos: Studien zur Poetik der Bettine Brentano-von Arnim.* Heidelberg: Carl Winter Universitätsverlag, 1989.

Linley, Margaret. "Sappho's Conversions in Felicia Hemans, Letitia Landon, and Christina Rossetti." *Prism(s)* IV (1996): 15–42.

Lipking, Lawrence. *Abandoned Women and Poetic Tradition.* Chicago: University of Chicago Press, 1988.

Lokke, Kari. "Children of Liberty: Idealist Historiography in Staël, Shelley, and Sand." *PMLA* CXVIII (May 2003): 502–20.

—— "Sibylline Leaves: Mary Shelley's *Valperga* and the Legacy of *Corinne*," in *Cultural Interactions in the Romantic Age*, Gregory Maertz (ed.). Albany: State University of New York Press, 1998, pp. 157–76.

Looser, Devoney. *British Women Writers and the Writing of History, 1670–1820.* Baltimore: Johns Hopkins University Press, 2000.

Lovell, Ernest J., Jr. "Byron and Mary Shelley." *Keats–Shelley Journal* I (January 1952): 35–49.

Lukacher, Maryline. *Maternal Fictions: Stendhal, Sand, Rachilde, and Bataille.* Durham: Duke University Press, 1994.

Lyotard, Jean-François. *The Differend: Phrases in Dispute*, Georges Van Den Abbeele (trans.). Minneapolis: University of Minnesota Press, 1988.

Mahlendorf, Ursula R. *The Wellsprings of Literary Creation: An Analysis of Male and Female "Artist Stories" from the German Romantics to American Writers of the Present.* Columbia: Camden House, 1985.

Martin, Biddy. "Feminism, Criticism, and Foucault," in *Feminism and Foucault: Reflections on Resistance*, Irene Diamond and Lee Quinby (eds). Boston: Northeastern University Press, 1988, pp. 3–20.

Martin, Judith. "Between Exaltation and Melancholy: Madame de Staël's *Corinne* and the Female Artist Novel." *Journal of the Association for the Interdisciplinary Study of the Arts*, II (2000): 29–50.

—— "Nineteenth-Century German Women's Reception of Madame de Staël," *Women in German Yearbook*, XVIII (2002): 133–57.

Massardier-Kenney, Françoise. *Gender in the Fiction of George Sand*. Amsterdam: Rodopi, 2000.

—— "Textual Feminism in the Early Fiction of George Sand." *George Sand Studies* XIII (Spring 1994): 11–17.

Mee, Jon. *Romanticism, Enthusiasm, and Regulation*. Oxford: Oxford University Press, 2003.

Mellor, Alec. *La vie quotidienne de la franc-maçonnerie française du XVIIIe siècle à nos jours*. Paris: Hachette, 1973.

Mellor, Anne K. "English Women Writers and the French Revolution," in *Rebel Daughters: Women and the French Revolution*, Sara E. Melzer and Leslie Rabine (eds). New York: Oxford University Press, 1992, pp. 255–72.

—— *Mothers of the Nation: Women's Political Writing in England, 1780–1830*. Bloomington: Indiana University Press, 2000.

—— *Romanticism and Gender*. New York: Routledge, 1993.

Miller, James. *The Passion of Michel Foucault*. New York: Simon & Schuster, 1993.

Miller, Nancy K. *Subject to Change: Reading Feminist Writing*. New York: Columbia University Press, 1988.

Modum, Egbuna. "Une Initiation à caractère maçonnique: L'exemple de *Consuelo* et *La Comtesse de Rudolstadt* de George Sand." *Nineteenth-Century French Studies* XI (1983): 268–77.

Moers, Ellen. *Literary Women: The Great Writers*. New York: Doubleday, 1976.

Moltmann-Wendel, Elisabeth. "Bettina von Arnim und Schleiermacher." *Evangelische Theologie* XXXI (1971): 395–414.

Moretti, Franco. *The Way of the World: The Bildungsroman in European Culture*. London: Verso, 1987.

Mortier, Roland. *Madame de Staël et l'Europe*. Paris: Klincksieck, 1970.

Moses, Claire Goldberg and Leslie Wahl Rabine. *Feminism, Socialism, and French Romanticism*. Bloomington: Indiana University Press, 1993.

Naginski, Isabelle Hoog. *George Sand: Writing for her Life*. New Brunswick: Rutgers University Press, 1991.

Nietzsche, Friedrich. *Thus Spoke Zarathustra: A Book for All and None*, Walter Kaufmann (trans.). New York: Random House, 1954.

O'Sullivan, Barbara. "Beatrice in *Valperga*: A New Cassandra," in *The Other Mary Shelley: Beyond Frankenstein*, Audrey A. Fisch, Anne K. Mellor, and Esther Schor (eds). Oxford: Oxford University Press, 1993, pp. 140–58.

Oehlke, Waldemar. *Bettina von Arnims Briefromane*. Berlin: Mayer & Mueller, 1905.

Patterson, Rebecca. "Emily Dickinson's Debt to *Günderode*." *The Midwest Quarterly* VII (1967): 331–54.

Paulson, Ronald. *Representations of Revolution, 1789–1820*. New Haven: Yale University Press, 1983.

Peel, Ellen. "Corinne's Shift to Patriarchal Mediation: Rebirth or Regression?," in *Germaine de Staël: Crossing the Borders*, Madelyn Gutwirth, Avriel Goldberger and Kayna Szmurlo (eds). New Brunswick: Rutgers University Press, 1991, pp. 101–12.

Peterson, Carla. *The Determined Reader: Gender and Culture in the Novel from Napoleon to Victoria*. New Brunswick: Rutgers University Press, 1986.

Pocock, J.G.A. *The Machiavellian Moment: Florentine Political Thought and the Atlantic Republican Tradition*. Princeton: Princeton University Press, 1975.

Poulet, Georges. "The Role of Improvisation in *Corinne*." *ELH* XLI, 4 (Winter 1974): 602–12.

Powell, David. *While the Music Lasts: The Representation of Music in the Works of George Sand*. Lewisburg: Bucknell University Press, 2001.

Rainer, Ulrike. "A Question of Silence: Goethe's Speechless Women," in *Goethes Mignon und ihre Schwestern: Interpretationen und Rezeption*, Gerhard Hoffmeister (ed.). New York: Peter Lang, 1993, pp. 101–12.

Rajan, Tilottama. "Between Romance and History: Possibility and Contingency in Godwin, Leibniz, and Mary Shelley's *Valperga*," in *Mary Shelley in her Times*, Betty T. Bennett and Stuart Curran (eds). Baltimore: Johns Hopkins University Press, 2000, pp. 88–102.

—— "Mary Shelley's *Mathilda*: Melancholy and the Political Economy of Romanticism." *Studies in the Novel* XXVI, 2 (Summer 1994): 43–68.

Redfield, Marc. *Phantom Formations: Aesthetic Ideology and the Bildungsroman*. Ithaca: Cornell University Press, 1996.

Reynolds, Margaret. "'I lived for art, I lived for love': The Woman Poet Sings Sappho's Last Song," in *Victorian Women Poets: A Critical Reader*, Angela Leighton (ed.). Oxford: Blackwell, 1996, pp. 277–306.

Rieger, James. *The Mutiny Within: The Heresies of Percy Bysshe Shelley*. New York: George Braziller, 1967.

Rigney, Ann. *Imperfect Histories: The Elusive Past and the Legacy of Romantic Historicism*. Ithaca: Cornell University Press, 2001.

Roetzel, Lisa C. "Acting Out: Bettine as Performer of Feminine Genius." *Women in German Yearbook*, Sara Friedrichsmeyer and Patricia Herminghouse (eds), XIV (1998): 109–25.

Rogers, Nancy. "George Sand and Germaine de Staël: The Novel as Subversion," in *West Virginia George Sand Conference Papers*, Armand E. Singer, Mary W. Singer, Janice S. Spleth, and Dennis O'Brien (eds). Morgantown: West Virginia University, 1981, pp. 61–73.

Rose, Paul Lawrence. *Revolutionary Antisemitism in Germany from Kant to Wagner*. Princeton: Princeton University Press, 1990.

Ross, Marlon. *The Contours of Masculine Desire: Romanticism and the Rise of Women's Poetry*. Oxford: Oxford University Press, 1989.

Rossington, Michael. "Future Uncertain: The Republican Tradition and its Destiny in *Valperga*," in *Mary Shelley in her Times*, Betty T. Bennett and Stuart Curran (eds). Baltimore: Johns Hopkins University Press, 2000, pp. 103–18.

St. Armand, Barton Levi. "Veiled Ladies: Dickinson, Bettine, and Transcendental Mediumship." *Studies in the American Renaissance*. Charlottesville: University Press of Virginia, 1987, pp. 1–51.

Sand, George. *Consuelo [et] La Comtesse de Rudolstadt*, Léon Cellier and Léon Guichard (eds and intro.). Paris: Garnier, 1959. 3 vols.

—— *Consuelo: A Romance of Venice*. No trans. New York: Da Capo, 1979.

—— *Correspondance [de] George Sand*, Vol. VI, Georges Lubin (ed.). Paris: Garnier, 1969, 26 vols.

—— *The Countess Rudolstadt, Being a Sequel to "Consuelo."* Frank H. Potter (trans.). New York: Dodd Mead, 1891, 2 vols.

—— *Jean Ziska*. Oeuvres complètes. Vol. XIX. Genève: Slatkine, 1980, 35 vols.

—— *Lettres d'un Voyageur*, Sacha Rabinovitch and Patricia Thomson (trans.). London: Penguin, 1987.

Schaeffer, Gérard. "*Consuelo*, le temps et l'espace, lieux symboliques et personnages," in *La Porporina: Entretiens sur Consuelo*, Léon Cellier (ed.). Grenoble: Presses Universitaires de Grenoble, 1976, pp. 53–67.

—— *Espace et Temps Chez George Sand.* Neuchâtel: Baconnière, 1981.

Schiefelbein, Michael. "'The Lessons of True Religion': Mary Shelley's Tribute to Catholicism in *Valperga.*" *Religion and Literature* XXX, 2 (1998): 59–79.

Schierenbeck, Daniel. "'Lofty enthusiasm' and 'vulgar superstitions': Shelley, Hume, and Religion's Role in History." NASSR Conference, 24 August 2002: University of Western Ontario.

Schiesari, Juliana. *The Gendering of Melancholia: Feminism, Psychoanalysis, and the Symbolics of Loss in Renaissance Literature.* Ithaca: Cornell University Press, 1992.

Schiller, Friedrich. *Naïve and Sentimental Poetry and On the Sublime,* Julias Elias (trans. and intro.). New York: Ungar, 1966.

—— *On the Aesthetic Education of Man.* Reginald Snell (trans. and intro.). London: Routledge & Kegan Paul, 1954; reprinted New York: Ungar, 1977.

Schor, Naomi. *George Sand and Idealism.* New York: Columbia University Press, 1993.

Shelley, Mary. *The Last Man,* Anne McWhir (ed.). Ontario: Broadview, 1996.

—— "Madame de Staël, 1766–1817." *The Cabinet Cyclopaedia: Eminent Literary and Scientific Men of France,* Vol. 2. London: Longman, 1839.

—— *Mary Shelley's Journal,* Frederick Jones (ed.). Norman: University of Oklahoma Press, 1947.

—— *Valperga: or, The Life and Adventures of Castruccio, Prince of Lucca,* Tilottama Rajan (ed.). Ontario: Broadview, 1998.

Showalter, Elaine. *The New Feminist Criticism: Essays on Women, Literature, and Theory.* New York: Pantheon, 1985.

Showalter, English. "Corinne as an Autonomous Heroine," in *Germaine de Staël: Crossing the Borders,* Madelyn Gutwirth, Avriel Goldberger, and Karyna Szmurlo (eds). New Brunswick: Rutgers University Press, 1991, pp. 188–92.

Simpson, David. *Romanticism, Nationalism, and the Revolt Against Theory.* Chicago and London: University of Chicago Press, 1993.

Simpson, Patricia Anne. "Letters in Sufferance and Deliverance: The Correspondence of Bettina Brentano-von Arnim and Karoline von Günderrode," in *Bettine Brentano-von Arnim: Gender and Politics,* Elke P. Frederiksen and Katherine R. Goodman (eds). Detroit: Wayne State University Press, 1995, pp. 247–77.

Smith, Bonnie G. "History and Genius: The Narcotic, Erotic, and Baroque Life of Germaine de Staël." *French Historical Studies* XIX (Autumn 1996): 1059–81.

Smith, Orianne. "Romantic Women Writers and the Figure of the Improvisatrice." NASSR Conference, 24 August 2002: University of Western Ontario.

Soderholm, James. "Byron, Nietzsche, and the Mystery of Forgetting." *CLIO* XXIII, 1 (Fall 1993): 51–63.

Sonnenfeld, Albert. "George Sand: Music and Sexualities." *Nineteenth-Century French Studies* XVI (Spring–Summer 1988): 310–21.

Sourian, Eve. "L'Influence de Mme de Staël sur les première oeuvres de George Sand." *George Sand Studies* VII (1984–5): 37–45.

Spacks, Patricia Meyer. *The Female Imagination.* New York: Knopf, 1975.

Spencer, Sharon. "'Femininity' and the Woman Writer: Doris Lessing's *The Golden Notebook* and the *Diary of Anaïs Nin.*" *Women's Studies* I, 3 (1973): 247–57.

Staël, Germaine de. *Corinne, or Italy.* Avriel Goldberger (trans. and ed.). New Brunswick: Rutgers University Press, 1987.

—— *Corinne, ou L'Italie,* Simone Balayé (ed. and intro.). Oeuvres complètes, series II; Oeuvres littéraires, Vol III. Paris: Champion, 2000.

—— *Corinne, ou L'Italie,* New York: Leavitt & Allen, 1864.

—— *De l'Allemagne*, Simone Balayé (ed.). Paris: Garnier-Flammarion, 1968.

—— *De la littérature considérée dans ses rapports avec les institutions sociales*, Paul Van Tieghem (intro). Geneva: Librairie Droz, 1959, pp. vii–lxiv.

—— *An Extraordinary Woman: Selected Writings of Germaine de Staël*, Vivian Folkenflik (trans., intro. and ed.). New York: Columbia University Press, 1987.

—— *Reflections on Suicide*. Trans. from French. London: Longman, Hurst, Orme, & Brown, 1813.

Stambaugh, Sara. *The Witch and the Goddess in the Stories of Isak Dinesen*. Ann Arbor: University of Michigan Research Press, 1988.

Starobinski, Jean. "Suicide et mélancolie chez Madame de Staël," in *Madame de Staël et l'Europe*, Roland Mortier (ed.). Paris: Klincksieck, 1970, pp. 41–8.

Steedman, Carolyn. *Strange Dislocations: Childhood and the Idea of Human Interiority, 1780–1930*. London: Virago, 1995.

Sunstein, Emily. *Mary Shelley: Romance and Reality*. Boston: Little Brown, 1989.

Swallow, Noreen J. "The Weapon of Personality: A Review of Sexist Criticism of Mme de Staël, 1785–1975." *Atlantis* VIII (Autumn 1982): 78–82.

Sychrava, Juliet. *Schiller to Derrida: Idealism in Aesthetics*. Cambridge and New York: Cambridge University Press, 1989.

Taillefer, Michel. *La franc-maçonnerie toulousaine sous l'Ancien Régime et la Révolution, 1741–1799*. Paris: E.N.S.B.-C.T.H.S., 1984.

Thomson, Patricia. *George Sand and the Victorians: Her Influence and Reputation in Nineteenth-Century England*. London: Macmillan, 1977.

Thorslev, Peter. *The Byronic Hero*. Minneapolis: University of Minnesota Press, 1962.

Thurman, Judith. *Isak Dinesen: The Life of a Storyteller*. New York: St. Martin's, 1982.

Vallois, Marie-Claire. "Old Idols, New Subject: Germaine de Staël and Romanticism," in *Germaine de Staël: Crossing the Borders*, Madelyn Gutwirth, Avriel Goldberger, and Karyna Szmurlo (eds). New Brunswick: Rutgers University Press, 1991, pp. 82–97.

Varsamopoulou, Evy. *The Poetics of the Künstlerinroman and the Aesthetics of the Sublime*. Aldershot: Ashgate, 2002.

Vierne, Simone. "Le mythe de la femme dans *Consuelo*," in *La Porporina: Entretiens sur Consuelo*, Léon Cellier (ed.). Grenoble: Presses Universitaires de Grenoble, 1976, pp. 41–52.

Vincent, Patrick Henri. *Elegiac Muses: Corinne and the Engendering of the Romantic Poetess, 1820–1840*. Hanover: University Press of New England, 2004.

Waldstein, Edith. *Bettine von Arnim and the Politics of Romantic Conversation*. Columbia: Camden House, 1988.

Waller, Margaret. *The Male Malady: Fictions of Impotence in the French Romantic Novel*. New Brunswick: Rutgers University Press, 1993.

White, Daniel E. "Mary Shelley's *Valperga*: Italy, and the Revision of Romantic Aesthetics," in *Mary Shelley's Fictions: From Frankenstein to Falkner*, Michael Eberle-Sinatra (ed.). New York: St. Martin's, 2000, pp. 75–94.

Wolf, Christa (ed.). *Karoline von Günderrode: Der Schatten eines Traumes*. Darmstadt: Luchterhand, 1981.

—— "Your Next Life Begins Today: A Letter About Bettine," in *Bettine Brentano-von Arnim: Gender and Politics*, Elke P. Frederiksen and Katherine R. Goodman (eds). Detroit: Wayne State University Press, 1995, pp. 35–67.

Woolf, Virginia. *A Room of One's Own*. London: Harcourt Brace Jovanovich, 1929.

Index